MEMORY-ENHANCING TECHNIQUES FOR INVESTIGATIVE INTERVIEWING

MEMORY-ENHANCING TECHNIQUES FOR INVESTIGATIVE INTERVIEWING

The Cognitive Interview

By

RONALD P. FISHER, PH.D.

*Florida International
University*

and

R. EDWARD GEISELMAN, PH.D.

*University of California,
Los Angeles*

CHARLES C THOMAS • PUBLISHER
Springfield • Illinois • U.S.A.

Published and Distributed Throughout the World by

CHARLES C THOMAS • PUBLISHER
2600 South First Street
Springfield, Illinois 62794-9265

© *1992 by* CHARLES C THOMAS • PUBLISHER
ISBN 0-398-05800-8 (hard)
ISBN 0-398-06121-1 (paper)
Library of Congress Catalog Card Number: 92-6195

Printed in the United States of America
SC-R-3

Library of Congress Cataloging-in-Publication Data

Fisher, Ronald P.
    Memory-enhancing techniques for investigative interviewing : the
cognitive interview / by Ronald P. Fisher & R. Edward Geiselman.
        p.   cm.
    Includes bibliographical references (p.   ) and indexes.
    ISBN 0-398-05800-8. — ISBN 0-398-06121-1 (pbk)
    1. Interviewing in law enforcement.   2. Police questioning.
3. Memory.   I. Geiselman, R. Edward.   II. Title.
HV8073.F523   1992
363.2'54 – dc20
                                                                        92-6195
                                                                        CIP

Dedicated to my father, Reuben Fisher, and mother, Fay (Fisher) Braunstein, whose love and guidance are forever appreciated (R.P.F.).

Dedicated to my wife, Cynthia Jay-Geiselman, whose inspiration has made my efforts worthwhile (R.E.G.).

PREFACE

Our interest in memory-enhancement interviewing techniques developed rather innocently. In casual conversations, we often found that we could help neighbors and family members to remember where they had lost or misplaced objects, like keys and eyeglasses. Similarly, we sometimes alleviated friends' distress by helping them to remember the names of people, telephone numbers, or addresses they had temporarily forgotten.

Initially, we were unaware that our ability to help stemmed from our professional training in the science of cognition (memory, perception, attention, speech, and other mental activities). Later, in retrospect, we realized that many of the techniques we used to prompt memory came directly from the scientific, laboratory research we lectured about in our college classrooms. We soon realized that such knowledge could be valuable for those professionals who regularly conduct investigative interviews where memory and ability to describe details are critical. Naturally, we thought about police detectives who are constantly interviewing victims and eyewitnesses to probe their memories for detailed descriptions. With encouragement from the Los Angeles Police Department, and later from the Metro-Dade Police Department, we began to pursue the issue more systematically and started on a program of laboratory and field research to develop the Cognitive Interview.

Since the early developmental stages, we have worked closely with several police departments conducting training workshops or interviewing victims and eyewitnesses in particularly interesting criminal cases. The present book is our attempt to share the knowledge we have gained in the past ten years with others who will conduct investigative interviews in the future.

Much of the work described in this book has appeared in other professional, research-oriented sources: either in journals, book chapters, or conference lectures. Our goals here are to organize all of this material into one coherent work, and to present it in a handbook form so it can be used by applied investigative interviewers. We provide some conceptual background about memory retrieval and communication, so readers will have a better understanding of why and how the practical suggestions work. The main focus, however, is on practical application.

Most of the sample interviews that appear in the book have been excerpted from real police cases. In these instances, all identifying information (names, telephone numbers, license plate numbers, etc.) has been changed so that any resemblance between the information provided here and the original case is purely coincidental.

Although only two authors' names appear on the cover of this book, many individuals and institutions contributed their knowledge and resources. We wish to acknowledge the National Institute of Justice (grants USDJ-83-IJ–CX-0025 & USDJ-85-IJ–CX-0053) without whose support the research to develop the Cognitive Interview could never have been undertaken. We also would like to extend our thanks to the many local police officers who assisted in the research, especially to Chief John Farrell and the members of the Robbery Division of the Metro-Dade Police Department, Captain Mike Nielsen and Dr. Martin Reiser of the Los Angeles Police Department, and Detective Tom Sirkel of the Los Angeles Sheriff's Department.

The burden of collecting and analyzing the data during the research phase was borne by a devoted set of research assistants: David MacKinnon, Heidi Holland, Kim O'Reilly, Gail Bornstein, David Raymond, Michael Amador, Lynn Jurkevich, Monica Warhaftig, Kathy Quigley, David Tacher, Alex Torres, Michelle McCauley, and Denise Chin. Many of our current ideas have evolved as a result of having presented training workshops to police and other investigative agencies. We are particularly grateful to Detective Sergeant Richard George of the City of London Police Department, the members of the polygraph division of the Israeli Police Department, and the investigators from the National Collegiate Athletic Association, who have provided valuable feedback during these presentations. A significant portion of this book was written while one of us (RPF) was on sabbatical leave at the University of Haifa, where excellent working conditions (minus a few Scud attacks) and a collegial atmosphere were provided. Finally, we would like to thank Drs. Brian Cutler, Alan Fisher, and Janet Fisher, who have given us valuable feedback on earlier drafts of this book.

CONTENTS

MEMORY-ENHANCING TECHNIQUES FOR INVESTIGATIVE INTERVIEWING

Chapter 1

INTRODUCTION

Despite the obvious importance of eyewitness information in criminal investigation, police receive surprisingly little instruction on how to conduct an effective interview with a cooperative eyewitness (Sanders, 1986). In a study by the Rand Corporation (1975) more than half of the police departments polled reported that they had no formal training whatsoever for newly appointed investigators[1] (see Cahill & Mingay, 1986, for a comparable lack of systematic training for British police). Most text books in police science either completely omit the issue of effective interviewing techniques or provide only superficial coverage (e.g., Harris, 1973; Leonard, 1971; More & Unsinger, 1987; O'Hara & O'Hara, 1988). Reflecting this lack of formal training, police often maintain a less-than-rigorous attitude toward this phase of investigation. As one police officer described his interviewing approach, "You just ask them what, where, why, when, and how." It is not surprising, therefore, that police investigators often make avoidable mistakes when conducting a friendly interview and fail to elicit potentially valuable information. The intent of this book is to provide the police interviewer (*INT*) or any other investigative *INT* with a systematic approach so that he can elicit the maximum amount of relevant information from cooperative eyewitnesses (*E/Ws*).[2]

The language of this book is couched in terms of police investigations, primarily because our research has been conducted with police par-

---

1. Our informal survey of police officers in the Miami and Los Angeles areas revealed that almost none had any scientific training in interviewing cooperative eyewitnesses. What training they had received focused primarily on the formal and legalistic requirements of the investigative interview. Some detectives received scientific training in interrogating potential suspects, but clearly, different techniques ought to be used to elicit information from suspects than from cooperative witnesses.

2. Two notes about writing style: Because the terms "eyewitness" and "interviewer" appear so frequently, we use the handier abbreviations, *E/W* and *INT,* for economy. Throughout the book we use the feminine terms *she* and *her* to refer to the eyewitness (*E/W*) and the masculine terms *he* and *him* to refer to the interviewer (*INT*). We make this distinction only to avoid ambiguity, so that it will be clear whether we are referring to the *E/W* or the *INT.* In our research, both men and women served as *E/Ws* and *INTs*. As such, our conclusions are intended for both men and women *E/Ws* and *INTs*.

ticipants. However, since the Cognitive Interview is based on general principles of cognition, it should be useful by anyone conducting an investigative interview, whether a police detective, fire marshal, state-, defense-, or civil attorney, private investigator, etc.[3] The central problem is identical in all investigative interviews, to extract relevant information from the mind of the respondent. Non-police investigators, who are as likely as police to be untrained in the science of memory, can therefore benefit equally from the Cognitive Interview. We suggest that they simply modify the general concepts to make them compatible with their particular investigative conditions.

There are, unfortunately, a variety of factors that limit the amount of information reported by *E/Ws*. Many people simply "don't want to get involved"—they are afraid of the potential consequences, they find court appearances inconvenient, etc. Other seemingly innocent *E/Ws* are, in fact, suspects and prefer to divulge as little information as possible. Still others have such poor communication skills as to make effective interviewing impossible. Practically, little can be done to overcome those hurdles; they are built into the system. Our concern is to focus on an investigative problem that can be remedied, one where we can make detective work more efficient. One such universal problem is the limitation imposed by human memory, a problem faced by all *E/Ws,* caring or unconcerned, cooperative or uncooperative, victims or innocent bystanders, . . . As opposed to the other insurmountable obstacles of investigation, eyewitness memory definitely can be enhanced by appropriate interviewing techniques. The focus of this book is to describe an interviewing technique that can assist the investigative process by increasing eyewitness recollection.

The Cognitive Interview has evolved over the past several years and reflects a multidisciplinary approach. We have relied heavily on the theoretical, laboratory research in cognitive psychology (hence the name "Cognitive Interview") that we and other psychologists have conducted over the past thirty years. In addition, we have borrowed concepts from other disciplines of investigative interviewing: journalism, oral history, medical interviews, psycho-therapeutic interviews, etc. Having established a sound, theoretical basis for memory-enhanced interviewing, we sharpened these principles with a heavy dose of practical research. Some

---

3. See Fisher and Quigley (1991), summarized in Appendix B, showing how the technique can be modified to improve public health interviews about recalling foods eaten at an earlier meal.

of this practical experience reflects our "ride-alongs" with police detectives in the field. We have conducted several interviews ourselves, either for police or for private investigators. Most of our practical research stems from intensive listening and analysis of hundreds of hours of tape-recorded interviews conducted by experienced police detectives. Finally, we interviewed several of the police detectives who participated in our experiments to elicit their views on different interviewing techniques. The Cognitive Interview, therefore, is an eclectic approach, making use of ideas found across a variety of people, research approaches, and disciplines.

Because of our scientific training, one principle that we have upheld steadfastly throughout the entire research program is that we would recommend the Cognitive Interview only if its merit could be demonstrated scientifically. Regardless of how intuitively reasonable our approach was and regardless of how many "experts" endorsed our ideas, our ultimate concern was always whether or not the effectiveness of the Cognitive Interview was supported by objective data. When tested, does the Cognitive Interview actually elicit more information than a standard, police interview?

Since we assume that many of our readers will take such a healthy, skeptical position, we present in Appendix B a summary of the scientific evidence documenting our claims. We recommend that the serious investigator read the original, detailed journal articles for a more thorough description of the research. In brief, experimental tests of the Cognitive Interview showed it to increase substantially the amount of information gathered in many different settings. It worked with student and non-student E/Ws; it worked with novice and experienced investigators; it worked with criminal and civil investigations; it worked in the laboratory, and more important, in the field, with actual victims and witnesses of crime.

Thus far, two independent studies have been conducted to test the Cognitive Interview in the field, with victims and witnesses of crime. One study was conducted in the United States, with the Metro-Dade (Miami) Police Department (Fisher, Geiselman, & Amador, 1989), and one study was conducted in England, with investigators from various police departments (George, 1991). In the American study, experienced detectives elicited 47 percent more information after training on the Cognitive Interview than they did before training. In the British study, the detectives elicited 55% more information after training than before training. Interestingly, the only detective who did not improve with training in the Cognitive Interview (in the U.S. study) is the one detective who did not change his style of interviewing.

How does the Cognitive Interview compare with other attempts to enhance memory, specifically hypnosis? An overview of the scientific literature shows hypnosis to be unpredictable. Some researchers show that hypnosis enhances memory, whereas others find no effect (see Smith, 1983; Orne, Soskis, Dinges, & Orne, 1984, for reviews). On the negative side, a major reservation about using hypnosis in forensic investigations is that *E/Ws* become highly suggestible to leading or misleading questions (Putnam, 1979). By comparison, the Cognitive Interview is relatively immune to the effects of leading questions (Geiselman, Fisher, Cohen, Holland, & Surtes, 1986). Furthermore, while hypnosis requires a lengthy training period and also significantly lengthens the interview session, the Cognitive Interview can be learned within a few hours, and lengthens the effective interview time by only a few minutes. Overall, then, the Cognitive Interview is more reliable as a memory enhancer than is hypnosis, it induces less distortion, and it is more easily learned and implemented.

The only other technique we are aware of that has been tested scientifically is Conversation Management, a procedure used in some British police departments. As described by George (1991), Conversation Management "seeks to equip interviewers in the social and communication skills required to open, and keep open channels of communication in order to find out facts." (p. 4). In a formal test of Conversation Management, George (1991) found that it enhanced recall of witnesses and victims of crime, but only slightly and considerably less so than did the Cognitive Interview. Furthermore, more time was required to train investigators in Conversation Management (five days) than in the Cognitive Interview (two days) (see Appendix B for more details of the research). In defense of Conversation Management, its primary focus is on interrogating suspects, not on interviewing cooperative witnesses.

Although the Cognitive Interview is an effective investigative instrument, its utility will vary from one situation to another. Its primary contribution will be in cases like commercial robbery or battery, where the bulk of the evidence comes from *E/W* reports, as opposed to crimes where there is an abundance of physical evidence. Second, the Cognitive Interview was designed to be used with cooperative *E/Ws*. Witnesses who intentionally wish to withhold information will not be "broken" by the Cognitive Interview. Third, the Cognitive Interview may take some-what longer to conduct than the standard police interview.[4] Thus, it can be used to greatest effect when there is ample time to conduct the interview. Finally, the Cognitive Interview requires considerable mental concentration on the part of the *INT*. He must make more on-line decisions and show greater flexibility than is typically demonstrated in police interviews. In that sense, it is more difficult to conduct the Cognitive Interview than the standard interview. With practice, however, most of the mental concentration required initially will be handled auto-matically (see Chapter 13 for an effective training program to learn the Cognitive Interview).

One striking, although not unexpected, finding in our research is that some *INTs* consistently elicited more information than others. While some of the differences between good and poor *INTs* no doubt reflect personality traits that cannot be altered readily, the real concern is whether other important interviewing skills can be learned. Our research demonstrates that most *INTs* can learn new techniques and increase their effectiveness. The goal of this book is to describe these successful techniques so that all *INTs* can elicit more *E/W* information.

Because this book is geared primarily to the practicing investigator, it is written in a how-to-do-it style, with emphasis on practical techniques rather than on theories of cognition. However, we also feel that readers should understand the scientific principles on which the suggested tech-niques are based. We therefore describe the background scientific reason-ing and provide the literature references for readers who wish to explore the theories in more depth. In order to maintain the practical orientation, however, we have presented the underlying theories and laboratory findings as extensive footnotes. Those who wish to understand why the technique works are encouraged to read the footnotes carefully. We especially recommend that attorneys read the footnotes, as we discuss there several legal practices that either violate well-established prin-ciples of cognitive psychology or are incompatible with recent experi-mental findings.

The following is a brief summary of the topics covered in each chapter. In The Complexity of Eyewitness Memory (Chapter 2), we provide an

---

4. In the two field studies conducted thus far, the Cognitive Interview did ***not*** take any longer than did standard, police interviews (Fisher, Geiselman, & Amador, 1989; George, 1991). The Cognitive Interview did take somewhat longer in some of the laboratory studies, however, the additional time was not the cause of its superiority (see Fisher & McCauley, in press).

analysis of memory and forgetting, specifically how it applies to eyewitness recall. We examine the *INT's* role in facilitating memory, and conclude with an overview of the Cognitive Interview. The Dynamics of Interviewing (Chapter 3) focuses on the interactive nature of interviewing. We look at some of the differences between the *INT's* and the *E/W's* expectations of the investigation, how to bridge some of these differences, and, in general, how each member of the interview team affects the other. Overcoming Eyewitness Limitations (Chapter 4) describes some of the major factors that limit eyewitness recall (anxiety, confidence, and communication skill) and indicates several techniques that can be used to overcome these limitations.

The next two chapters examine some of the more practical aspects of interviewing. Logistics of Interviewing (Chapter 5) addresses the questions of where and when to conduct interviews, and explores issues that arise from conducting multiple interviews with the same *E/W*. Mechanics of Interviewing (Chapter 6) deals with the nuts and bolts of interviewing, how to word questions, and the advantages and disadvantages of different question formats (e.g., open-ended vs. direct, closed questions).

Principles of Cognition (Chapter 7) examines the fundamental principles of cognition: how knowledge is represented in the *E/W's* mind, and how it is retrieved from memory. The following, companion chapter, Practical Techniques to Facilitate Memory (Chapter 8) converts these principles of cognition into practical interviewing techniques that can be used to increase the amount of information recalled. In the next chapter, Witness-compatible Questioning (Chapter 9), we develop a cardinal, but often-violated, rule of effective interviewing. Because all of the relevant information resides in the *E/W's* mind, she, not the *INT,* should play the central role in the interview. The *INT* simply assists her to recall the information. Assisting the *E/W* to recall the information, however, depends on how it is stored in her mind. Probing Image and Concept Memory Codes (Chapter 10) describes techniques to elicit this information, whether it is stored in the form of a mental image or an abstract idea. Having presented all of the individual components of the technique, we turn to the Sequence of the Cognitive Interview (Chapter 11), which develops a systematic, sequential structure of the entire interview and indicates the different approaches and techniques to be used at the beginning, middle, and end of the interview. This chapter integrates the information from the preceding chapters and, in a sense, puts it all together in one package.

The remaining chapters are intended primarily to sharpen the skills previously learned and to assist in applying the Cognitive Interview in an actual case. Sample Interviews with Analysis (Chapter 12) provides excerpts of two interviews, along with our comments to highlight good and poor interviewing techniques. In the final chapter, Training Program to Learn Cognitive Interviewing (Chapter 13), we describe an effective procedure to learn the Cognitive Interview. This chapter reflects our experiences in conducting training workshops with various police departments and other investigative agencies and is directed both to investigators who wish to teach themselves and to trainers who will teach others. A Reference Guide to Conducting the Cognitive Interview (Appendix A) is provided for investigators to use as a handy reference. Investigators may find this guide particularly helpful as a last-minute review before conducting an interview. Finally, a Summary of Research (Appendix B) is presented to document our claims about the technique. The studies described were conducted in the United States, Germany, and England by research psychologists and police detectives trained in scientific research.

Chapter 2

THE COMPLEXITY OF EYEWITNESS MEMORY

The Beverly-Chase has just had its vault lightened by $1,500,000 worth of valuables. Within 20 minutes, a miniature army of uniformed police officers and detectives has imposed some control over the crowd and its work begins. No physical evidence of the robbery exists other than the impressions of eight bewildered eyewitnesses: a half-alert security guard; a teller who directly confronted one of the criminals, and another teller who viewed the criminals only out of the corner of her eye; a white-haired grandfatherly depositor and his 5-year old companion; a bewildered tourist; and a curious passer-by. What a motley crew of observers! But that's all there is to work with. No fingerprints, no shreds of clothing, no tire-marks . . . nothing, other than eight frightened eyewitnesses.

The key to solving the Beverly-Chase robbery will, like most others, depend on extracting as much objective information as possible from the eight available *E/Ws* and then piecing together the crime. In this case, there will be no assistance from the crime lab. In other cases, even where physical evidence exists, the success of the investigation still balances on the quality and extent of *E/W* accounts.

The importance of *E/W* evidence in the criminal investigation process cannot be underestimated. It maintains a central position from the initial stages of the process, when attempting to apprehend the criminal, to the concluding courtroom setting, where the *E/W's* memory often becomes the focus of the litigative drama. In a comprehensive study of criminal-investigation processes, the Rand Corporation (1975) reported that the principal determinant of whether or not a case is solved is the completeness and accuracy of the *E/W's* account. This official document mirrors the feelings unofficially held by many law enforcement agents (Sanders, 1986). On the other side of the coin, defense attorneys have made comparable claims (e.g., Visher, 1987) about the importance of *E/W* testimony. The more *E/W* evidence an attorney can marshal to support a client, the more potent is the defense. In short, all concerned profit from having more complete and stronger *E/W* evidence. The criminal is more effectively pursued and tried, and the innocent person is less likely to be arrested and convicted falsely.

Because the potential for *E/W* evidence to determine the outcome of a criminal case is so great, it is critical that the information be extensive and accurate. In the ideal world, *E/W* reports would be detailed, accurate and complete, so that police could easily apprehend criminals without interfering with the lives of innocent people, and jurors could easily decide to convict the guilty and acquit the innocent. Unfortunately, there is a wide gap between the complete reports of ideal *E/Ws* and the fragmented, sometimes inaccurate reports of real *E/Ws*. Anyone who has ever listened to an *E/W* account of a crime realizes quickly that what seemed like an unforgettable experience has faded from consciousness, not unlike other life experiences. Gaps in memory abound, sometimes left simply as a void, at other times filled in with reasonable guesses. Worst of all, memories are sometimes distorted, so that, although they appear sharp and convincing, in fact, they are incorrect. Alas, real-world *E/Ws* are a far cry from the ideal. Their testimony is known to be partially inaccurate, incomplete, and unreliable (Loftus, 1979, although see Appendix B, Footnote 2).

Several legal approaches have been adopted in response to the problem of *E/W* memory. One "solution," often subtly introduced by the prosecution, is simply to deny the problem. Because the event in question was so meaningful and unique, they claim, it must have been etched permanently into the *E/W's* mind with the resulting recollection perfect. An alternative and equally misused approach—this time by defense counsel—is to flaunt the problem. The fallibility of *E/W* recollection is recognized and often highlighted, leading to the conclusion that almost all resulting testimony is baseless. A more promising, but seldom pursued, approach is to recognize the limitation of *E/W* recollection, and more important, take action to improve it.

There are two approaches to improving *E/W* recollection of a criminal event. One possibility is to train the general public to become more careful observers of their environment. While such an approach is theoretically possible, it requires such a massive expenditure of personnel and financial resources as to be impractical. In addition, recent studies have shown that crucial aspects of *E/W* behavior (e.g., face recognition) cannot be trained effectively (Ellis, 1984). Even if the appropriate skills could be trained, it is unlikely that they would be used during the trauma of a crime. Our goal, then, was to improve *E/W* recollection by developing a technique that is (a) affordable, (b) trainable, and (c) conducted at a time when *E/Ws* are calm enough to control their mental activities.

MEMORY AND FORGETTING

In order to understand the mechanics of the Cognitive Interview, it is first necessary to appreciate how memory works and what causes forgetting. Most psychologists divide memory into three phases: encoding, storage, and retrieval (Melton, 1963). In the encoding phase an event is perceived and represented in the *E/W's* mind. Following this initial registration phase the mental record of the event is kept in storage for later use. At the retrieval phase the stored, mental record is activated, bringing about the conscious phenomenon of recollection.

In some ways, we can think of memory as being similar to a mechanical filing system, where a file is initially created (encoded), it is maintained for later use (storage), and finally, it is retrieved from the system (retrieval). It should come as no surprise that the simple filing system is not nearly as complex and dynamic as is human memory. The mental record of an event is not an exact replica of the event, as sometimes thought. Rather, it reflects an intricate web of interactions between the event, the surrounding context, the observer's mood and thoughts at the time, general knowledge of related experiences, and a host of other forces. For example, the mental record of a bank robbery may reflect the *E/W's* sense of fear, her physiological state, whether she recently saw a movie of a bank robbery, her thoughts of being detained for an important meeting, etc.

After the crime has been encoded, the stored mental record may be altered as it comes into contact with other stored information. Stereotypes of how a typical bank robbery occurs, conversations with other *E/Ws,* and simply thinking about the robbery or suppressing it from conscious recollection may change the mental record. The last phase of memory, retrieving the mental record, may well be the most difficult part of the task. The human mind is capable of storing billions of facts (Landauer, 1986). The sheer magnitude of the task, searching through an inventory of billions of detailed, oftentimes similar, events is overwhelming.

Although there is extensive scientific knowledge about the encoding and storage phases of memory, most of this knowledge cannot be applied to improve the *E/W's* recollection of the typical crime. There is little warning that a crime is about to take place, so that *E/Ws* are not prepared to select an effective encoding strategy when the crime does occur. During the storage phase most of the forces acting on the mental record are at a subconscious level, so again, little can be done to alter the process. The retrieval phase, on the other hand, is largely under conscious control (Klatzky, 1980). It is the phase in which the *E/W* is most likely to think about the crime scene intentionally. Thus, despite the apparent difficulty of retrieving the details of a traumatic event, it is the phase of memory that is most easily altered and improved. Not surprisingly, the Cognitive Interview seeks to improve *E/W* recollection by enhancing the retrieval phase of memory.

A popular misconception about memory is that recollection depends entirely on whether or not a learned event is "in the memory store." Many people believe that information is either "in the memory store," in which case it will be recalled correctly, or it is "not in the memory store," in which case it will not be recalled. While it is certainly true that some things are learned better than others—and are thus more likely to be recalled—many people overlook the possibility that forgetting may occur even though the information is in the memory system. In terms of our filing system analogy, we may fail to pull out a file even though it is in the system. An obvious explanation is that we are looking in the wrong part of the filing system. We have all had occasions in which we have forgotten someone's name, only to remember it later. We did not recall the name initially because we did not search for it properly, not because it was "not in the memory store."[1] It may be that all events are stored somewhere in memory and that all forgetting is caused by inappropriate retrieval. Although such a claim is obviously speculative, we do know for certain that at least some acts of forgetting are caused by inappropriate retrieval. This fact is critical for investigative interviewers because, through their interviewing procedures, they indirectly control the *E/W's* retrieval plan, and the more efficiently they guide the *E/W* to search through memory the more information they will uncover.

---

1. Several laboratory experiments have also reported this phenomenon of retrieval-based forgetting. In a classic series of experiments, Tulving and his colleagues (Tulving, 1974; Tulving & Thomson, 1973) showed that previously forgotten information can be recalled when a different retrieval cue is provided. (A retrieval cue is a hint about the to-be-recalled information, e.g., "The last name begins with the letter *L*.") In the most extreme case, events that were not recognized initially could later be recalled correctly when an appropriate retrieval cue was provided. For example, an *E/W* might not recognize which license plate she had seen when shown a list of several license plates, but she might be able to recall the license plate at another time, when she is shown a picture of the get-away car.

THE COGNITIVE INTERVIEW

The Cognitive Interview focuses on two major components of *E/W* testimony: memory and communication. The *E/W* must first draw into consciousness all of the details of the crime event; then she must communicate the information to the investigator. Only if both of these processes function properly will a successful interview take place.

The core memory principle of the Cognitive Interview is the notion of guided retrieval. Because all of the relevant information resides in the *E/W's* mind, the goal of the interview is to assist her to access that information. It is critical to note that it is the *E/W*, not the *INT*, who will or will not access the desired information. As a result the interview must be directed by the mental operations of the *E/W*. All too often the investigator becomes the central character in the interview and the *E/W* plays only a secondary role (Fisher, Geiselman, & Raymond, 1987). The successful *INT*, by contrast, is one who can infer how the *E/W* has stored the relevant knowledge and then gently guide her search through memory to retrieve that knowledge. The Cognitive Interview enhances memory by (a) assisting the *INT* to infer the *E/W's* mental representation of the event, (b) suggesting techniques to ensure that the *E/W* becomes the central personality of the interview, and (c) providing retrieval strategies to facilitate the *E/W's* accessing specific memories.

Although the information is stored in the *E/W's* mind, simply activating that knowledge does not necessarily guarantee a successful interview. The second hurdle is to communicate the information effectively to the *INT*. If we think of the witness-interviewer interaction as a simple communication system we can isolate two problem sources: the *E/W's* converting the conscious memory into a verbal description, and the *INT's* comprehending and recording the *E/W's* description. Furthermore, since this is a communication system, and not simply two isolated people, each communicator must be aware of the other's needs and abilities. The productive *E/W* must be able to generate a complete description of her conscious memory, and also must present the description in a form that is comprehensible and meaningful to the *INT*. Similarly, the *INT* must become an efficient listener and be aware of the *E/W's* psychological needs and abilities. The Cognitive Interview enhances communication by (a) helping the *E/W* to formulate a complete, intelligible response, (b) helping the *INT* to comprehend and record the *E/W's* response, and most important, (c) helping the *INT* to understand the *E/W's* psychological needs and, conversely, to convey his investigative needs to her.

The Cognitive Interview is not intended as a recipe. One cannot simply memorize a set of predetermined questions and expect to conduct an effective interview. As will be mentioned repeatedly in this book, interviews should be highly interactive and spontaneous. To be an effective *INT,* just like being a good navigator, one must be flexible enough to use good judgment and change directions as unexpected conditions arise. We offer the Cognitive Interview as a general guiding principle, but always to be used in concert with sound judgment and the flexibility to respond to the unanticipated.

Chapter 3

DYNAMICS OF THE INTERVIEW

Let us begin our examination of the interview by stating the obvious. At the outset, all of the relevant information is stored in the *E/W's* mind and the *INT's* goal is to elicit as much of this knowledge as possible. At a simplistic level, the problem sounds very much like reading a book. All one needs to do is understand the code in which the book is written and then read through the entire text. Unfortunately, this simple analogy breaks down when describing an interview with a human being. Whereas a book is passive, an *E/W* is active and her relationship with the *INT* is dynamic. The *E/W* participates and alters the course of the interview. Most important for our concern, both the *E/W* and the *INT* alter each other's behavior. How the *INT* conducts himself will affect the *E/W's* ability and willingness to share information. Perhaps a more appropriate analogy is that the *E/W* and the *INT* form a working—or nonworking—relationship during the interview and they construct a final product as a team effort.

Some of the topics we shall examine in this chapter are: (a) encouraging the *E/W's* active participation in the interview, (b) developing rapport with the *E/W,* (c) understanding the differences between the *E/W's* and the *INT's* needs and expectations, (d) altering the *E/W's* behavior, and (e) promoting positive community-police relations.

ENCOURAGING THE EYEWITNESS'S
ACTIVE PARTICIPATION

In the typical investigative interview, especially if it takes place shortly after the crime has been committed, the *E/W* will regard the investigator as the person who should control the interview. In most cases the *E/W* has recently been victimized or she has played a passive role as an observer to the crime. As a result, her self-confidence is probably low. The investigator, on the other hand, is perceived as an authority figure who represents a powerful institution—the police. The police investigator can solve the crime, or so it may appear to the *E/W*. In some ways, the situation is similar to the medical patient who expects the physician to take charge, ask the appropriate questions and solve her health problem. The dynamics of the situation dictate that, at the outset of the interview, the investigator is in control and the *E/W* is in a secondary role. Because of these expectations, the investigating officer cannot present himself as being overly meek when he first meets the *E/W*. He must take charge initially and actively direct the interview.

For several reasons, the investigator is more likely to guide the interview successfully than is the *E/W*. Most important, he should be much calmer than the potentially traumatized *E/W*. This will be especially so when the *E/W* is a victim, as opposed to a bystander, and even more so if she has been personally violated, as in cases of sexual battery. Because the *INT* is in greater control of his emotions, he should be more flexible and open to exploring unexpected leads that arise during the interview. The *INT* also has greater experience and knowledge of criminal behavior. He is therefore in a better position to judge which aspects of the crime are relevant and deserve more in-depth probing. The average citizen has relatively little knowledge about crime and cannot discriminate well between important and unimportant information. Similarly, because the *INT's* profession is to investigate crime, he can be pre-trained to conduct effective interviews. By comparison, *E/Ws* are not professional witnesses so they are untrained about effective interviewee behavior. As a result of the *INT's* perceived role, his greater self-control and professional expertise, he has the potential to lead a more effective interview than the *E/W*.

There is only one factor suggesting that the *E/W* is better qualified to lead the interview, and that is that *she has all of the relevant information.* Since the *E/W's* information is the target of the investigation, she should be doing most of the mental work during the interview, not the *INT*.[1] For the *E/W* to do most of the mental work, however, she must feel that she is a vital and essential part of the interview. If she perceives the investigator as being the leader and solely in control, she will become passive and expect him to do most of the work. She will wait for him to ask questions instead of her volunteering information. When the *E/W*

---

1. This does not imply that the *INT* can relax and allow the *E/W* to control the interview, talking about whatever she wishes. The *INT* has many decisions to make during the interview, as will be evident throughout this book, and must guide the *E/W's* narration so it does not stray from the target. Ultimately, however, the burden of providing the information should rest on the *E/W*.

plays such a passive role, less information will be collected.[2] *THE KEY TO EFFECTIVE INTERVIEWING IS TO CONVEY TO THE E/W THAT SHE PLAYS A CENTRAL ROLE IN THE INTERVIEW AND THAT SHE MUST TAKE AN ACTIVE PART IN GENERATING INFORMATION.*

On the surface, it may appear as if the *INT* is giving up control of the interview by encouraging the *E/W* to do most of the talking. In fact, the *INT* always retains control. He can terminate the interview or shift the topic of discussion as he chooses. Nevertheless, to maximize the amount of information generated, the *INT* should lead the *E/W* to *believe* that she is directing the flow of information.

A few specific techniques can be used to induce the *E/W* to play a more active role in the interview and encourage her to speak more freely. The most direct method is for the *INT* to *tell the* E/W *explicitly that she has all of the relevant information and therefore, he expects her to do most of the talking.* The *INT* can use the following as a guide:

> Mary, you're the only person who saw the crime. I didn't see it, so I'm depending on you to tell me what happened. Don't wait for me to ask you lots of questions. I'm expecting you to do most of the talking here. Now, try to tell me everything you can about what happened earlier today.

Compare this approach to the one used in the following excerpt, transcribed word for word from an actual interview with a robbery victim.

INT: Can you give me a description of the subject?
E/W: He was a Latin boy, more or less 23 to 25 years old.
INT: How tall was he?
E/W: Let's say 5-foot 3 . . . And with a blue overcoat.
INT: Let me ask the questions and you give me the answers.

Not surprisingly, following the *INT's* last statement, the *E/W* did not volunteer any more information than was absolutely necessary during the remainder of the interview.

---

2. Even though *INTs* often believe that they must ask many questions to elicit extensive, detailed information, in fact, the most effective interviewers are those who ask the fewest questions and encourage the *E/Ws* to do most of the talking. In a laboratory test of the Cognitive Interview (Geiselman, Fisher, MacKinnon, & Holland, 1985), we counted the number of questions asked by those *INTs* conducting the Cognitive Interview and those conducting a standard police interview. On the average, the Cognitive Interviewers asked fewer questions than did the standard interviewers (54.9 vs. 68.9, respectively). Nevertheless, the Cognitive Interviewers elicited considerably more information than did the standard interviewers (41.15 vs. 29.40 correct facts, respectively). A similar, but even more dramatic, pattern of results (fewer questions elicits more information) was found with British police (George, 1991).

In addition to a direct statement, *INTs* can encourage *E/Ws* to participate actively in the interview by phrasing questions properly. In general,
open-ended questions, (e.g., "Can you describe his face?") are much
more likely to encourage the *E/W's* active participation than closed,
short-answer questions (What color were his eyes? Did he have any scars?
How long was his hair? . . .). Open-ended questions, almost by definition,
encourage the *E/W* to provide a lengthy response, whereas closed questions encourage responding in one word or a short phrase. When giving
a lengthy answer requested by the open-ended question, the *E/W* adopts
the role of being an active participant. By contrast, after responding with
the one word or phrase to the closed question, the *E/W* waits passively
for the *INT* to ask the next question (See "Closed vs. Open-ended
Questions" in Chapter 6 for a more in-depth analysis). The moral of the
story: *Ask primarily open-ended questions.*

Notice in the following excerpt that, as a result of the *INT* asking
closed questions, the *E/W* appears to be passive, and volunteers only the
minimal amount of information.

> *INT:*   About how much taller was he than you?
> *E/W:*   He was a tiny bit taller than me.
> *INT:*   Was he very thin? Was he heavy?
> *E/W:*   He was about medium.
> *INT:*   Was he white or black?
> *E/W:*   Black.
> *INT:*   Did he have long hair or short hair?
> *E/W:*   Short hair.
> *INT:*   Was it very short, like close to the scalp?
> *E/W:*   Yeah.

A second interviewing error, *interrupting the* E/W *in the middle of a
response, also discourages the* E/W *from taking an active role in the
interview. This error is probably the most common and the most severe
error* INTs *make,* because it establishes the *INT,* not the *E/W,* as the
focus of the interview. By contrast, allowing the *E/W* to complete her
response, and then pausing before asking the next question to allow the
E/W to embellish her response, helps to place the *E/W* in the central
role.

In our analysis of tape recorded interviews (Fisher, Geiselman, &
Raymond, 1987), the most effective *INTs* asked many open-ended
questions, interrupted infrequently, and in general, permitted the *E/W*

to do most of the talking. Unfortunately, this approach was not used by most police investigators. In the typical interview *INTs* asked 26 closed questions and only 3 open-ended questions. This phenomenon, which was observed with American police, is also characteristic of British police (George, 1991.) To compound the error, police interrupt repeatedly. Following their initial request for a description of the crime, on the average, police *INTs* interrupted within 7.5 seconds after *E/Ws* began their narration. Because the tendency to make these errors is so great, *INTs* should pay particular attention to asking more open-ended questions and to avoiding interruptions.

The following excerpted interview of an *E/W* to a shooting exemplifies this problem. In this interview, the first interruption occurred within approximately 4.5 seconds after the *E/W* began her open-ended narration. The next two interruptions were impossible to measure with an ordinary stop-watch because it took longer to start and stop the watch than it took the *INT* to interrupt.

INT: Can you tell me in you own words, in a story fashion, what happened to you and your boyfriend about 45 minutes ago?

E/W: We were sitting in the car. I was laying in his lap.

INT: (interrupts) Approximately what time was it? Do you know?

E/W: It was twelve-something. I really don't remember the time.

INT: OK.

E/W: Um

INT: (interrupts) Your car was parked where we find it right now, on the north-east corner of the park there?

E/W: Yes.

INT: OK.

E/W: Uh

INT: (interrupts) You were in the front seat . . .

DEVELOPING RAPPORT

One obstacle inherent in police interviews, especially with victims who have been physically or psychologically violated, is that much of the requested information is highly personal. It is the type of information that people are often reluctant to disclose except to close friends. Before trying to elicit such personal statements the police investigator needs to develop within the *E/W* a sense of trust and rapport (see also Prior &

Silberstein, 1969; Wicks, 1974). In that regard, the investigator's task is similar to that of the clinical psychologist, who must initially develop a personal bond with his or her client before any intimate feelings are exposed. One important difference is that the police investigator usually has only one or two opportunities to interview the *E/W,* whereas the clinician can plan the therapy over the course of many sessions spanning weeks or months. Unfortunately, the police investigator does not have the luxury to use the same type of sophisticated, time-consuming techniques as does the psychotherapist. Instead, he must rely on those that are easily implemented. Equally important, he must avoid making those errors that alienate the *E/W* early in the interview. In line with these goals, we suggest two guiding principles to help develop rapport: personalizing the interview, and developing and communicating empathy.

Personalizing the Interview

One of the hurdles to overcome is the tendency for the police investigation to become depersonalized. Frequently, both the *INT* and the *E/W* respond to each other as if they were playing expected roles. From the *E/W's* perspective, the investigator is just a representative of the police force doing his job. For the investigator, this may be just another typical home invasion and the victim is just one of the many he sees over the course of a year. Whenever people start to respond to each other as stereotypes and not as individuals, they erect barriers to effective communication. One key ingredient in any successful interview is for the *INT* to personalize the interview as much as possible. *The* INT *must treat the* E/W *as an individual with a unique set of needs. He must also present himself as a genuine, identifiable person, and not simply as a representative of an official organization.*

The most direct way to personalize the interview is to *refer to the* E/W *by name as much as possible.* Children and young adults should be referred to by their first names; older adults may be referred to either by first or last name, whichever seems appropriate. If in doubt, the *INT* should use whichever name the *E/W* used when introducing herself, or simply ask how she would like to be called.

Personalizing the interview requires that the *INT* develop active listening skills, forcing himself to listen attentively to the *E/W's* message. One helpful technique is periodically to *repeat the last idea the* E/W *mentioned and follow it up with a relevant comment or question.* For example, if the *E/W* reports that she was "scared when she first saw the killer pull out the gun," then the *INT* might follow up by saying: "You said that you were scared when you first saw the killer pull out the gun. That is a scary event. What can you remember about that scene?" Repeating the *E/W's* words conveys to her that the *INT* has been attentive to her story.

Since active listening requires a considerable amount of concentration, *the* INT *should take care of all incidental matters before the interview has begun* so he can listen with undivided attention. If the *INT's* mind is distracted with another task while listening to the *E/W,* he will not be able to listen effectively.

While preparing for the interview, either in reading the police report or in speaking to the investigator who interviewed the *E/W* earlier, the *INT* will become familiar with some details of the case. This information may provide some clues for the *INT,* however, it may also prevent him from listening actively to the *E/W's* entire report. The INT *should try to avoid being overly biased by these pre-interview expectations so he can listen more actively to the* E/W (see also Stone & DeLuca, 1980).

Because the task of interviewing is done repeatedly, *INTs* tend to develop pet expressions that they use repeatedly. For example, one of the *INTs* we studied used the following expression in several interviews: "Is there anything else you can tell me that might further assist me in this investigation?" This is obviously a memorized line and is easily detected by the *E/W.* Such *memorized, stylistic speech depersonalizes the interview and should be avoided.*

To encourage the *E/W* to respond to the *INT* as a unique individual and not simply as a police investigator, he will have to present himself as such. In the initial conversation he strikes up with the *E/W,* the *INT* can *inject some personal, biographical information about himself that the* E/W *can relate to* (Chelune, 1979). For example, if he knows from the preliminary investigation or from a picture on the wall that the *E/W* has children, the *INT* can indicate that he has children about the same age.

At some time during the interview, investigators generally collect background, biographical information for official police records. Because that is such an impersonal activity, and the *INT* seems more like an official census-taker than a unique, concerned individual, he should try to separate himself from that official role. *While conducting this official part of the interview, the* INT *can appear to dismiss it as a "police requirement,"* as if he had little to do with it. The *INT* might say:

I need to ask you some questions about background information, first. This is a standard police procedure and we have to do this in all of our cases.

Developing and Communicating Empathy

Whether or not the *E/W* relates highly personal events to the *INT* partially depends on whether she believes that he understands her plight. The classic example is the teen-age child who responds in one- or two-word answers to questions posed by her parents, because "they don't understand." Yet this same teenager can talk at length to her friends. The information is there. Extracting it means conveying to the *E/W* that the *INT* can identify with her feelings and can understand the problem from her perspective.[3] There are no simple techniques for developing empathic skills. It is more of a general attitude of trying to see the event from the *E/W's* perspective, as if the *INT* were "standing in her shoes." This can be particularly difficult in many police investigations, because crime is a routine event for the investigator, but it may be a once-in-a-lifetime experience for the *E/W*. Nevertheless, *to engage the* E/W's *trust, the* INT *must view the event from her perspective.* Investigators may find it helpful to take a minute or two before the interview simply to think about what the victim has gone through and to imagine himself in her position.

Empathizing with the *E/W's* plight is only half of the task. For the *E/W* to reveal her story, she must be made aware that the *INT* understands her feelings. The second step in the process, then, is for the *INT* to communicate his empathy to the *E/W*. *He must provide some type of feedback to indicate his understanding. The most straightforward way to do this is, periodically, to make comments like, "I can understand your feelings [of fear, of injustice, of helplessness . . .] about the attack."*

For some investigators statements of concern will be natural, whereas for others this approach will seem awkward. Once the *INT* gets into the habit of injecting these comments regularly into his interviewing style, it will seem as automatic and as natural as any other appropriate comment.

In addition to personalizing the interview and developing and com-

---

3. The ability to empathize is so essential that it is viewed as a necessary ingredient for all successful psychotherapists, whether one practices behavior modification, psychoanalysis, or humanistic therapies (Rogers, 1942).

municating empathy we suggest the following simple techniques to establish a sense of trust. The general theme of these recommendations is to *convey the feeling of personal closeness, that the* INT *is concerned about the* E/W's *welfare, and that he is interested in her message* (see also, Wicks, 1974).

At the outset of the interview, the *INT* should try to *establish some minimal physical contact,* e.g., a handshake, with the *E/W* (Alagna, Whitcher, Fisher, & Wicas, 1979). He should be careful though, especially if he and the *E/W* are of opposite sexes, that the contact is not seen as overly familiar.

If there is any type of visible injury, the *INT* should *examine the injury, even if only superficially, and inquire about any discomfort.* He might ask whether the *E/W* has gone to a physician to examine the injury and if anything has been done to make her feel more comfortable. Even if he already knows about the status of the injury, perhaps from the hospital report, he should inquire just as a show of concern. Similarly, if he knows beforehand about an injury that is not immediately visible he should inquire about it.

Compare the following two interviews in terms of the rapport—or sense of alienation—between the *E/W* and the *INT* in the first few moments of the interview. Not surprisingly, the first *INT,* who simply showed human concern for the *E/W,* elicited considerably more information later in his interview than did the second *INT,* who sounded as uncaring as possible.

Interview # 1: *E/W-INT* Rapport Properly Developed

INT: How are you feeling today? Are you feeling a little better?
E/W: Yeah.
INT: Did you soak your knees?
E/W: Yeah, and I took a hot bath last night.
INT: OK, did you cancel your credit cards and everything?
E/W: Yes
INT: You haven't heard from anybody who might have found your property?
E/W: No.
INT: All right, what I want you to do is just relax . . .

Interview # 2: *E/W* Alienated by Uncaring *INT*

INT: OK, your name is . . . ?
E/W: Louisa Turner.
INT: Louisa Turner. And you live at 134 Lincoln Road?
E/W: Yes.
INT: How long have you lived there?
E/W: About a year and a half.
INT: OK, who do you live with?
E/W: My daughter.
INT: Now, the person who got shot last night was . . .

The fact-finding portion of most interviews is often begun with an open-ended question, to establish the general framework of the incident (see Chapter 11). *If the* INT *has had any experiences similar to those described, he should convey them to the* E/W. The following can serve as a guideline: "I know what you're feeling now, because I was once burglarized myself." This statement should be relatively brief. Otherwise it runs the risk of making the *INT* the focus of the interview.

Unless there are particularly strong reasons to suspect the credibility of the E/W's *story, it should be treated as a truthful statement.* If the *E/W* is not innocent, but is truly involved in the crime, that will be uncovered eventually during the investigation and there will be ample time to re-interview her. If an innocent *E/W* is treated with suspicion, her cooperation may be compromised for the entire investigation. For related reasons, *the* INT *should avoid making judgmental comments and asking confrontational questions,* unless he is certain there is some deception (see also Prior & Silberstein, 1969; Wicks, 1974). Similarly, if conflicting stories arise, the *INT* should not challenge the stories immediately, since that may inhibit the *E/W* from speaking freely later in the interview. To the contrary, the *INT* wants to encourage the *E/W* to say everything that might be relevant and not edit anything from her report (see "Overcoming Eyewitnesses' Suppressing Information" in Chapter 4). *If a contradiction arises, or there is some inconsistency between the statements of two* E/Ws, *the conflict should be dealt with later in the interview, after the* INT *has extracted most of the* E/W's *statement.*

The *INT's* interest in the *E/W's* statement is conveyed by the quality of his questions and also by his non-verbal behavior. *Eye contact should be maintained, especially in the early phase of the interview, when trying to develop rapport* (although see "Focused Concentration" in Chapter 4 for eye contact as a source of distraction later in the interview). If appropriate, the *INT* should try to *sit during the interview facing the* E/W, *perhaps with a slight forward lean, to indicate his interest.*

INTERVIEWER'S vs. EYEWITNESS'S EXPECTATIONS AND GOALS

In the ideal interview, the *INT* and the *E/W* have the same expectations and goals, and they coordinate their efforts toward one common solution. In reality, however, the *INT* and the *E/W* probably have different concerns. The *INT's* primary goal is to elicit a detailed description of the crime and specifically of the assailant. His concern is mainly to gather information that will help close the case. By comparison, most *E/Ws'* immediate concerns, especially if they are victims, are not relevant for the investigation. Generally they need to vent their outrage or their fear. They have just experienced a terrifying act, and may have been physically violated in the process. Often, they feel a strong sense of injustice—"That guy had no right to take my money. I work hard for it and earned it. He just took it." Their focus is that the world is unfair, and that decent behavior is not rewarded. Others blame themselves for the crime having been committed; either they should not have put themselves into such a vulnerable position, or they did not resist strongly enough. Whether or not their concern is defensible—usually not—their focus is on their actions and not on the assailant's. In either case, *E/Ws* often focus on some aspect of the crime that is immaterial for the investigation.

Since the view adopted here is that the *E/W* and the *INT* are working as a team, with a common goal, what can be done to merge the two players' expectations and focus? Clearly, each side must become more aware of the other's perspective. The *INT* must become sensitive to the needs of the *E/W* who, in turn, must become redirected toward the needs of the investigator. Although we conceptualize the task as a team effort, where each of the players adopts a common goal, the burden of merging the actions of the two players will probably fall only on the *INT*. He subtly controls the flow of the interview and he is likely to be the only participant who is calm enough to see the overall picture. Thus, although it would be desirable if each member of the interview team was concerned about the common goal, in reality, the *E/W* will probably be concerned only with her individual needs, leaving the investigator to play the dual role of both interviewer and mediator. He must understand the *E/W's* concerns and also convey his own investigative needs to the *E/W*.

UNDERSTANDING THE EYEWITNESS'S CONCERNS

Before the *INT* can induce the *E/W* to describe the event in adequate detail, he must first give the *E/W* an opportunity to express her concerns. The *E/W's* fears and sense of injustice and inadequacy may hold no investigative insights for the *INT*. Nevertheless, if these emotions are not expressed, they may block the path toward a successful investigation. Therefore, the *INT* should *encourage the* E/W *to express these emotions at the beginning of the interview.* After the *E/W* has "let go" of these emotions, the *INT* can use them as lead-ins to develop his investigative needs. Suppose the *E/W* has been focusing on the injustice of the crime. The *INT* can use those feelings about injustice to develop his approach. He might suggest: "That's what the police are here for, to ensure that people who commit crimes are brought to justice." Similarly, if the *E/W* is concerned about the loss of her property, the *INT* can suggest that her property may be recoverable, depending on the success of the investigation. In general, the investigator's role is to make a convincing claim that he empathizes with and is working toward the *E/W's* stated goals.

Once the *E/W* is aware that she and the investigator are working toward a common goal, the *INT* can inform the *E/W* about the kind of information he needs in order to conduct the investigation successfully. For example, the *INT* can tell the *E/W* directly that, in order to apprehend the assailant, he needs a detailed description of the assailant and the get-away vehicle. The more finely the *E/W* can describe the assailant the more likely the police are to apprehend him. Again, the general idea is to *convince the* E/W *that she and the* INT *share the same concerns, and that in order to meet her stated needs, it is vital for her to provide the kind of information the* INT *requests.*

ALTERING THE EYEWITNESS'S BEHAVIOR

Conducting an interview successfully requires not only influencing the *E/W's* general attitude toward the *INT* but also her overt behavior. As we shall discuss in later chapters, she will have to relax in order to probe memory effectively. She may also have to slow her rate of speech so the *INT* can understand and record her description accurately. The most direct method of change is for the *INT* to state explicitly what he needs. For instance, he may state: "Please try to speak a bit slower so I can write down everything you say." Such a direct approach may work for some requests, perhaps to slow down her speech rate, but it may backfire and exaggerate other symptoms. Telling the *E/W* that she seems anxious and that she should try to relax may cause her to become even more anxious. In such cases, an indirect method of control may be more effective.

It has been found that, during the course of a two-person interaction, each person's behavior will tend over time to resemble that of the other person (Matarazzo & Wiens, 1985; Webb, 1972). Thus, when one person's speech rate slows down so will the other's, much like the tendency of two people walking together to conform to each other's pace. This phenomenon, which is manifested in a variety of verbal and non-verbal behaviors, is referred to as the Principle of Synchrony. The *INT* can use the principle of synchrony to influence the *E/W's* behavior simply by modeling the desired behavior himself. *By speaking in a calm, even-keeled voice and behaving in a relaxed manner, the* INT *can subtly guide the* E/W *to do so as well.* Similarly, if the *INT* wants to encourage the *E/W* to sit down while describing the incident, he should find two seats and sit down on one.

ESTABLISHING FAVORABLE COMMUNITY-POLICE RELATIONS

Since it is unlikely that the *E/W* has had any contact with the *INT* prior to the investigation, her initial attitude toward him will reflect her general attitude toward the local police department. If the police are seen as being effective and sensitive to the needs of the community, the *E/W* will be more helpful. On the other hand, if the police are not trusted or are seen as being insensitive to civilian needs, the *INT* will start off at a disadvantage and will have to work harder to gain the *E/W's* trust. Obviously, it is to the *INT's* advantage if he starts off in a positive light.

How does one establish favorable community-police relations? As this handbook is intended for the individual *INT* and not as a general work on police administration, we shall restrict our comments to the individual. Most *INTs* interact with civilians in the community when interviewing victims and witnesses of crime. Practically speaking, their ability to promote effective community-police relations depends upon how well they conduct these interviews. How can an *INT* affect an entire community simply by conducting an interview with a single individual? Although the interview is conducted with only one respondent, many others will soon find out about it, as the *E/W* will probably communicate her impressions to friends, relatives, or neighbors. Both the crime and the investigation will be unique events in the *E/W's* life, and therefore will be the focus of many conversations. Thus, a well-conducted interview of an individual *E/W* has the potential to leave an impression on several people. Should any of these people be *E/Ws* in future investigations, their preliminary attitudes toward the police will reflect the *INT's* conduct in the current investigation. Interviews that are well conducted facilitate collecting information later. Poorly conducted interviews establish just one more barrier to overcome in future investigations.

What specific techniques convey a positive attitude to *E/Ws?* Other than actually closing the case, which is guided by solvability factors largely out of the investigator's control, the major factors are his diligence, empathy, and respectful attitude (see Los Angeles's recent Christopher Commission Report for the importance of a respectful attitude toward the public on developing community-police relations; Rohrlich, 1991). Diligence is conveyed by the investigator conducting a thorough interview, exploring all avenues to extract new information. *Sometime after the interview, perhaps a few days later, the INT should telephone the* E/W *to see whether she has thought of any new information.*

Whereas diligence requires more effort on the investigator's part, genuine empathy and compassion require virtually no work. It is simply a matter of understanding the victim's plight and expressing it. There are a variety of opportunities to express such empathy, at the outset when trying to establish rapport, or at the completion of the interview, when trying to create a positive last impression. Here, the *INT* can *introduce a word expressing his concern, a note of hope that the crisis will be resolved—if it can—or an informative message of what to do should a related emergency arise.* In general, the *INT* should convey the simple courtesies one would naturally extend to another individual, especially for one recently victimized. Finally, the *INT* should *reinforce the* E/W's *participation, explaining the value of her information in the investigation, expressing admiration for her recall under duress, and thanking her profusely.*

CHAPTER SUMMARY

1. All of the relevant information is stored in the *E/W's* mind. Therefore, she must be mentally active during the interview and generate information, as opposed to being passive and waiting until the *INT* asks the appropriate question before answering. The *INT* can encourage her to be mentally active by directly requesting her to do so, or indirectly, by asking open-ended (vs. closed) questions. He should avoid interrupting her answer to an open-ended question.

2. The *INT* must develop good rapport with the *E/W* so she feels comfortable conveying personal information. Developing rapport is accomplished by personalizing the interview and by developing and communicating empathy. Personalizing the interview requires that the *INT* listen actively and treat the *E/W* as a unique individual. The *INT* needs to empathize with the *E/W's* plight and also communicate this empathy effectively.

3. The *E/W's* and *INT's* expectations and goals of the interview differ from each other. The *INT* should convey to the *E/W* that she can best meet her goals if she provides information relevant to the investigation.

4. The *INT* can modify the *E/W's* behavior (e.g., slow her speech rate, induce relaxation) either by requesting it directly, or indirectly through the principle of synchrony, by his modeling the appropriate behavior.

5. Eyewitnesses will be more cooperative if favorable community-police relations have been established. Investigators should try to promote favorable relations by working diligently and by showing empathy, compassion, and respect for the *E/W*.

Chapter 4

OVERCOMING EYEWITNESS LIMITATIONS

U nder the best of conditions, with a motivated and articulate respondent, it is difficult to conduct a successful interview. Respondents who have never been interviewed before are somewhat anxious and their memories fail occasionally. Under the worst of conditions, which is more likely the case in a criminal investigation, the difficulties are compounded severalfold. Eyewitnesses are not only anxious over the prospect of being interviewed by an official law enforcement agent, but they may have just witnessed or been the victim of a terrifying act that endangered their lives.

Because of the fear associated with crime and the speed with which it occurs, most *E/Ws* can initially recall only a few details. This just compounds the problem, because now the initially anxious *E/W* may have lost confidence in her ability to describe the event, which further depresses her recollection. To make matters worse, *E/Ws* often suppress reporting events even though they are consciously aware of them and are confident of their accuracy. Finally, as if the basic memory task were not difficult enough, the police *INT* is asking a typical citizen, who may have only limited communication skills and minimal experience in crime-related activities, to describe a fleeting event as if she were a veteran news reporter. Indeed, the *E/W's* task is difficult, and the police *INT* must overcome several *E/W* limitations to do his job successfully.

CONTROLLING EYEWITNESS ANXIETY

The high arousal associated with observing or being the victim of a crime in most cases will interfere with initially perceiving the event (Loftus, 1979; Peters, 1988). The belief that criminal events are etched indelibly into the *E/W's* mind simply is not true. Criminal events, precisely because of their threat to our safety, are difficult to perceive and recall accurately. Although the *E/W's* fear at the time of the crime limits her ability to perceive the event accurately, this is of little concern

33

for the investigating officer. The crime has already occurred and the investigator has no control over the *E/W's* initial perception. The investigator's practical concern is that some residual anxiety may remain at the time of the interview, and this residual anxiety will interfere with the *E/W's* ability to recall the event (Lipton, 1977; Reiser, 1980). One of the *INT's* goals therefore is to minimize the *E/W's* anxiety at the time of the interview.

Eyewitnesses may show anxiety at the time of the interview because the interview is conducted shortly after the crime, so that the anxiety associated with the original crime has not yet subsided. Eyewitnesses may also be anxious even if the interview is conducted several hours or days after the crime because the act of remembering the crime, bringing it back to consciousness, will revive the anxiety associated with the crime.[1]

The debilitating effects of fear and anxiety occur, in part, because the *E/W* feels a loss of control over her emotional and mental activity. Part of the problem stems from the *E/W's* (mistaken) belief that her fear is unnatural, which may induce a sense of inadequacy. An effective technique to facilitate the *E/W's* coping with this feeling of inadequacy is to *acknowledge the fear and to indicate its naturalness,* in light of the circumstances. The *INT* may simply say, "I can imagine that you're pretty upset now." That provides an opportunity for the *E/W* to talk about her fears and bring them out in the open where they can be dealt with rationally.[2] Obviously, being afraid in an objectively dangerous situation is not unnatural. Nevertheless, if the *E/W* believes that her anxiety is unnatural, the *INT* must help her reshape that belief. Often, it is as simple as an outsider, especially an authority figure, defining the situation as dangerous and indicating that such fear is natural and acceptable. After having brought out into the open the *E/W's* fear, the

---

1. An event is encoded in memory along with the psychological context in which it occurred (see Chapter 2). This principle, called the encoding specificity principle (Tulving & Thomson, 1973), suggests that (a) recreating the *E/W's* original psychological state should facilitate remembering the event, and (b) remembering the event will cause the original psychological state to be revived. The first half (a) of the rule will be exploited to assist recalling the event in question (see "Recreating the Context of the Original Event" in Chapter 8). The second half (b) of this double-edged sword must be contended with, however, as it has potentially negative consequences in recalling traumatic events.

2. Many *INTs* will feel uncomfortable with bringing out in the open the *E/W's* emotions and would just as soon circumvent that issue. Note, however, that in the process of displaying her emotions to the *INT,* the *E/W* will have developed a stronger rapport with him, assuming he responds supportively, which will improve the quality of the remainder of the interview. Building rapport is especially important if the facts requested have personal significance as is often the case when a physical attack was perpetrated (Chapter 3).

INT may note, "That was a dangerous situation. Most people would react in just the same way as you." It is even more effective to provide a concrete example. The *INT* can describe how he felt in a threatening situation, or how other *E/Ws* reacted. These concrete examples do not have to be detailed or exacting; they simply need to convey the point that fear in an objectively dangerous situation is the norm and therefore acceptable.

Fear and anxiety are disruptive partially because they appear suddenly and without warning. Unpleasant experiences and their resulting emotional reactions are always most potent when they appear unexpectedly. This element of surprise will not occur for interviews conducted immediately after the crime, since the residual fear will still be present and the *E/W* will not expect to remain calm. It may be more problematic for interviews conducted several hours or days after the crime, when the *E/W* has had ample time to recover from the initial shock. This "surprise effect" may be combated, and the unpredictability minimized, by previewing for the *E/W* the fear or anxiety she may feel when describing the event. Before requesting a description of the crime, the *INT* can indicate to the *E/W* that in the act of describing the crime, she may feel some of the fear or anxiety as when the event originally occurred. It is important to *convey to the* E/W *at this time that if she does experience some of the original fear, it will not be nearly as intense as the original event and that she will be able to control this feeling now.* The *INT* may suggest the following:

> You might feel some anxiety when you think about the crime again, but it will be relatively mild compared to your original feelings. Also, you will be able to control your feelings better now than before. If at any time, you want to stop and relax, to compose yourself, that's fine. Just tell me and we'll stop. Remember, you are in control now.

A technique used by psychotherapists to assist clients in describing particularly traumatic experiences is to encourage them to describe the event as if it were happening to someone else (speaking in the third-person, using "him" or "her" instead of "me"). Thus, a victim would describe the event as if she were an observer, not a direct participant, watching the event from a safe distance. Instead of saying, "He pointed the gun at *me,*" she would say, "He pointed the gun at *her.*" This technique is appropriate with rape victims (Latts & Geiselman, 1991; Reiser, 1980) and abused children (Geiselman, Saywitz, & Bornstein, in press).

There is a slight disadvantage of this technique in that the memory will not be as detailed as if the description were done in the conventional (first-person) manner.[3] However, the technique can be used effectively in highly traumatic cases, where the *E/W's* emotional state is the primary barrier to a successful investigation.

It has been known for a long time that our feelings in part result from the interpretation we give to our behavior (James, 1890). Sensing that we are speaking quickly and our muscles are tensed, we experience and label ourselves as anxious. When our overt behavior changes, our feelings change to match the new behavior more closely. Therefore, the *INT* can help the *E/W* to become less anxious by changing her overt behavior. This can be accomplished by encouraging the *E/W* to breathe deeply and slowly. *At the beginning of the interview, before collecting any formal description of the event, the* INT *can suggest that the* E/W *try to relax and just take a few deep breaths, inhaling slowly and deeply, and exhaling slowly.*[4] The *INT* should demonstrate once or twice and go through the exercise with the *E/W* a few times.

A more subtle way to facilitate the *E/W's* relaxing and slowing down her pace is through the Principle of Synchrony (Chapter 3). That is, if the *INT* speaks calmly, slowly, and in a controlled manner, the *E/W* will tend to follow his pattern. In general, *the* INT *should try to set a relaxed tone by presenting himself in the same fashion.*

In any crime, some events will be seen as more stressful than others. Not surprisingly, questions about the most stressful aspects of the crime will lead to greater *E/W* anxiety than more innocuous questions. A question about the assailant threatening the victim will certainly induce more anxiety than biographical, background information (e.g., "Where do you work?"). Furthermore, the anxiety elicited by a question will not

---

3. When the *E/W* adopts the role of another person, some of the specific, personal-context cues will be lost and she will depend more on her general knowledge of related crimes to reconstruct the event. Accordingly, she may omit some details of the specific crime and substitute more typical activities that are characteristic of generic crimes (see Bartlett, 1932; Fisher & Chandler, 1991).

4. The relaxation methods suggested here seem similar to those used in hypnosis. Is the Cognitive Interview simply a fancy name for hypnosis? We can rule that out, as there are several experiments showing that hypnosis and the Cognitive Interview behave differently. For instance, hypnosis increases the respondent's suggestibility to misleading information (Putnam, 1979) whereas the Cognitive Interview does not increase suggestibility (Geiselman, Fisher, Cohen, Holland, & Surtes, 1986). Furthermore, Yuille and Kim (1987) have argued that the induction component of hypnosis is ineffective as a memory-enhancer. Rather, hypnosis enhances memory only because it also uses some of the techniques found in the Cognitive Interview, e.g., context reinstatement (see also Timm, 1983).

subside immediately after the question has been answered. The negative aftereffects of the stress produced will continue into the next several questions and may last the entire interview. In one interview we examined, the detective asked a question about the assailant's drawing a gun and threatening the victim. This question so upset the *E/W* that she lost her composure and, not only could she not answer the question posed, but she also could not provide answers to any of the next five questions. Obviously, to be thorough, an investigator must ask these stressful questions at some time during the interview; he cannot simply avoid them. He can minimize their negative aftereffect, however, by *saving the most stressful questions for later in the interview, after having elicited most of the important, detailed information.*[5]

If the *E/W* does show excessive fear or anxiety during the interview, it is imperative to respond to that anxiety immediately and not proceed with gathering new information. Requesting detailed information while the *E/W* is in a heightened state of anxiety will result in a less-than-adequate description, which may in turn lower her confidence and also induce her to give superficial descriptions later in the interview.

Presumably, the **INT** could re-interview the *E/W* at a later time, when she is less anxious, and ask the same questions again. However, having already made an incorrect response on the first interview decreases the chances of making a correct response on a later interview.[6]

Witnesses who are interviewed while in a heightened state of anxiety may perceive this as being insensitive to their emotional needs, and will feel alienated from the **INT**. *When the* E/W *shows excessive anxiety during the interview, the* INT *must attend immediately to the anxiety. Only after the* E/W *has regained her composure should the* INT *return to the description of the crime.* When the interview resumes, the **INT** should start off with a series of innocuous questions and gradually build up to the part of the interview that previously elicited the stress response. If the *E/W* is still extremely anxious, it is best to terminate the interview and resume at a later time rather than force the *E/W* to complete it at that time.

---

5. This technique is similar to the journalistic interview technique of saving the most revealing questions ("bombs") until later in the interview (Metzler, 1979). The underlying ideas are similar: not contaminating the remainder of the interview by asking a question that may terminate the interview prematurely.

6. Answering the original question alters the *E/W's* memory, making the incorrect response more likely to be given later (see Fisher & Chandler, 1991; Raaijmakers & Shiffrin, 1980).

INCREASING EYEWITNESS CONFIDENCE

It is easy to understand the difficulty of an *E/W's* task, to describe in detail a frightening event that occurred quickly and with no warning. In the face of such a difficult task, *E/Ws* may lose confidence in their ability to provide adequate descriptions. When the *E/W's* confidence drops, her task becomes all the more difficult, since lack of confidence blocks engaging the necessary mental activities (West, 1985). Instead of searching through memory properly, low-confident people terminate their memory retrieval prematurely, often responding "I don't know" almost immediately after hearing the *INT's* question. This is most evident with older *E/Ws,* who often lack confidence even in their everyday recall abilities, and with young children (Geiselman, Saywitz, & Bornstein, in press). As we shall see, the confidence level of everyone, whether young or old, will fluctuate somewhat from time to time. Most important for our purposes, the *E/W's* confidence partially reflects the course of the interview, which is under the *INT's* control. His success in orchestrating an effective interview depends on his ability to maintain the *E/W's* confidence and to prevent it from dropping too low.

Before describing some techniques that can be used to increase the *E/W's* confidence level, let us address one concern that probably occurred to the reader in the last paragraph. That is, if the *INT* raises the confidence level of a low-confident *E/W* won't that simply induce her to generate more mistaken information? First, there is no evidence that more errors are generated with the Cognitive Interview,[7] perhaps because of a built-in mechanism to discourage *E/Ws* from simply guessing (see "Overcoming Eyewitnesses' Suppressing Information" later in this chapter). However, even if there were a few more errors, that would be more than compensated by the additional correct information elicited, especially in cases where there are few leads to go on. The problem faced by most investigators is not that there are too many false leads, but that there is not enough correct information. Furthermore, the relationship between confidence and accuracy is often rather weak. Low-confident *E/Ws* frequently are just as accurate as those with high confidence

---

7. In all of the laboratory studies conducted thus far (see Appendix B), except for one (Kohnken, Finger, & Nitschke, 1991), the number of incorrect responses elicited by the Cognitive Interview was no higher than by a standard interview. If anything, the **percentage** of incorrect responses (number of errors divided by the total number of responses) was invariably lower for the Cognitive Interview than for the standard interview.

(Deffenbacher, 1980). Therefore, the *INT* does not want an *E/W* to withhold information simply because she is not very confident.

During the interview, *the* INT *can help to maintain the* E/W's *confidence by providing appropriate feedback to convey his interest in her description. Follow-up questions that ask the* E/W *to elaborate on a claim she has just made are also effective.* He may say, for instance, "That's interesting, can you tell me anything more about the hat the assailant was wearing?" At a more subtle level, the *INT* periodically can inject some nonspecific verbal reinforcement (as in "OK" or "mm-hmm"). Respondents are generally unaware of these cues; nevertheless, they can increase the amount of information generated (Greesnpoon, 1955).

Non-verbal signals can also be used to indicate the *INT's* interest and maintain the *E/W's* confidence. The *INT's* general posture of leaning forward slightly (in a non-threatening manner) and periodically making eye contact are two such techniques.

When providing feedback, *the* INT *should avoid giving direct, qualitative feedback (for example, "good" or "right") immediately after the* E/W *makes a specific statement,* as this may be interpreted as a sign that the *INT* agrees with her. This may alter the *E/W's* memory of the specific statement by increasing her confidence artificially. By the same token, *the* INT *should control his demeanor and not display surprise after a particular response,* as that may be taken as a sign that the response is incorrect (see also Flanagan, 1981).

In addition to responding to the *INT's* feedback, the *E/W's* confidence is affected by her performance during the interview. When she answers questions successfully her confidence increases; conversely, when she fails to answer questions, especially when she cannot provide an answer to several, successive questions, her confidence decreases. One situation to avoid therefore is asking several consecutive questions that the *E/W* is unable to answer. *If the* E/W *has not been able to provide an adequate response to the last few questions, the* INT *should switch to an easier line of questioning.* If necessary, he can return to the more difficult questions later, when the *E/W* has regained her confidence. If the *INT* switches topics, he should inject a short break—just a few seconds should suffice—and interrupt the interview with some unrelated activity (e.g., offering a glass of water). When the *INT* returns to the interview he should indicate clearly that he is going to change topics. For example, he might say something like, "OK, let's examine a different issue," and then proceed with a few simple questions that will elicit positive responses.

OVERCOMING EYEWITNESSES'S
SUPPRESSING INFORMATION

Oftentimes during an interview, *E/Ws* will think of an important event but will suppress reporting it. As we shall see, most excuses for suppressing information are invalid, and by and large, interviews could be improved by encouraging *E/Ws* to describe whatever thoughts come to mind.

Eyewitnesses, like most other people, do not want to appear unreliable, so they sometimes withhold information because it contradicts something they said earlier. Contrary to popular belief, however, inconsistency of reporting does not necessarily indicate inaccurate recollection. Under some conditions, inconsistent claims are as accurate or more accurate than consistent claims (Fisher & Cutler, 1991).[8]

If the E/W *does generate inconsistent stories, the* INT *should not challenge the story immediately,* as that will lower her confidence. Rather, the *INT* should wait until he has elicited as much information as possible in the current session, and then ask the *E/W* to explain the discrepancy. Unless the *INT* has good reason to doubt the credibility of the *E/W,* he should not attack the discrepancy too assertively (cf. Stone & DeLuca, 1980). The inconsistency may simply reflect an innocent error in the *E/W's* description, or a mistake in the *INT's* understanding of her statement. If done in a non-threatening manner, asking the *E/W* to elaborate on the different versions of the statement may even lead to additional, correct information (see "Multiple Retrieval Attempts" in Chapter 7).

A second reason why people sometimes edit out information is because it is either out of order or it seems unrelated to the issue they are

---

8. Although inconsistency of recollection is often used in the legal system as an indicator of the inaccuracy of an *E/W's* testimony, and it is a favorite tactic by successful attorneys to impeach *E/Ws* (see e.g., Bailey & Rothblatt, 1971), there are no experimental data to support this claim. In the only experimental test we are aware of (Fisher & Cutler, 1991), observers of a staged theft attempted to describe the "thief" on two separate occasions (interviews) and then tried to identify him from a photoarray or lineup. The relation between eyewitness consistency and accuracy of recall was surprisingly weak. Eyewitnesses who responded inconsistently across the two interviews were no less accurate than those who responded consistently. This weak relation held for both accuracy of description and also accuracy of identification in the photoarray and lineup.

Care must be taken in interpreting these results as our experimental *E/Ws* had no motivation to lie. Our findings—no relation between inconsistency and accuracy—therefore, hold only for those cases in which *E/Ws* are trying to be truthful, which may not obtain in many real-life cases.

currently describing. The typical way to describe a sequence of events is in a forward, chronological order (Burns, 1981). Sometime, in the middle of the description, people may think of an earlier event. If they are not encouraged to report events out of order, they may suppress reporting the event until after completing the entire description. By that time, they are in a different mental state and the once-available thought may have vanished into the recesses of the mind, perhaps never to be found again. This is particularly true for minute details, which are not closely tied to the main theme of the story. In a similar fashion, people sometimes suppress a fact because they are currently describing a different topic and the fact seems "out of place." Again, by not describing the fact when it comes to mind, but suppressing it for a "more appropriate" time, the fact may never again surface to consciousness.

Finally, *E/Ws* withhold information because they perceive it as being trivial, of no investigative value. This self-editing is more harmful than helpful since most civilian *E/Ws* are not knowledgeable about what does and what does not have investigative value. Even if the information is trivial, the act of recalling it may trigger off an associated fact that does have investigative value. In suppressing what they consider to be trivial, *E/Ws* may also be suppressing valuable information.

The rule is simple: *encourage the* E/W *to describe everything that comes to mind as soon as she thinks of it.* Toward the beginning of the interview, the *INT* should *indicate to the* E/W *that she should not edit anything out of her response, but rather, she should say everything when she thinks of it, whether it seems trivial, out of place, or inconsistent.* The *INT* can remind the *E/W* that he will sort out all of the details later, and that she should not worry about her story being well organized and systematic. The *INT's* primary concern is that the *E/W* generates as much information as possible, not that it is presented in an orderly fashion.

The instruction not to edit her thoughts may be misinterpreted by the *E/W* as encouragement to fabricate statements, whether true or not, simply to please the *INT.* Clearly, that is undesirable, as it generates misinformation. *The* INT *must explicitly warn her not to guess or fabricate.* He might suggest, "I don't want you simply to make up something, if you don't know," or more emphatically, "If you don't know something, that's OK. Just say that you don't know. Don't make up anything, though, just to give me an answer."

FACILITATING EYEWITNESS COMMUNICATION

Whether *E/Ws* have observed the crime carefully or only superficially, most will have only limited ability to describe it in detail. Other than news reporters, most civilians are not required to provide such elaborate, detailed descriptions in their regular lives, so they are unpracticed in the task. Regardless of the *E/W's* descriptive skills, whether good or poor, a carefully executed interview can enhance the quality of the description elicited.

Relative versus Absolute Judgments

One general tactic to improve *E/W* descriptions is to *provide a concrete reference point as a source of comparison.* Several studies have shown that virtually everyone can make better relative judgments than absolute judgments (Miller, 1956).[9] For instance, although most of us would have difficult indicating exactly how tall is any one person, we can all decide very accurately which of two people is taller. If the *E/W* cannot describe the suspect's height, the *INT* can ask how tall the suspect was compared to himself or someone else the *E/W* knows (see also, Rochester, N.Y.P.D. 1981). The more similar the reference point is to the object being described, the more accurate will be the judgment.

Making absolute judgments about color is particularly difficult, especially if the object being described is not one of the standard colors: white, black, brown, red, pink, orange, yellow, green, blue, or purple-violet (Rosch, 1973). Nevertheless, although people may not have adequate vocabularies to describe an aquamarine blue, they will be able to indicate accurately whether the object was bluer or greener than a specific reference. To assist in describing colors, *INTs* can carry a simple color chart (patches of various color, available at paint stores) and ask the *E/W* to indicate how the object compared to the reference colors.

---

9. In a classic study Miller (1956) showed that, across a variety of perceptual dimensions (judgments of loudness, brightness, hue, etc.), experimental participants could discriminate accurately only approximately seven (plus or minus two) categories. For example, participants could categorize sounds along loudness into one of approximately seven different categories without making an error. With more than seven categories, participants started to make errors in categorizing the sounds. However, even though participants were limited to these seven categories when making *absolute* judgments, they could make much finer discriminations when the task required making *relative* judgments, e.g., which of the following two sounds is louder?

Recognition versus Recall

A related phenomenon is that people can recognize objects better than they can recall them (Kintsch, 1970).[10] For instance, an *E/W* may be unable to describe whether a weapon was a revolver or an automatic. Nevertheless, she might be able to select the correct alternative from a picture of a typical revolver or automatic. Similarly, an *E/W* who is unfamiliar with the different styles of cars may be unable to describe a particular car, but she may be able to select it from a sketch. We suggest that INTs *carry pictures or sketches of typical weapons, vehicles, and other technical objects, and ask* E/Ws *to select the appropriate figure or to indicate how the target item differs from one of the alternatives.*

When sketches or pictures are unavailable, which is usually the case, the *INT* can provide the alternatives verbally. For example, if the *E/W* is trying to describe the assailant's hat, the *INT* may offer suggestions as to the various possibilities (baseball, sailor's, etc).

Whenever the *INT* provides a set of alternatives, he must be careful not to bias the *E/W's* response. If only a few alternatives exist, the *INT* should *suggest all of the possible alternatives.* If a large number of alternatives exist, so that it is impossible to list all, the *INT* should either not suggest any, or state explicitly that the alternatives indicated are just examples of the wide variety of possible alternatives.

Non-Verbal Responding

Most of the information in an interview is conveyed verbally. The *INT* uses words to ask the questions, and the *E/W* uses words to convey the response. Although the verbal medium may be the typical means of communication, it may not be suitable for all events. Some events, like complex actions or unfamiliar objects, may be difficult to describe in words. For such difficult-to-describe events and objects, it may be preferable for the *E/W* to act out the event, draw a sketch of the object, or in some way, respond non-verbally.[11]

---

10. Although people usually recognize objects better than they recall them, there may still be some occasions when objects, people, or events can be recalled but cannot be recognized (Tulving & Thomson, 1973).

11. Even familiar objects may be difficult to describe verbally, but easily described non-verbally. For example, people make gross errors when expressing verbally the size of a dollar bill, but they can very accurately discriminate through the sense of touch whether a given piece of paper feels larger or smaller than a standard bill (Leibowitz & Guzy, 1990).

In one particularly interesting interview we monitored, of a witness to a plane crash, the *E/W* had considerable difficulty expressing in words which way the plane banked as it lost control. Had the *E/W* been given a model plane to demonstrate the plane's motion, he certainly would have provided a more accurate and comprehensible description. Similarly, in eliciting descriptions of traffic accidents, *INTs* might elicit more accurate and comprehensible descriptions if they (a) asked the *E/W* to draw or gave her a sketch of the intersection, (b) gave her models to represent the cars involved, and (c) asked her to move the models to reflect the movements of the cars involved. If the *E/W* was an active participant in the event, e.g., if she was the pilot of the plane, and it was important to determine her actions, then ideally, she should be interviewed in a similar plane and she should convey her actions by re-enacting what she had done originally (see Greenwald, 1970).

Non-verbal responding is particularly helpful when interviewing *E/Ws* whose verbal skills are limited, such as young children (see "Populations with Unique Communication Disabilities" in this chapter.)

INDUCING DETAILED DESCRIPTIONS

Most people are not trained or well practiced at giving elaborate, detailed descriptions. For our everyday affairs, superficial descriptions are generally adequate. We ask others to pass the "cup of coffee," not the "4.5-inch ceramic vessel with narrow, blue, vertical stripes on the outside and containing a dark, brown liquid with the consistency of water." As a consequence, most *E/Ws* have little skill in describing events in detail, an essential ingredient for a successful investigative interview.

Elaborate, detailed responses take longer to formulate than superficial responses. The *INT* must therefore *suggest to the* E/W *toward the beginning of the interview that she should take as much time as is necessary to answer* (see also Prior & Silberstein, 1969). We have noticed that, often, *INTs* suggest that the interview will take "only a few minutes." That type of introduction conveys to the *E/W* that superficial responses are acceptable, which certainly does little to promote detailed responding.

One of the major obstacles the investigator faces is that the *E/W* may not realize that he needs a detailed description, specifically of the suspect. The *E/W's* primary concern is that she has just been personally violated, so her description of the event focuses on general actions, not on specific details.[12]

Although action information is important to the investigating detective, his primary concern is to elicit person (suspect) or object information (e.g., weapons, vehicles). *IT IS IMPERATIVE THAT THE* INT *EXPLICITLY REQUEST THE* E/W *TO PROVIDE DETAILED, PERSON INFORMATION.*

In the hundreds of interviews we have listened to, we have yet to hear an *INT* state definitively that he needs a detailed response. Invariably, his request is minimally demanding, usually something like, "Tell me what happened." This is not the time to be subtle. If the *INT* truly wants to elicit a detailed response, he must state so boldly. He might say something like:

> In order for us to solve this case, we need as detailed a description as possible of the person who committed the crime. Try to describe his face to me in as much detail as you can. Imagine that I am trying to paint a picture of this person, but the only information I have is what you say. Tell me everything you can about him.

Informative Responses

Sometimes, *E/Ws* do not describe an important feature of an action, object, or person simply because they do not realize its importance. For example, an *E/W* may not know that gun handles can have various shapes. Consequently, she may fail to describe the handle of the gun used in the crime, not because her memory has failed, but simply because she believes it is uninformative. *If the object to be described is technical—or anything the* E/W *may not be familiar with—the* INT *should indicate what are the important properties to describe.*

Typically, police investigators request information about height, weight (or body build), and other global characteristics. Whereas these characteristics are easily accessed by *E/Ws* (see "Probing Concept Codes" in Chapter 10), only in rare cases are they discriminating. When an *E/W* describes the assailant as being about 5-foot 10-inches tall, and around 170 pounds, she has described a large percentage of all males. Unless the assailant is unusually short or tall, or unusually thin or heavy-set, this global description will be of little value. This is particularly so because

---

12. In a typical interview of a robbery victim, 64% of all the facts elicited were about the actions that took place; only 30% of the facts were about the people involved (Fisher, Geiselman, & Raymond, 1987).

many civilians are notoriously bad judges of height and weight (Yuille & Cutshall, 1986). Therefore, although it is usually required that investigators extract such information, it is a mistake to pursue it with much vigor because of its unreliability and lack of discrimination.

More informative than these global characteristics are descriptions of the face and any features that are idiosyncratic or highly distinctive. Among the facial features, the most informative features are those in the upper portion, in particular, the hair and the hairline (Ellis, 1984). Thus, *in probing about facial features, the* INT *should start with the hair and top of the head and proceed downward, toward the chin.*

By definition, idiosyncratic features are the most desirable to elicit because they are distinctive. If the *E/W* does not volunteer this information to an open-ended question, it is often difficult to elicit (see "Closed versus Open-ended Questions" in Chapter 6). One could target this type of idiosyncratic information with the question, "Was there anything unusual about the robber's appearance?" In our analysis of police interviews, many detectives asked this question. In almost all cases, however, it elicited a "no" response. We suspect the question is not particularly valuable—and should be used only as a last resort—because it is vague and so does not serve as an effective retrieval cue. Also, it suggests implicitly that the *INT* will accept a "no" response. Instead, to elicit a more positive response, we suggest that the *INT* rephrase the question slightly and ask, "What was the *most* distinctive feature about the robber's appearance?" Everyone, no matter how bland, has some feature that is more distinctive than others. If the *E/W* provides a positive response to this question, the *INT* can follow up with, "What was the next-most distinctive feature," and continue along that line until the *E/W* no longer provides a positive response.

Sometimes, when trying to describe a person or object, *E/Ws* provide subjective descriptions, like, "The guy looked angry," or "The guy looked like a farmer." Although such a description may not hold up in court, it can be useful for the investigator if it is converted into a more objective form. *The* INT *should follow up a subjective description by requesting the* E/W *to elaborate on it in objective terms.* A simple formula to convert subjective into objective comments is to ask: "What about the guy made you think he looked _____ [angry; like a farmer]?" If the *E/W* is given ample time to respond, this question almost always leads to an objective description.

Populations with Unique Communication Disabilities.

While many civilians have some deficiencies generating a detailed description, they can usually provide at least a marginally acceptable description. Some people, however, have such impoverished communication skills that they seem incapable of contributing any useful information toward the investigation. They have not had adequate formal education; or English is not their native language; or they may be intoxicated at the time of the interview. On first questioning, it may seem that such people can provide little valuable information. With proper interviewing techniques, these same people may provide surprisingly informative responses.[13]

Intoxicated Witnesses

Unique problems are posed by intoxicated *E/Ws,* because their expressive abilities are impaired as well as their ability to organize a coherent response (Eich, 1977). Some of these limitations can be overcome by providing alternatives to choose from and by indicating the relevant characteristics to describe. Furthermore, since intoxicated *E/Ws* also have difficulty organizing their response, the *INT* should try to segment the report, requesting information about a specific topic, then moving on to another topic. Only by providing such guidance will the report be complete. If too much latitude (very open-ended questions) is given to the intoxicated *E/W* — normally a desirable strategy with sober *E/Ws* — entire sections of information may be missing. Thus, whereas an *INT* might ask a sober *E/W* to describe the assailant's clothing, when interviewing an intoxicated *E/W* the *INT* should ask separate questions about the assailant's shirt, jacket, shoes, etc. *The key to interviewing intoxicated* E/Ws *is to provide as much structure as possible.*

An obvious question here is: Isn't it preferable to wait until the *E/W* has become sober and conduct the interview then? If the event occurred recently, and the *E/W* was intoxicated at the time, it is preferable to interview her immediately, even while intoxicated, than to postpone the interview until she becomes sober. Even if the *INT* plans to interview her later, after she becomes sober, it is still preferable to interview her immediately, while intoxicated, and then re-interview her later while

---

13. Brown & Geiselman (1991), e.g., found that the Cognitive Interview produced a 32% increase in amount of correct recall with people who were mildly, mentally retarded.

sober (Yuille & Tollestrup, 1990).[14] Naturally, this depends on the degree of inebriation. We are assuming, obviously, that, although intoxicated, the *E/W* is still reasonably coherent.

Non-Native English Speakers

Obviously it is best if the *INT* and the *E/W* speak the same language. Sometimes, however, this is impossible, and an interpreter must be used. If the *E/W* understands the *INT's* language, but simply cannot respond in that language, the *INT* should speak directly to her, not through the interpreter. It is best to avoid speaking through an interpreter, as many non-professional interpreters will distort the message somewhat. When speaking directly to the *E/W,* the *INT* should *use short sentences and simple vocabulary, and speak slowly and distinctly.*

If the *E/W* neither comprehends nor speaks the *INT's* language, so that an interpreter must be used, the *INT* should speak in short phrases and request that the interpreter translate phrase by phrase, as opposed to waiting until the *INT* finishes a complex question and translating all at once. Similarly, the *INT* should request that the *E/W* speak slowly and in short phrases, and that the interpreter translate for him phrase by phrase.

If the *E/W* is not an American and is more familiar with the metric system of measurement (meters, grams, liters) than the American system (feet, pounds, gallons), she should describe important people and objects using the system she is familiar with (metric). Requesting the *E/W* to use an unfamiliar system of measurement, especially if she is anxious at the time of the interview, could lead to gross errors (see Smith, Jobe, & Mingay, 1991).

Children[15]

Children differ from adults in important ways in their cognitive skills and social perceptions and it is essential to modify the interview accordingly. These differences revolve principally around three themes: (a) children are more uncomfortable in the presence of adults they do

---

14. This occurs for three reasons. First, memory declines with the passage of time, so some of the information available immediately after the event occurred will be lost in postponing the interview. Second, as noted earlier (Chapter 4, Footnote 6), attempting to recall the event on the initial interview makes the event easier to remember later. Third, being in the same physiological state (intoxicated) at the time of the first interview as the original event enhances recall (see Chapter 7).

15. This section was written with Michelle McCauley.

not know, especially in an unfamiliar environment, (b) children's verbal skills are far less developed than are adults', and (c) children's expected roles in the interview are more easily influenced by the *INT's* behavior.

The first rule of interviewing young children is to make them comfortable with the environment and with the *INT.* If the interview is conducted at a site other than the child's house, the interview room should be equipped with items familiar to the child: toys, games, coloring books, etc. *The first several minutes of the interview should be devoted exclusively to developing rapport between the* INT *and the child* (Dent, 1982; Saywitz, 1988). This means showing genuine interest in understanding the child's world. The *INT* might engage the child in conversation about her friends or family, her favorite games, toys, television shows, movies, or school. Building rapport here requires that the *INT* interact meaningfully with the child, contributing as an interested party, not simply asking a series of census-like questions about "What is your favorite t.v. show?" and "What grade are you in?"

Young children may also have poor verbal skill, as evidenced by their inability to understand the *INT's* question and in their inability to describe the relevant event (see Saywitz, 1988; 1989). In general, INTs *should simplify their communication. This entails using shorter sentences and limiting their vocabulary to words the children know.* This is particularly important when interviewing children about instances of sexual abuse, as children may use idiosyncratic terms to refer to sexual body parts. When children identify a concept by an idiosyncratic name, the *INT* should use that name exclusively during the interview.

Children often provide very short, unelaborated descriptions of events or objects (Chi & Ceci, 1986), especially if they have not yet developed adequate rapport with the *INT.* Interviewers can help to overcome this limitation by *encouraging the child to speak uninterruptedly, especially during the initial rapport-building stage when she is describing a familiar event, e.g., favorite game.* Follow-up comments, such as, "That sounds like fun. Tell me more about how to play that game," have a dual role of helping to increase rapport and also priming the child to provide detailed, elaborated responses. Once the child has provided such a detailed, elaborate response in the rapport-building phase, the *INT* can refer to it later as a standard. For example, if the child initially described in detail how she plays her favorite computer game at home, the *INT* can say later in the interview, "Now, tell me about when he (the assailant) touched you. But try to tell me everything that happened, like when you told me how to play the computer game."

While it is preferable for the *E/W* to elaborate on the information following open-ended questions (see Chapter 6), children typically require more directed questioning from the *INT* for elaboration (Saywitz, 1988). The *INT* should first try to elicit the information with an open-ended question, and use the directed question afterward.

Even under the best of conditions, children will be unable to describe in words many events. In such instances, *INTs* should encourage the children to rely on other, non-verbal forms of communication (see "Non-Verbal Responding" in this chapter). Children might act or draw simple sketches to convey what they observed. Care should be taken to ensure that, if props are used (e.g., anatomically correct dolls), they are not used in a manner that is overly suggestive (Goodman, Bottoms, Schwart-Kenney, & Rudy, 1991).

Like adults, but even more so, children may misinterpret the *INT's* intentions and fabricate information to please him. For example, asking a question a second time may be a cue for a child that the *INT* was unhappy with her first response, thereby inducing her to change the response (Geiselman & Padilla, 1988; Geiselman, Saywitz, & Bornstein, in press). Similarly, an overly zealous *INT* may encourage children to fabricate answers by repeatedly asking, "Is that all you can remember? Can you remember anything else?" When probing in depth, *INTs* should explicitly tell children at the beginning of the interview that they should not make up answers, but should tell only the truth. This type of instruction can be reinforced by providing the child with the option of responding "I don't know" to a question. The *INT* should also ask the child to tell him if she does not understand a question, so he can reword it.

CHAPTER SUMMARY

1. The *E/W's* anxiety at the time of the interview may be minimized by the *INT's* acknowledging it and indicating that it is natural, given the objective situation. Other techniques to minimize the detrimental effects of heightened anxiety include (a) previewing it (to reduce the "surprise effect"), (b) encouraging the *E/W* to describe the event as if it were happening to someone else, and (c) inducing a relaxation response, either by directly or indirectly motivating the *E/W* to breathe slowly

and deeply. Interviewers should save the most stressful questions for later in the interview.

2. The *INT* should try to maintain the *E/W's* confidence throughout the interview by (a) verbally or non-verbally conveying his interest in her response, and (b) avoiding asking several successive questions that she cannot answer.

3. Eyewitnesses often withhold information, even though it may be valuable for the investigation. Interviewers should encourage them to describe everything that comes to mind as soon as they think of it. Interviewers should explicitly warn *E/Ws* not to fabricate responses.

4. Interviewers can assist *E/Ws* to provide detailed descriptions by (a) presenting them with concrete reference points to guide their responses, (b) encouraging relative judgments over absolute judgments, and (c) recognition over recall. Interviewers can present pictures or sketches of typical objects to facilitate description. If alternatives are presented for recognition, the entire set of possible alternatives should be indicated.

5. Descriptions of actions and complex objects can be improved by encouraging *E/Ws* to respond non-verbally, acting out or sketching the event or object.

6. The *INT* must indicate explicitly his need for detailed, person information.

7. Facial features and idiosyncratic features are the most important for person description. The hairline and upper-facial features are the most distinctive. Idiosyncratic features can be elicited by requesting *E/Ws* to indicate "the most" distinctive feature.

8. Subjective responses can be converted to more useful, objective descriptions by rephrasing the *E/W's* response.

9. Populations with unique communication limitations (e.g., intoxicated, non-native English speakers, and children) require special techniques to help overcome their limitations.

Chapter 5

LOGISTICS OF INTERVIEWING

Before examining some of the more complex interviewing strategies, let us look at the basic nuts-and-bolts decisions that must be made about the logistics of interviewing. In this chapter, we shall focus on two such issues: where and when to conduct interviews. We shall also examine a related problem that arises often in police investigations, interviewing the same *E/W* several times. Finally, we shall describe a simple procedure to lengthen the functional life of the interview.

WHERE TO CONDUCT THE INTERVIEW

Investigators generally select an interview site because of its convenience for the *E/W's* schedule. Although convenience is certainly a practical criterion, it is important to realize that not all interview sites promote equally good interviews. If a site is chosen to maximize the amount of information gathered, the primary concern is: Where will there be the fewest distractions? When external distractions disrupt the *E/W's* concentration, the amount of information gathered will be lessened and the description elicited will be more superficial and less detailed.

There will always be some external sources of distraction that the *INT* will have little control over once the interview begins. Usually these will be associated with the particular location of the interview, e.g., spectators milling about at the crime scene. Although the *INT* may not have perfect control over these distractions, he can do several things to minimize them.

The first rule is to try to **conduct the interview with just one** E/W **at a time**[1]. If there are two or more **E/Ws,** the **INT** should separate them

---

1. Group interviews have several risks. When two or more people participate at the same time, there is a good chance that one of them will interrupt in the middle of another's response, causing the same kind of distraction as if the *INT* interrupted. Second, the statements of one *E/W* may alter the memory of another, which can open the door to a host of legal problems on the acceptability of each *E/W's* testimony. Third, the *E/W's* confidence in her recollection may be artificially raised or lowered depending upon whether the other *E/Ws* agree or disagree with her description.

and talk to each individually (see also Rand, 1975; Wells, 1988). If the interview is conducted at the crime scene and potential *E/Ws* may leave the site before the interview is conducted, *the* INT *should ask anyone who must leave immediately for her name, telephone, and address, so that he can interview her at another time.*

If the *E/W* refuses to be interviewed alone, because of fear or other personal reasons, the *INT* should try to arrange the interview location so that the requested third person is near, but out of the *E/W's* sight. *The third person should be told explicitly not to talk or interrupt the interview in any manner until the* INT *terminates the interview.* For interviews that require an interpreter, see Chapter 4.

Once the general interview site has been determined, the interview should be conducted in the quietest location possible, away from potential sources of distraction (see also, Wicks, 1974). The *INT* must consider whether or not other people are likely to pass by, whether there will be distracting noises (telephones, cars, etc.) and whether the *E/W's* presence will be requested by others during the interview. Since these decisions are unique to each interview location, let us examine the various interview sites separately.

Detective interviews generally are conducted at one of the following locations: the crime scene, police headquarters, the *E/W's* residence, or her place of employment. What are the advantages and disadvantages of each?

Interviews Conducted at the Crime Scene

In this section, we refer to crimes that occur at a location other than one's residence or at one's place of business, for example, while shopping, or walking in the street. Interviews conducted at one's residence or place of business, if they are also the scene of the crime, will be covered later under the headings of "Residence" or "Place of Business."

Interviews generally take place at the crime scene because the investigator has arrived there before the *E/W* has left. There are two potential advantages associated with interviews conducted at the crime scene. They usually take place shortly after the crime has occurred, so that the *E/W's* memory of the crime has had little time to fade. In addition, the context of the interview site typically is very similar to the context of the crime itself, a factor that often promotes good memory (see "Memory Retrieval" in Chapter 7).

In theory, interviews conducted shortly after the event and at the interview site should be the most effective. In practice, however, there are several factors that usually detract from these interviews. First, if the crime has just recently occurred, the *E/W* may be in a highly anxious or fearful state. Second, depending upon the type of crime, there may be several bystanders or other potential *E/Ws*. The presence of others interferes with conducting the interview privately and increases the chances of unnecessary distractions. If other *E/Ws* are present, the *INT* may be tempted to terminate the interview prematurely, since he does not want to lose these other potential *E/Ws*. Interviews conducted at the crime scene shortly after the crime are also compromised by the *E/W's* and the *INT's* inability to prepare beforehand. Thus, the *E/W* may have to interrupt or terminate the interview prematurely because she needs to contact a family member or because she has another commitment to fulfill.

The major problem of conducting interviews at the scene of the crime is that there is minimal control over distractions. Traffic noises, passersby, weather, and a host of other distractions often make it virtually impossible to induce sufficient concentration to conduct an effective interview. If the investigator does conduct the interview at the crime scene, he should **select the most remote location, one that is least affected by extraneous distractions and one that allows the greatest privacy.** Often the squad car fills this role, since the *INT* can shut out most other influences.

It has often been suggested that taking the *E/W* back to the scene of the crime can refresh her memory of the original event (e.g., Wicks, 1974). Although this is probably true (see "Memory Retrieval" in Chapter 7), we do not generally recommend this technique because one can often accomplish the same memory boost in a more convenient way, simply by imagining the crime scene mentally (Smith, 1979). This is especially so for crimes that occur in a location well known to the *E/W*. Furthermore, the details of many crime scenes change from the time the original event occurred until the later interview. For example, if a crime occurred outside, it is unlikely that the weather or lighting conditions will be the same, that the traffic or street sounds will remain constant, or that the same passersby will be available at the interview. To the extent that these details differ from the original event to the interview, memory will be impaired (Loftus, Manber, & Keating, 1983). We recommend returning to the scene of the crime only if the crime occurs in a location not well known to the *E/W,* so that she cannot reconstruct it mentally, and if the environment is likely to remain unchanged. In most other cases, imagining the scene mentally will suffice.

The overall success of interviews conducted at the crime scene shortly after the crime has been committed depends primarily on the *E/W's* emotional state and on the ability to control external distractions. If the *E/W* is reasonably calm and the interview can proceed without interruption, the crime scene is potentially an excellent site, especially for collecting detailed information which will be forgotten quickly with the passage of time. Conversely, if the *E/W* is still anxious or there are uncontrolled distractions, interviews conducted at the crime scene will be incomplete and perhaps even incorrect. In such instances, it is preferable to conduct interviews under more controlled conditions, even if that means delaying the interview.

Interviews Conducted at Police Headquarters

Interviews conducted at police headquarters generally take place several days after the event has occurred, so that the *E/W's* memory of the crime has faded somewhat. As a result, she must concentrate more intensely to recall the event than interviews conducted shortly after the crime. On the other hand, the *INT* has much greater control of the interview environment than interviews conducted at other sites. With the proper precautions, the *INT* should be able to minimize distractions and induce more effective memory retrieval operations. Furthermore, because of the passage of time, the *E/W* should be in better control of her emotions.

The *INT's* primary concern is to **prepare the interview room so it is as free as possible from distractions.** If it is feasible, one or a few rooms should be set aside in each police station to be used exclusively for *E/W* interviews. These rooms should be as remote as possible in order to isolate them from other noises in the building. If the facilities are adequate to set aside a room exclusively for interviewing, it should be furnished only minimally, with a table, two chairs and any necessities (e.g., ashtray and writing pad). The *E/W's* chair should be comfortable enough for her to sit for a long session without having to reposition herself frequently. Telephones and other auditory distractions, e.g., intercom systems, should be disconnected or eliminated. Similarly, anything that might be visually distracting (mirrors, clocks, pictures, posters, etc.) should be removed or covered, if possible. A sign should be placed on the outside of the door to indicate when the room is being used, so that no one else is tempted to enter in the middle of an interview.

Interviews Conducted at the Eyewitness's Residence

Interviews are conducted at the *E/W's* residence typically because of their convenience for the *E/W*. They also appear to be the natural interview site for crimes committed at the *E/W's* residence, especially if the interview is conducted shortly after the crime has occurred.

One advantage of conducting an interview at the *E/W's* residence is that it gives her a great degree of control over the physical environment. If the *INT* is able to gain her confidence early he can use it to control the physical environment and create a distraction-free interview. In order to accomplish this, the *INT* must spend some time at the beginning of the interview developing rapport and engaging the *E/W's* trust. Once the *INT* has gained her trust, he can request her to follow the same general pattern as setting up a distraction-free environment at police headquarters. That is, the interview should be conducted in a room that is free from auditory and visual distractions. If other family members are present, the interview should be conducted in a room that is remote from their traffic. Finally, the family members should be requested to refrain from interrupting in the middle of the interview. The *INT* should tell them that they will have the opportunity to speak with him either before or after the interview is conducted.

If the crime occurs at the *E/W's* residence and the interview takes place shortly after the crime, the dynamics of the interview are similar to interviews conducted at the scene of a crime. That is, the *E/W* may still be in a highly anxious state, in which case the *INT's* first concern is to overcome this anxiety. If other *E/Ws* are present, the general directions proposed earlier still hold: separating them and interviewing them individually.

Interviews Conducted at the Eyewitness's Place of Business

Interviews are conducted at the *E/W's* place of business either because she was at work and the crime has occurred recently, i.e., it is the crime scene, or because it is a convenient location. If it is the scene of a recently committed crime, the same principles hold as mentioned earlier.

In general, the *E/W's* place of business is a poor location to conduct the interview. The workplace is often noisy and there is little opportunity to control the noise. We have listened to scores of interviews conducted at fast-food restaurants or 24-hour convenience stores and, invariably, there were interruptions from customers asking questions or unavoidable noises associated with the business (doors opening and closing, cash registers ringing, etc.).

Even if the environment is reasonably quiet, the *E/W* may be unable to concentrate fully on the details of the interview because she is preoccupied with business matters. If she is an employee, she may feel that the time spent away from work is being monitored, leading her either to terminate the interview prematurely or give a less detailed response than if time were not a factor. Interviews with the employer, owner, or manager of the business face additional problems. If she has decision-making responsibilities or possesses important information, other workers may be tempted to interrupt because they need her advice immediately. Similarly, she may feel obligated to be available to her co-workers. In either case, she too may prefer to terminate the interview prematurely or give superficial answers.

For all of the above reasons, we advise against conducting interviews at the *E/W's* place of business, except if the crime has recently occurred there and it is important to conduct the interview immediately. If it is not conducted immediately after the crime, it is preferable to hold it either at the *E/W's* residence or, if that is not possible, at police headquarters.

Interviews Conducted on the Telephone

Because of its extraordinary convenience, the telephone is used frequently to conduct interviews. Our experience with telephone interviews suggests that they can be used effectively to follow up earlier face-to-face interviews, but only for facts that are easily retrieved. Telephone interviews might be used to elicit global characteristics of the assailant or perhaps to elicit general, background information, like the *E/W's* work schedule. Phone conversations should not be used, however, as a substitute for face-to-face interviews. Because telephone interviews are impersonal, *E/Ws* who have not yet met face-to-face with the *INT* will not reveal much information. Also, it is particularly difficult to induce *E/Ws* to engage the mental operations necessary for focused memory retrieval (see Chapter 8).

WHEN TO CONDUCT THE INTERVIEW

As a rule, E/Ws *should be interviewed as soon as possible after the event has occurred* (Lipton, 1977; Wells, 1988), since forgetting begins immediately and the longer the delay the more will be forgotten. Details of the crime, e.g., color of clothing, will be forgotten the most rapidly; meaningful actions will be forgotten more slowly.

Although, in principle, memory generally decreases with the passage of time, there may be good reason to postpone an interview. Specifically, the ability to recall information depends not only on its availability in the *E/W's* memory store, but also on other incidental factors, for example, the *E/W's* ability to follow instructions and retrieve information properly. A highly anxious *E/W* who has just recently been traumatized may have a considerable amount of information stored in memory, but she may be unable to access that information because her tremendous anxiety interferes with the retrieval process of memory (Reiser, 1980). For an *E/W* in such a heightened state of anxiety, it may be more profitable to wait until she has calmed down and conduct the interview later. The *INT* will have to make a reasoned judgment weighing the heightened-memory advantage against the heightened-anxiety disadvantage of interviewing shortly after the event. *If the* E/W *is reasonably calm, seems capable of following instructions, and can perform intensive memory retrieval operations, the interview should be conducted as soon as possible after the event. If, however, the* E/W *is extremely anxious, has difficulty following even simple instructions, and appears incapable of doing intensive memory retrieval, it is better to postpone the interview for a while.*

In addition to the *E/W's* level of anxiety, there may be other practical reasons to postpone the interview. The *E/W* may have other commitments at the time that she cannot cancel; the present interview scene may be so chaotic and full of distractions that it is practically impossible for the *INT* and the *E/W* to concentrate properly. If the current conditions are so disruptive that they would lead to a less-than-satisfactory interview, it is preferable to postpone the interview for a while to guarantee more favorable conditions. Unless the interview can be conducted immediately after the crime, there will be little memory loss in postponing the interview somewhat (Wells, 1988). Thus, whereas there may be a large decrement caused by postponing the interview from one hour to two hours after the crime, there will be relatively little loss by postponing the interview from two days to three days after the crime. If anything, postponing the interview for a limited time to establish a more favorable environment will probably elicit more information.

When scheduling the interview, the *INT* should try to *select a time slot that provides considerable padding in case the interview runs longer than expected* (see also, Wicks, 1974). One thing to avoid is having to terminate the interview prematurely because the *INT* or the *E/W* has another commitment. If the interview is successful and the *E/W* has a wealth of relevant information, terminating the interview before she has the opportunity to completely exhaust her memory may lead to a less-than-complete investigation (see also Wicks, 1974). If the interview must be resumed at a later time, it is unlikely that the *E/W* will be able to put herself back into the same efficient memory retrieval mode as earlier.[2]

CONDUCTING MULTIPLE INTERVIEWS
WITH EYEWITNESSES

In a typical police investigation, *E/Ws* may be interviewed several times: by a uniformed officer shortly after the crime, by a detective after a few hours or days, by a member of the state or district attorney's office, by defense and prosecuting attorneys after several weeks or months, etc. Such repeated testing has unique effects on both the *E/W's* and the *INT's* approaches toward the interview, and on the amount and quality of information elicited. Many of the participants involved see the multiple-testing format as a burden and inefficient—why not simply interview the *E/W* once and get all the information then, as opposed to asking the same questions repeatedly and eliciting the same answers?

Despite the *E/W's* belief that she has told the initial investigator all she can remember, there is good theoretical reason and an ample supply

---

2. This does not imply that follow-up interviews will not elicit new information. As the next section on multiple interviews states, follow-up interviews should generate new information. However, some of the information that might have been elicited in the original interview will have been lost.

of data (see Payne, 1987, for a review) to believe that a carefully conducted follow-up interview should elicit new information.[3] Therefore, if used properly, the multiple-testing format provides an excellent opportunity to extract more information than a single interview. Before making use of this opportunity, several obstacles must be overcome. We shall consider these obstacles from the *E/W's* and the *INT's* perspectives separately.

The major *E/W* hurdle to overcome is lack of motivation. Many *E/Ws* are opposed to even a single interview. They would prefer to forget about the unpleasant event and they do not want to take time from their schedules to participate in the investigation. No doubt these problems are compounded when *E/Ws* are asked to participate in a second interview. Because they believe that they have already told the earlier investigator everything they know, many *E/Ws* expect the follow-up interview to be a further waste of their time. Why then should they bother repeating the interview? The investigator's first task, therefore, is to convince the *E/W* that it is valuable to conduct a follow-up interview. The *INT* must convey to the *E/W* that there will be something different about the present interview, something not covered earlier. The *INT* might indicate that he has uncovered some new information since the initial interview and would like to pursue these leads. Alternatively, the *INT* might try to motivate the *E/W* to feel that she is a part of the investigative team, and that her testimony is instrumental in solving the case.

Once the *INT* has secured the *E/W's* participation, he is still faced with the task of actually collecting the new information. For a variety of psychological reasons, when interviewed a second time, many people

---

3. Some of the reasons to expect new information are: (1) the *E/W* is likely to be in a more controlled emotional state for the later interview, so that her initial anxiety is less of an impediment; (2) the *E/W* has had more time to think about the crime, which should make more information available (Roediger & Payne, 1982); (3) the context of the interview has changed somewhat from the initial to the follow-up interview, which should also make available new recollections (see "Multiple Retrieval Attempts" in Chapter 8 for a more detailed analysis).

This has interesting legal implications, as it suggests that *E/Ws* may remember certain details of a crime at a later interview (e.g., courtroom testimony) that they failed to report at an earlier interview (e.g., deposition). Often, when this occurs, opposing counsel tries to discredit the *E/W's* "newfound" memory, suggesting that she must have been told this detail by someone else. "After all," argues the opposing attorney, "we all know that memory decreases with time, so how could she have possibly remembered something at a later date (in court) that she did not remember earlier (deposition)?" While this may seem like a convincing argument to the lay person, it is indefensible on psychological grounds.

simply repeat whatever they said before.[4] Since this information has already been gathered, it does not further the investigation. We shall shortly describe some techniques *INTs* can use to circumvent this problem.

In addition to the problems created by uncooperative *E/Ws,* limitations are sometimes imposed on the multiple-interview format by inappropriate attitudes held by investigators. Many of these self-imposed limitations stem from the fact that investigators often know what the *E/W* reported in the initial interview. With this as a guide, they concentrate on trying to verify the *E/W's* earlier testimony by asking the same questions as the original *INT.* While this approach may filter out some respondents who are fabricating stories, it also severely limits the potential of follow-up interviews to generate new information.[5] Rather than trying to validate the earlier interview, the *follow-up investigator should conduct the interview to elicit as much new information as possible.*

Another problem of the investigator's knowing what was reported in the initial interview is that he may have several expectations about the *E/W's* knowledge and about potential suspects. These expectations may reduce the effectiveness of the interview because (a) the *INT* is more likely to ask leading questions (see "Wording Questions" in Chapter 6), (b) the *INT* may become so concerned about verifying his expectations that he blocks out other possible considerations, which might be revealed with a more open-minded approach (see also Stone & DeLuca, 1980), and (c) the *INT* may rely so heavily on his pre-interview expectations that he listens less actively and misses some of the subtle cues available in the present interview. Interestingly enough, we have often observed that

---

4. There are social, cognitive, and emotional reasons that account for the *E/W's* tendency simply to repeat what she said earlier. There is social pressure to be consistent, so that the *E/W* is not thought of as being unreliable (Festinger & Carlsmith, 1959). Cognitively, it is easier for the *E/W* to repeat her earlier statement than to retrieve from memory the original crime event. The facts recalled on the first interview have become more memorable as a result of their earlier recall (Raaijmakers & Shiffrin, 1980). Therefore, less mental effort is required to retrieve facts already recalled than to retrieve new information. Finally, it is more emotionally disturbing to recreate and relive the original event than to review the events of the earlier interview. Since the *E/W* was probably under high stress during the original event, she would likely try to avoid thinking about it again. As an alternative to rethinking the original event, the *E/W* may opt for the psychological safety of rehashing the earlier interview.

5. By asking the same questions as the original investigator, the *INT* may invoke the same mental operations, and therefore the same recollections, as those used earlier, which defeats the purpose of the reliability check. Also, by using the same questioning strategy, the quality of the follow-up interview is limited by the conditions of the original interview, which is almost assuredly less efficient. This is particularly problematic when the initial interview has been conducted by a uniformed officer shortly after the crime, since (a) the uniformed officer generally is less experienced and hence less skillful than the follow-up investigator, (b) the *E/W* was probably in a more stressful emotional state in the earlier interview, and (c) more severe time constraints are generally imposed on the initial interview.

INTs who had no prior familiarity with the case conducted the most effective interviews. To make the best use of pre-interview information, *the* INT *should act as if he had no prior knowledge of the case, thereby forcing himself to (a) ask fewer leading questions, (b) keep open other possible solutions to the crime, and (c) listen more actively.*

The following specific suggestions are offered to maximize the amount of information gathered in the multiple-interview format. Note the distinction between investigators who conduct the initial interview and those who conduct the follow-up interview.

One cardinal rule stands when conducting the initial interview: even though a follow-up interview is expected, perhaps under better conditions, *the initial interview should be comprehensive and should be conducted as efficiently as possible. The* INT *should not rely on the follow-up investigator to elicit information not gathered initially.*[6]

When conducting the follow-up interview, the investigator should avoid asking the exact same questions and in the same order as used in the first interview. This tactic is likely to generate the same answers as given on the first interview. This repeated information is not particularly valuable precisely because it has already been collected. Instead, the *INT's* goal should be to elicit new information not yet uncovered in the original interview. To discover such new information, the *INT* should *explicitly instruct the* E/W *to think about the original crime and not to consider the answers she provided at the earlier interview.* The *INT* should tell her that she may think of new facts now that she did not report earlier, and that it is OK if her recollections now are inconsistent with or even contradictory to those reported earlier (see Chapter 4). To assist the *E/W's* recalling from the memory record of the original event and not simply repeating her comments from the first interview, the *INT* should *recreate the circumstances of the original event,* putting the *E/W* back into the same psychological frame of mind that existed at the original event (for more details, see "Recreating the Context of the Original Event" in Chapter 8).

Infrequently, in the follow-up interview, all attempts will fail in trying

---

6. There is no guarantee that the *E/W* will submit to a follow-up interview. Whether or not she does participate in a second interview depends partially on how much she recalls on the initial interview. The more she recalls, the more psychologically involved she will be in the investigation and the more likely she will be to participate later (Festinger, 1957). If the *E/W* does participate in the follow-up interview, the amount she recalls will be directly related to the amount recalled on the initial interview. The more information recalled initially the greater will be the increment on the follow-up interview (Roediger, Payne, & Gillespie, 1982).

to elicit a specific recollection of the original event by directing the *E/W's* attention to the event. Should this happen, as a last resort, the *INT* can suggest that the *E/W* try to remember what she mentioned at the earlier interview. Because this indirect method tends to duplicate the information gathered in the earlier interview, it should be used only after more direct methods of activating the original memory are exhausted. If the *E/W* can recall what she said at the earlier interview, the *INT* should then try again to direct her back to the original event by using her previous recollection as a guide. Let us say, for example, that at the follow-up interview, the *E/W* cannot remember anything about the get-away car. However, when asked, she can recall having told the first *INT* that the car was in "beat-up" condition. The second *INT* can now follow up on this comment with the following directions:

> You said that you remembered telling the uniformed officer that the car was "beat-up." Try to think back to when you first saw the car. Where were you when you saw the car? Which parts of the car did you look at? (Recreate the original context) What aspect of the car made it look like it was "beat up"?

PROLONGING THE INTERVIEW

Many detectives carry heavy case loads and have only limited time to conduct each interview, especially if the crime is not serious and the solvability factors are unfavorable. Nevertheless, we recommend that detectives try to spend a few more minutes on each interview and use their limited time more profitably by *lengthening each interview by a few minutes,* even if at the expense of spending less time on the road.[7]

In the interest of using their limited time more efficiently, detectives could increase the functional life of the interview without being physically present. It is natural for *E/Ws,* especially victims, to continue to think about the crime long after the interview has been terminated. During that additional time, she will recall new information (see footnote 3). The efficient *INT* can make use of that additional mental effort by *encouraging the* E/W *to tell him any new information that she recalls after the interview has ended.* Most of the detectives in our sample made

---

7. In our sample, the typical interview lasted only 10 minutes. (The actual interview time may have been a few minutes longer. We measured only the amount of time that was captured on the tape recorder.) In George's (1991) study, the average interview time was 16 minutes. By comparison, each detective spends considerably more time "on the road," filling out crime reports, appearing in court, giving depositions, etc.

an effort to do this by saying something like, "If you think of anything relevant after I leave, give me a call." That kind of claim suggests some uncertainty ("*if* you think of something"), as though the detective does not truly expect her to think of new information. If the *INT* conveyed the idea more strongly, that he does expect the *E/W* to remember more information, she is more likely to make the return call. To develop that expectation, the *INT* should close the interview with a stronger statement, such as,

> I am sure you will continue to think about the crime after I leave. *When* you think about it, you will also remember some information that you can't remember just now. Write it down and call me as soon as you think of anything new, even if it seems trivial. Here's my card.

If the *E/W* has thought of valuable information after the interview terminated, it is the *INT's* obligation to find out what she remembered. He should not rely on her telephoning him. Sometime after the interview, perhaps a day or two later, the *INT* should contact her, either by telephone or in person if it is convenient, and ask her whether she has thought of anything new. As a show of common courtesy, he should also inquire about her physical or emotional state.

CHAPTER SUMMARY

1. Regardless of the site, interviews should be conducted with one *E/W* at a time, if possible.

2. Interviews conducted at the crime scene are subject to many uncontrolled distractions. Interviewers should select the most remote location, allowing for the greatest privacy.

3. If possible, a separate interviewing room should be set aside at police headquarters to minimize distractions.

4. Interviews conducted at the *E/W's* residence permit control over the environment. To maximize this advantage, the *INT* must develop rapport with the *E/W* and engage her trust at the beginning of the interview.

5. Interviews conducted at the *E/W's* place of business are subject to many uncontrolled distractions, and as such, are not recommended.

6. Interviews conducted on the telephone are adequate as a follow-up to a personal interview, but they should not be used as the primary interview format.

7. In general, interviews should be conducted as soon as possible after the event to minimize forgetting. However, if the *E/W* is extremely anxious, has difficulty following instructions, or is incapable of doing intensive memory retrieval, it is better to postpone the interview.

8. Interviewers should motivate *E/Ws* to participate in follow-up interviews, because new information is likely to be uncovered. The follow-up *INT* should avoid being overly biased by preliminary information he knows about the case, so he can listen actively. The follow-up *INT* should avoid asking the same questions as the earlier *INT*. Repeat questions induce the *E/W* simply to repeat whatever she reported earlier.

9. The functional life of the interview can be extended by encouraging the *E/W* to tell the investigator new facts she has thought of following the interview. The *INT* should contact the *E/W* a few days after the interview to inquire about any new information she may have recalled.

Chapter 6

MECHANICS OF INTERVIEWING

In this chapter, we examine some of the mechanics of interviewing, including methods of formulating questions, techniques to improve the *INT's* comprehension of the *E/W's* responses, and suggestions to improve the *INT's* note-taking.

The distinction is often made between an interrogation, where the goal is to extract a statement of confession from a suspect, and an interview, where the goal is to elicit relevant, descriptive information from an innocent *E/W* (e.g., Flanagan, 1981). Although both can be classified generically as interviews, the goals and dynamics of interviews and interrogations are extremely different. For an interrogator to be effective, he must overcome the motivational problem posed by a reluctant respondent. In contrast, an interviewer must overcome the communication and memory problems of a willing respondent. The techniques and approaches employed by interrogators and interviewers are therefore radically different.[1] The successful interviewer must adopt the perspective that the *E/W* wishes to share valuable information with the *INT;* however, she must overcome the limitations imposed by imperfect communication and memory.[2] Unless there is good reason to believe otherwise, the investigator should adopt the general approach that the

1. Unfortunately, many police detectives use similar styles of interviewing when conducting interrogations and interviews with cooperative *E/Ws.* They use the more-aggressive interrogation style in all interviews, with the result that potentially cooperative *E/Ws* do not volunteer as much information as they might. Part of the problem, we suspect, stems from their training, where they often receive some formal skills in interrogation but little or none on interviewing cooperative *E/Ws.* As a result, they use their only trained skills (interrogation) in all interviews. Surprisingly, even some police-investigator manuals (e.g., Stone & DeLuca, 1980) do not distinguish adequately between the styles to be used in the two types of interview and, consequently, recommend several techniques that are dysfunctional when conducting interviews with cooperative *E/Ws* (e.g., introducing misleading information, asking many forced-choice questions.)

2. There are a variety of interview situations in which *E/Ws* are not as cooperative as the ideal we have described, as for example, in drug investigations, where *E/Ws* frequently are also suspects. In those situations, the *INT's* goals are to encourage the *E/W* to participate fully in the investigation and then to induce her to remember and describe the relevant information. In this handbook, we examine only those problems imposed by the limitations of communication and memory.

E/W is trying to be cooperative and that the two share a common goal. The general mood should be supportive and non-intimidating. If the investigator starts by assuming that the *E/W* is a potential suspect, that sense of mistrust will be conveyed to the *E/W* and will make the interview all the more difficult.

WORDING QUESTIONS

There are many ways to formulate and word questions or comments, some of which elicit more extensive and accurate responses and some of which elicit only simple, incomplete, and perhaps even incorrect responses. Questions that differ only minimally in wording may still elicit very different responses. For example, "Was he carrying the bag under his right arm?" seems similar enough to "Was he carrying a bag under his right arm?" In case you missed it, the first question used the expression *the bag* whereas the second question used *a bag*. Although seemingly negligible, this minute change in wording can have drastic effects on the *E/W's* recollection. In the above case, the first question (*the bag*) is generally interpreted as implying that there was a bag, and that the intent of the question is to determine under which arm it was carried. In the second question (*a bag*), the existence of the bag is not assumed. Experiments comparing responses to questions like this show that *E/Ws* are more likely to recall later that a bag was present when asked the first question (*the bag*) than the second question (*a bag*) (Loftus & Zanni, 1975). The moral of the story is that *INTs* must be careful how they word questions, since even simple changes can alter the *E/W's* recall.

Leading versus Neutral Questions

Questions vary in terms of what can be inferred from their wording. As in the above example, *E/Ws* may reasonably infer the existence of a bag from one question but not from the other. Similarly, listeners can also sometimes infer the *INT's* motivation from the question's wording. For example, if an *INT* asks, "Did the assailant have a blue shirt?" the *E/W* can infer that the *INT* suspects that the assailant had a blue shirt, and that the purpose of the question is to verify his suspicion. On the other hand, if the *INT* asks, "What color was the assailant's shirt?" the *E/W* can not infer the *INT's* belief about the shirt's color. We refer to this distinction as leading versus neutral questions, where "leading" refers to questions that permit the *E/W* to infer some knowledge about the world (there was a bag) or the *INT's* beliefs (he thought the shirt was blue), whereas neutral questions do not permit such inferences.

What difference does it make whether the *INT* asks a leading or a neutral question? Because of the mental operations in retrieving information from memory[3] and the social dynamics of the interview,[4] leading questions may bias what the *E/W* remembers and also how she reports her recollection. As such, leading questions do not accurately elicit the *E/W's* knowledge, which defeats the purpose of the interview: to determine what the *E/W* knows about the event.

There are also practical concerns associated with leading questions. They can be challenged legally by the opposing attorney—assuming, of course, that he or she can reliably reconstruct the *INT's* question. Leading questions also misdirect the investigation by generating incorrect information when the investigator's information is incorrect (there was no bag involved) or his expectations are wrong (the assailant was not wearing a blue shirt). If the investigator's knowledge and expectations are correct, they will not be invalidated by asking leading questions. However, the investigator can elicit the same information with a carefully worded neutral question. The advantage of a neutral question is that it is less likely to generate misleading information when the investigator's expectations are incorrect.

Wells (1988) offers several suggestions to develop non-leading, neutral questions.

1. The indefinite article, (e.g., *a* gun) should be used instead of the definite article (e.g., *the* gun), unless the object's existence has already been affirmed by the *E/W* (see also, Deffenbacher, 1988).

2. Questions about a person's or object's characteristics should use the

---

3. Recollection is not simply a passive search through one's memory bank for stored information. Rather, the rememberer combines the information contained in the retrieval probe (the *INT's* question) with the information stored in memory to construct a recollection (Tulving, 1983). The more information the *E/W* can infer from the question, the less her recollection reflects the contents of her memory.

4. In the typical police interview, and in many other investigative interviews, the *INT* is perceived as the expert and therefore may have some information unavailable to the *E/W*. Within the context of this two-person group, he has greater social status than the respondent. As a consequence, respondents tend to agree with the *INT's* expectations and give confirming responses (Smith & Ellsworth, 1987). Thus, the *E/W* may agree with the *INT* whether he asks, "Was he wearing a blue shirt?" or "Was he wearing a green shirt?"

noun form of the characteristic (e.g., "What was the assailant's *height?*") instead of the adjective form (e.g., How *tall* was the assailant?"). Frequently, the adjective form conveys the expected answer. [If the *E/W* has already used the adjective form (e.g., the *E/W* already said, "He was tall"), then repeating the adjective to elicit a more detailed response (e.g., "How tall was he?") is acceptable.]

3. Similar to Number 2, above, the question should not direct the *E/W* to confirm or disconfirm a specific trait ("Did he have a *red* beard?"). Instead, the question should be about the general dimension ("What *color* was his beard?").

The E/W *should use neutral wording and try to conceal his private expectations* whenever possible (see also, Deffenbacher, 1988; Flanagan, 1981; Prior & Silberstien, 1969; Rochester, N.Y.P.D., 1981; Wells, 1988). In order to do so effectively, the *INT* must learn to keep separate his expectations—especially those derived from a source other than the *E/W*—from those claims explicitly made by the *E/W.* And, whereas he need not be so careful about repeating statements claimed earlier by the *E/W,* he must use great caution about not implicitly communicating his own, private expectations. It is difficult, especially at first, to ask insightful questions that are not leading (Yarmey, 1979). However, by concentrating on proper wording and periodically monitoring one's interviews the technique can be mastered.

Negative Wording

We have often noticed that when the *INT* believes the *E/W* does not know the answer to a question, he asks the question in a negative form. He might say something like, "You don't remember the license plate, do you?" Questions using such negative wording, similar to leading questions, convey the *INT's* belief that the *E/W* does not know the answer, and that the *INT* will not be terribly disappointed with the *E/W's* inability to remember. This subtle message discourages the *E/W* from concentrating on the memory retrieval task and almost always elicits a "No" or "I don't remember" response. *Questions should be worded positively ("Do you remember . . . ?), even if the* INT *believes the* E/W *does not know the answer.*

Multiple Questions

Investigators need to develop thorough descriptions. Therefore, they must request information about many different characteristics of the event, especially about the assailant's appearance. In response to this need for extensive information, *INTs* sometimes ask overly complex questions containing many sub-questions. For example, the *INT* may ask, "Can you remember anything else? Did he have any scars, or tattoos, or glasses, a ring, any jewelry, any gold teeth, . . . ?" In fact, there are several mini-questions embedded in this one complex question: Did he have any scars? Did he have any tattoos? Did he have glasses? Did he have a ring? . . . Because it is difficult for *E/Ws* to process all of these mini-questions and simultaneously search through memory for the answers, *E/Ws* often make mistakes in answering such questions.[5] *Instead of asking a complex question,* INTs *should ask several simple questions, each about one or two related characteristics rather than one complex question* (see also Levie & Ballard, 1981). In the above example, the *INT* can ask one question about whether the assailant had any scars or tattoos. After the *E/W* responds, he can ask a second question about whether the assailant had glasses. The *INT* continues in such fashion to ask about small groups of related items until he has exhausted the list of questions.

The above example was constructed by us simply to demonstrate the point. Note a comparable problem in a real-life interview with an *E/W* to a crime. In examining the following complex question, try to think of a less-complex way to request the *E/W* to provide a detailed response.

> OK, if I can take you back to when the people first came into the shop. . . . try and focus in as much detail as possible as to the exact words that were said and what they look like and what they wore and if you can just describe exactly what happened.

---

5. The difficulty in answering such questions is that the *E/W* must do two things simultaneously. She must (a) remember the questions and (b) search through memory for the answers. Each of these tasks requires mental resources which compete with one another for the limited pool of resources available (see "Limited Mental Resources" in Chapter 7; Baddeley, 1986; Kahneman 1973). If the *E/W* concentrates on the memory retrieval part of the task, she may forget some of the details of the question. She may forget to indicate that the suspect had gold teeth because, in searching through memory to look for scars, tattoos, glasses, etc., she forgot the mini-question about gold teeth. On the other hand, if the *E/W* uses her mental resources to remember all of the components of the question, she may have more difficulty searching through memory for the relevant facts.

If the crime is complex and involves several perpetrators, the *INT* should *request the* E/W *to describe one perpetrator at a time. The goal is to exhaust all of her knowledge about each perpetrator before proceeding to the next.* Questions about many perpetrators induce a less-detailed response about each. In addition to making it easier for the *E/W* to search through memory, asking about one person at a time also makes it easier for the *INT* to keep track of the *E/W's* response. Listening to the *E/W* describing four or five people simultaneously can be extremely confusing and sometimes leads to the *INT's* blending together the characteristics of different suspects, attributing some characteristics of Suspect # 1 to Suspect # 2. One can easily imagine an *INT* confusing two or three suspects on hearing:

> The driver was wearing a blue jacket. The guy sitting in the back had the gun. He was wearing a red hat. The other guy was in the passenger's seat. I think he got out of the car first. The guy with the gun was the tallest. The guy with the red hat walked with a limp, but he seemed to be the leader, since he was yelling orders to the guy with the gun. He was the youngest. In a way, he looked like the driver, but thinner, and much younger.

Grammatically Complex Questions

Some questions are difficult to understand, not because the information is complex, but because the wording of the question is grammatically complex. A question like, "What did the tall guy with the shotgun that was pointed at the woman say when he heard the alarm?" is difficult to follow. The same question would be less confusing if it were stated in two short sentences: "The tall guy had a shotgun that was pointed at the woman. What did he do when he heard the alarm?" *Interviewers should avoid using long, grammatically complex sentences. It is preferable to break up the one long sentence into two or more short sentences.* Introductory sentences establish the general scenario and who was doing what. The final, critical question should be as simple as possible, focusing on only the person or object in question.

Jargon and Technical Terminology

Police investigation, like other professional work, has its own set of jargon. Although jargon may be useful, and certainly provides some color for informal conversations among members of the profession, it may be misunderstood by people outside of the group. Thus, a "black-and-white" is easily understood by some police officers as a reference to a marked patrol car; however, it may not be understood by a civilian. Failure to understand the question may lower the *E/W's* confidence and perhaps alienate the investigator. Worse than not being understood, jargon may be misinterpreted to mean something other than intended. Such misunderstanding may lead to confident, but incorrect, responses because the *E/W* is answering a question other than the one intended by the *INT.*

A similar problem arises when using technical terminology, which may be commonplace for the police investigator but foreign to the civilian. Asking whether the weapon is a revolver or an automatic may be a source of embarrassment to an *E/W* who is unfamiliar with the distinction. This may further lead to the *E/W's* losing confidence and giving less detailed and elaborate responses.

Interviewers should avoid using jargon and technical language, when-ever possible. Instead they should use everyday language, unless the E/W *has indicated that she is familiar with the technical terminology* (see also Flanagan, 1981).

CLOSED VERSUS OPEN-ENDED QUESTIONS

Questions can be categorized as either closed or open-ended. Closed questions elicit narrowly defined responses, whereas open-ended questions permit the *E/W* to give a more encompassing, more elaborate response. Examples of typical closed questions are "What color was the gun?" and "Was the gun black or a steel-blue color?" Yes-no questions ("Was the gun black?") also fall into this category. In each case, the expected response is only one word or perhaps a short phrase. An open-ended request for the same information is "Describe the gun in as much detail as you can." Here, the response might contain any-where from a one-word description to several sentences of informa-tion, depending on the *E/W's* memory of the gun and her descriptive abilities.

Both categories of question have some advantages and disadvantages, so the two should be used strategically for maximum efficiency. Closed questions have the advantage of eliciting relevant information and keeping the *E/W's* description from going far afield. They also pos-sess many limitations. Most notably, *E/Ws* search through memory superficially when answering these questions.[6] The *E/W's* memory may contain a detailed record of the event, but the closed-question format does not encourage her to access this knowledge. Even worse, closed questions elicit more incorrect answers (Cady, 1924; Geiselman, Fisher, Firstenberg, Hutton, Sullivan, Avetissian, & Prosk, 1984; Hilgard, & Loftus, 1979).

Another limitation of closed questions is that all of the elicited information is tied to the specific request. Questions about the suspect's height elicit information only about height; questions about the color of the gun elicit just that, the color of the gun. The focus of the question is well defined, which encourages the *E/W* to terminate her response as soon as she has provided the requested information. As a consequence, only explicitly requested information is gathered; no unsolicited information is generated. If the *INT* forgets to ask a relevant question, that information will not be gathered.[7] Even if the *INT* does ask all of the standard questions, idiosyncratic information, which the *INT* cannot reasonably anticipate but which may be vital, may go unreported. In one interesting robbery case, where we conducted a follow-up interview, the *E/W* remembered that one of the robbers had a physical deformity and that he walked on the outside of his right foot. Since it would be impossible for an *INT* to anticipate this condition and ask the appropriate closed question ("Did he walk on the outside of his right foot?") this kind of information can be elicited only with an open-ended question (see "Informative Responses" in Chapter 4). As a final note, in addition to being a superior information-gathering technique, open-ended questioning also is preferable from a legal perspective because it is less likely to be attacked by the opposition.[8]

---

6. We evaluate the depth of the memory search with two criteria: quality and latency of the response. Quality of the response, whether extensive-and-detailed or shallow-and-uninformative, is a direct reflection of the memory record activated. Latency to respond, whether slow or fast, has been found to be related to the nature of the response. Extensive, detailed responses typically have longer latencies, as more time is required to formulate the response (Johnson, 1972). Answers to closed questions, compared to open-ended questions, are generated after a relatively short latency. The answers are also briefer and less detailed.

7. Note that, by asking primarily closed questions, the burden of the mental activity ("If the *INT* forgets . . .") is on the *INT* instead of the *E/W*. This is counterproductive because the *E/W* has all of the relevant information not the *INT*. Therefore she, not the *INT*, should be doing most of the mental work.

8. Whereas it is easy to fall into the trap of asking closed questions that are leading, open-ended questions are less problematic, as they lend themselves more naturally to neutral wording (see "Wording Questions" in this chapter). Also, open-ended questions, especially when followed by long pauses, elicit more information than do closed questions (George, 1991). Therefore, *INTs* need not ask many questions when they rely primarily on open-ended questions. An *INT* can hardly be accused of asking leading questions or committing other improprieties if he spends most of the interview simply listening to the *E/W* generate information.

The advantages and disadvantages of open-ended questions are just the opposite of those of closed questions. That is, whereas closed questions keep the *E/W's* description on target, open-ended questions permit the *E/W* to generate irrelevant information. This type of problem can be minimized, however, by (a) giving the *E/W* permission to vent some of these irrelevant concerns early in the interview, before the information-collection stage (see Chapter 11), (b) prefacing the question with a description of the type of information that the *INT* considers relevant (see Chapter 4), and (c) framing the question so that it constrains the *E/W* to address only relevant details. For example, the *INT* might state:

> I'd like you to think about when you first saw the gun. You said that the robber held it in his right hand when he pointed it at you. Go back to that mental picture you have of his holding the gun in his right hand and pointing it at you. Now, try to focus in on the gun, . . . and describe to me in as much detail as you can exactly what the gun looked like from this picture.

Because the advantages of open-ended questions far outweigh any possible disadvantages, the *INT* should try to ***STRUCTURE THE INTERVIEW SO THAT MOST OF THE INFORMATION IS GATHERED THROUGH THE* E/W's *NARRATIVE RESPONDING TO OPEN-ENDED QUESTIONS RATHER THAN THROUGH BRIEF ANSWERS TO MANY CLOSED QUESTIONS*** (see also Levie & Ballard, 1981; Flanagan, 1981; Prior & Silberstein, 1969).

Although we discourage asking too many closed questions, they do play a valuable role in the interview. They ensure that the *E/W* directs her memory toward relevant facts. When the *INT* asks, "What color were the assailant's eyes?" either the *E/W* will provide relevant information or she will say that she does not remember. It is unlikely that she will waste the *INT's* valuable time with irrelevant information. On the other hand, open-ended questions, precisely because they give more freedom to the *E/W,* are more likely to elicit irrelevant information—although this can be reduced by framing questions properly. Furthermore, even though they have the potential to elicit a more complete response, open-ended questions seldom generate all of the information the *INT* needs. When asked an open-ended question to describe the assailant, the *E/W* may well generate a long list of attributes. Nevertheless, she may fail to provide an essential ingredient, like the color of the assailant's hair.

Strategic Use of Closed and Open-Ended Questions

In order to make best use of the unique contributions of closed and open-ended questions, and to minimize the deficiencies of each, we suggest the following strategy. Once the *INT* has identified the target information, e.g., the assailant's face, he should **begin by asking an open-ended question,** encouraging the *E/W* to develop as elaborate an answer as possible. If the *E/W* has not described some relevant detail after having generated a richly detailed answer, the *INT* should **follow up with closed questions** (see also Deffenbacher, 1988; Wicks, 1974; Wells, 1988).

The following sample interview exemplifies this approach of initiating the probe with an open-ended question and then following up with direct questions. Suppose the *INT* wants to extract a detailed description of the assailant's face, including information about hair (color, length, texture, hairline), eyes (color, size), and skin (color, markings). As in the following example, he begins the questioning with an open-ended probe, and then, depending on which of the features the *E/W* describes (and omits), he follows up with directed, closed probes.

INT: Tell me in as much detail as you can what the assailant's face looked like.

E/W: Well, he had a round face. It was kind of dark. I didn't notice any scars or anything like that. He had unusually big eyes, almost like a baby's . . . you know how their eyes really stand out, because they're so big for the size of their heads. And that's about all I can remember.

[Thus far, the *E/W* has provided the two relevant facts about skin (color and markings), one of the two relevant facts about eyes (size, but not color), and none of the relevant facts about hair (color, length, texture, and hairline). The *INT* therefore follows up with specific questions about the remaining fact about eye color and then probes about the hair.]

INT: You just said that he had unusually big eyes. Try to picture his eyes again. . . . [pause] . . . What color were they?

E/W: I'm not sure, but I think they were dark, maybe black or brown.

INT: You haven't mentioned anything yet about his hair. Tell me everything you can about his hair.

[Note how this is an open-ended question, although it is directed at a specific, as-yet-undescribed detail.]

E/W: It was also very dark, almost pitch black. It wasn't parted, but was combed straight back. It was medium length, not very short.

[Two of the four dimensions about hair (color and length) have been described, plus one additional fact not requested (combed straight back). The remaining two facts (texture and hairline) will have to be probed with direct, short-answer questions.]

INT: Can you describe the texture of his hair?
E/W: Yes, it was straight.
INT: What can you tell me about his hairline?
E/W: He had a pretty high forehead, and his hairline was slightly receding.

PACE AND TIMING OF QUESTIONS

The quality of a response is affected not only by the question's content, but also by its manner of delivery, especially its pace and timing. The often-used approach of asking questions in a rapid, staccato style elicits responses of poor quality.[9] This rapid-fire style of questioning interferes with memory retrieval and also with the *E/W's* communicating her recollection. When questions are presented quickly and abruptly, the *E/W* will search through memory superficially in order to produce a quick reply. As a result, either the search will end prematurely and no relevant memory record will be found, or only the most easily accessed memory record will be activated. In the first case, the *E/W* simply will not provide an answer ("I don't know"); in the second, she will provide a superficial description.

In addition to the memory-retrieval problem invoked, rapid-fire questioning (asking a question immediately after the *E/W* stops responding) limits the amount of time the *E/W* has to describe her

---

9. Our analysis of police interviews (Fisher, Geiselman, & Raymond, 1987) indicated that, more often than not, the *INT* asked a follow-up question within one second after the *E/W* terminated her response to the previous question. In several instances, the *INT* started his follow-up question even before the *E/W* had completed answering the previous question, and both were speaking at the same time! It is difficult to imagine that much information was conveyed during that period of simultaneous speech. Certainly the *INT's* time is not that precious that he cannot afford to wait another two or three seconds to extract a more thorough description.

recollection. In so doing, it interferes with the *E/W's* providing a detailed response.[10]

Rapid-fire questioning not only limits the current response, but if done repeatedly, it can abbreviate descriptions given later in the interview. When the *E/W's* responses are cut short by an impatient *INT,* she may come to expect that, for the remainder of the interview, she will have only a short period of time to respond to questions. With this expectation, she may abridge future responses in order to fit them into the expected time allotted. Once the *E/W* has developed such an expectation, she will conduct only those (superficial) memory retrieval operations that can be completed quickly. Both of these self-editing processes work to the *INT's* detriment.

To avoid these negative consequences, ***THE*** INT ***SHOULD SLOW HIS PACE OF ASKING QUESTIONS, AND ALLOW FOR AN EXTENDED PAUSE BETWEEN THE END OF THE*** E/W's ***RE-SPONSE AND HIS NEXT QUESTION*** (see also, Wicks, 1974). By an extended pause, we mean only a few seconds. It may feel uncomfortable to be in the middle of an interview and hear nothing but silence, however, if used properly, this silence will work to the *INT's* advantage.

As opposed to rapid-fire questioning, which limits the *E/W's* memory retrieval and descriptions, pauses do just the opposite; they enhance these processes (Dillon, 1982). Silence conveys to the *E/W* that the *INT* expects her to continue describing the object in question, which in turn, encourages her to do an even more intensive search through memory than she might have done otherwise.

Silence also has a direct effect on the *E/W's* willingness to speak. Most of us have been socialized to interrupt long periods of silence in a social situation by injecting a relevant thought. We feel uncomfortable at a party if there is no conversation, and so we try to think of something relevant to say, if only to break the silence. In the interview format, silence works to the *INT's* advantage by encouraging the *E/W* to speak more freely. Remember that the *E/W* also feels uncomfortable with the long silence, especially if she believes that she is responsible for generating the information during the interview (see "Encouraging the Eyewitness's Active Participation" in Chapter 3). Her discomfort with the silence will force her to break the silence by introducing new information.

---

10. In the course of describing an event, people pause slightly to organize their answers (Johnson, 1972). A pause in the *E/W's* response, therefore, does not necessarily indicate that the information has been exhausted. If the next question is asked during this pause, it may terminate the *E/W's* description prematurely.

The following excerpt, taken from an interview conducted with an elderly victim of a purse-snatching, illustrates how additional information can be gathered simply by a well-timed pause. The excerpt begins in the middle of the *E/W's* narration, which was elicited by the *INT's* request for an open-ended description of what happened.

> *E/W:* I turned around and observed a black man walking up our walk . . . He just walked toward me and started grabbing my purse. He just grabbed the strap and threw me around and I fell down and he got the purse. He ran across the street. I didn't notice him driving away, but I did observe an older-model car across the street in front of my neighbors. I came into the house and informed my husband about what happened. And he immediately called the police. And that's it.

> *INT:* (pauses here, without interrupting; silence lasts approximately 4.5 seconds)

> *E/W:* The man looked to me around five-foot ten or five-eleven. He was very husky looking. He had very broad shoulders, and was wearing a navy-blue shirt with what looked like white piping around the neck and some white trim over the shoulders. He was wearing dark pants. His hair was sort of wavy and flat. And his face was rather square, as I recall. He had sort of wide-set eyes and his lips were rather thick . . .

Notice how all of the additional information about the assailant's appearance came after the uninterrupted pause. Had the *INT* not kept silent here, but asked a follow-up question, he may not have elicited some of the following information. In listening to the tape recording, it appears as if the pause is very pronounced; however, when measured it lasted less than 4.5 seconds. Admittedly, investigators have busy schedules and cannot afford to waste precious time, but it is unlikely that any investigator does not have 4.5 seconds to "waste."

Investigators who feel uncomfortable even with a 4- or 5-second period of silence can substitute a word or short phrase encouraging the *E/W* to continue. Any of the following expressions may be used effectively: "continue," "keep going," "what else" or even a simple nod and "mm-hmm" (see also, Flanagan, 1981; Miner, 1984). Whatever phrase is used, it should be said unobtrusively, so that it does not disrupt the *E/W's* mental processes. It is immaterial whether the *INT* uses silence, a nod of the head, a word, or a short phrase to encourage the *E/W* to continue.

The important ingredient is that *the* INT *encourage the* E/W *to extend the search through memory and elaborate on her answer.*

TONE OF VOICE

The *E/W's* role in the interview, whether she or the *INT* becomes the central character, is determined in part by what the *INT* says, but even more so by the *INT's* non-verbal behavior, mainly in his tone of voice. If the *INT* speaks in authoritative tones, he will establish control over the interview and the *E/W* will play a more passive, peripheral role. If he speaks in a more relaxed, even tone of voice, he will encourage the *E/W* to play a more active, voluntary role in the interview. Ideally, during the information-collection phase, the *E/W* should play the central role, as she is the one with the relevant information. Once the information-collection phase has begun, and the *E/W's* memory becomes the focus of the interview, the *INT* should moderate his voice so that he does not become the focus of the interview.

The *INT's* voice can affect the outcome of the interview, especially during the information-collection stage, because it is an external signal that may be attention-demanding. If he speaks in a loud voice, it will act like any other source of distraction and will deflect the *E/W's* concentration from her own mind—the source of information—to the *INT's* voice. Therefore, *when the* E/W *is searching through memory, especially when she is concentrating intensely, the* INT *should speak softly.*

Some investigators may find it difficult to master the art of speaking softly at first, since they are not used to playing their professional roles as soft-spoken figures. Again, a minimal amount of practice combined with concentration and self-monitoring should promote better interview habits.

The *INT's* voice should not be so soft that the *E/W* will have to ask him to repeat the question, since that too is distracting. Our observations of police interviews have shown that not to be a problem. The more common error, which we observed frequently, is that the *INT* spoke loud enough to disturb the *E/W's* concentration on the memory retrieval task.

INCREASING THE INTERVIEWER'S COMPREHENSION AND RECORDING OF THE EYEWITNESS'S STATEMENT

One surprising finding in our field study (Fisher, Geiselman, & Amador, 1989) is that occasionally a relevant fact reported by the *E/W* was not included in the official police report.[11] In one such case, the *E/W* mentioned that the assailant was wearing brown, corduroy pants, but the police report indicated only the color of the pants, without mentioning the fabric. While there may be several reasons for such omissions, some probably occurred because the *INT* simply did not comprehend or record all of the information in the *E/W's* statement. What can be done to enhance the *INT's* understanding and recording of the message?

Slowing the Eyewitness's Speech Rate

The most common, technical reason for the *INT's* failing to comprehend the *E/W's* message is that her speech is too fast. Shortly after the crime, victims are more anxious than usual which induces them to speak faster than normal (Siegman, 1978). This is especially problematic if the *E/W* speaks with an accent or in some nonstandard dialect.

The *INT* can improve communication by encouraging the *E/W* to slow down her rate of speech. The *INT* can suggest that he is very interested in what the *E/W* has to say because her information is important in solving the case. However, in order for him to understand fully all of the details, it is important that she speak slowly and distinctly. The *INT* must convey—assuming it is true—that he has ample time to listen to all of the details of her story and that he is not in a rush to complete the interview. Similarly, the *INT* might indicate that he will be taking notes so he can include everything in his report, and it will be helpful if the *E/W* speaks slowly. As described earlier, a more indirect way to slow down the *E/W's* rate of speech is for the *INT* himself to speak slowly, deliberately, and calmly (see "Principle of Synchrony" in Chapter 3).

Sometimes, despite the *INT's* efforts to slow down the *E/W's* speech rate, it will still be too fast to note everything she says. When that happens, the *INT* can simply write a brief, one-word note (e.g., *jewelry*) to remind himself what the *E/W* spoke about. After the *E/W* has completed

---

11. We know what the *E/W* said, because we tape recorded the interview. In a recent study by Kohnken, Thurer, & Zoberbier (1991), almost one third of all of the relevant information was not recorded in the *INT's* notes.

a burst of information, the *INT* can ask her to repeat it slowly, so he can record all of the information. If the *E/W* has just described several facts, it is unlikely that she will omit any when asked to repeat them shortly thereafter, as long as the *INT* can provide the appropriate cue. For example, the *INT* might say, "You just described in great detail the jewelry the robber was wearing. Can you go over that description again, a bit slower this time, so I can write down all of the details?"

Taking Notes

Since even the most cooperative *E/Ws* speak faster than *INTs* can write, *INTs* need to develop some type of shorthand method of note-taking. One handy source of effective abbreviations is other, more experienced *INTs*. We suggest that investigators within a department simply pool their personal abbreviations into a master list that everyone can share.

Interviewers should keep in mind that their notes need not resemble Shakespeare; they only have to preserve the important details of the interview long enough so they can be converted to more conventional longhand script. If the notes written during an interview are particularly illegible or cryptic, they should be converted into legible, longhand script as quickly as possible after the interview, while everything is still fresh in the *INT's* mind. The more cryptic the notes are, the more important it is to convert them into conventional script shortly after the interview. Otherwise, the *INT* may be lulled into the false sense of security that, since his cryptic notes were comprehensible during the interview, they will be equally good in a few hours, when it comes time to write an official report. All too often, previously comprehensible markings are reduced to undecipherable scribbles later, when it is time to write the report.

Using Tape Recorders

One way to improve note-taking is to use a tape recorder (see also, Stone & DeLuca, 1980; Wells, 1988). When used properly, tape recorders guarantee virtually error-free recording. In addition, because the *INT* need not worry about taking notes, he can concentrate better on the *E/W's* responses and develop a more probing interview. As such, the tape recorder is a particularly valuable tool when investigating a complex event, with many suspects, victims, or actions.

In one such complex case, we tape recorded an interview of an *E/W* to a robbery that involved six suspects. Many of the details that were unclear in our notes, e.g., which suspects carried guns, became obvious when we replayed the tape recording after the interview. Presumably, we could have slowed down the interview to clarify some of the ambiguities in the *E/W's* description; however, that would have disturbed the natural flow of her narration and may have compromised the interview. Having a reliable copy of the interview which could be replayed repeatedly at our leisure allowed us to capture more facts than had we used only our on-line notes.

One note of warning when using the tape recorder: If the *E/W* is asked to act out a response or provide some other non-verbal response, the *INT* must translate the action into a verbal response that can be recorded on tape (see "Non-Verbal Responses" in Chapter 4). After the *E/W* has conveyed a non-verbal act, she should try to say in words what she has just acted out. If she omits an important component of her action, e.g., which direction she is turning, the *INT* can state verbally what she is portraying and ask her to verify his statement.

Some concerns have been raised about using tape recorders. Eyewitnesses may feel uncomfortable or self-conscious if they are being tape recorded and may inhibit their responses. Our experience has been that, for the first few seconds of the interview, *E/Ws* are aware of the tape recorder and they may even inhibit or modify some of their comments. After a very short time, however, they seem to be oblivious to its presence and respond naturally, as if there were no tape recorder.

Another problem, which is a more practical concern for police investigations, is that, depending on the jurisdiction in which cases are tried, the tape recording may be reviewed as evidence by the opposition. If there are any questionable issues recorded on the tape, e.g., leading questions, they may be used to help the opposition. With practice in the recommended interviewing technique, the *INT* should be able to minimize some of these errors, especially asking leading questions. Nevertheless, there may still be some unanticipated statements which can be used by the opposition to weaken the prosecution's argument. These are legal issues, and as such, we recommend consulting with expert legal opinion on the advisability of using tape recorders.

Given the technical sophistication of today's equipment, most battery-operated tape recorders are sufficiently portable to be used anywhere. Since almost everyone is familiar with using this kind of equipment, we offer only a few reminders.

1. Check to see that the batteries operate properly. To be sure, take along extra batteries.
2. Test the machine and the tape before conducting the interview.
3. Begin the interview by stating the case number, the *INT's* name, the *E/W's* name, the date, the time, and the place of the interview. When starting a new tape, leave a few seconds' of blank tape before recording, as sometimes, the first few seconds of tape do not record properly.
4. Label the cassette with the case number.
5. If taping starts in the middle of a cassette, be sure to leave enough room on the tape in case the interview lasts longer than expected. (Note: If one interview is recorded on one side of a cassette and a second interview is recorded on the other side, remember to rewind the tape back to the beginning for the second interview.)

REVIEWING THE EYEWITNESS'S DESCRIPTION

If the *E/W* provides extensive information, especially if it includes considerable detail, it is best to *review periodically the details provided*. This allows the *INT* to check the accuracy of his notes (see also, Stone & DeLuca, 1980). It also provides an additional opportunity for the *E/W* to think of extra details not mentioned in her initial description. When reviewing his notes, the *INT* should request the *E/W* to listen carefully and interrupt him immediately if (a) she notices any errors, or (b) she thinks of any new details not reported earlier. In order to assist the *E/W,* the *INT* must read his notes slowly and distinctly.

The *INT* should review the *E/W's* story both from his notes and from any details he remembers but did not record. If, in reviewing, the *INT* does remember some unrecorded details, he should write them down immediately. Otherwise, he runs the risk of forgetting them later.

It is best to review the *E/W's* statement after she generates a particularly detailed description. In doing so, the *INT* should be careful not to interrupt the *E/W* in the middle of an extended response. To avoid such an interruption, the *INT* should wait for a few seconds after the *E/W* has completed her description before reviewing his notes.

CHAPTER SUMMARY

1. Slight changes in wording can alter an *E/W's* testimony. Interviewers should ask neutral (non-leading) questions. They should also word questions simply and use non-technical language.

2. Open-ended questions are generally preferable to closed questions, although best use is made by combining the two strategically, with open-ended questions asked initially, and then followed up with closed questions.

3. Interviewers should avoid asking questions in a rapid-fire fashion. They should wait several seconds after the *E/W* has terminated her response before asking the next question.

4. Questions should be asked in a moderate tone of voice, so the *INT* does not intrude on the *E/W's* concentration and become the central character in the interview.

5. The *INT's* comprehension of the *E/W's* responses can be improved by (a) slowing down her speech rate, (b) using shorthand notes, and (c) using a tape recorder.

Chapter 7

PRINCIPLES OF COGNITION

Before examining specific techniques to enhance recall (Chapter 8), let us examine some of the underlying principles of cognition. We present these general principles so that the reader can better understand why the recommended procedures work. With this conceptual background, the innovative investigator should be more flexible in using the Cognitive Interview. If he understands the general principles behind the suggested techniques, he should be able to modify them as the specific needs of the situation change and develop new techniques on his own. If, however, at this point you wish to learn only the technique, without the background theory, skip to Chapter 8.

In order to understand how memory works, we need to focus on three basic issues of cognition: (1) the limitations of mental resources, (2) how knowledge is represented, and (3) how memories are retrieved. We address these three areas of cognition individually, however, they are very much intertwined (Haber, 1969). Some of the topics raised in one section will therefore extend into other sections.

LIMITED MENTAL RESOURCES

Although the human mind in some ways is far superior to the most powerful computers, there are still limits to our mental abilities. The primary limitation is in how many things we can be consciously aware of at any one time (Broadbent, 1957). Because you are reading this book now you are unaware of other messages in your environment, for example, dim noises in the background. Take a moment and listen to all of the background noises that can be heard if you attend to them. Once you start to attend to this other background information, you can no longer concentrate on the book, or at least not as intensely as when you focused exclusively on the book. (We apologize for bringing those background noises to your attention, but if you continue to concentrate on the book, the background noises will drop out of conscious awareness once again.)

Generally people can devote their full conscious awareness to only one information source at a time. If you have ever tried to listen to two conversations at the same time, you know that it is impossible to do that. When forced into such a situation, either you concentrate on one conversation at a time, switching attention back and forth between conversations, or you listen to both simultaneously, but with less than full concentration on each. You can extract some meaning from each conversation, but you also miss some of the subtle, hidden cues from each. Similarly, people cannot concentrate fully on two internal messages at the same time. Try doing two math problems at the same time: 240 divided by 16, and 126 minus 88. Again, you can do only one at a time. Now, you might think that there are some tasks that you can do simultaneously. You can chew gum and think about your name at the same time. That is because both tasks are relatively easy and thoroughly practiced. When either task is very difficult or is unpracticed, you can no longer do both at the same time (LaBerge & Samuels, 1974). If you try to listen to a news report at the same time you are balancing your checkbook, you can expect to make a mistake on one or both tasks.

That only one difficult message can be processed effectively at any time poses problems for both the *E/W* and the *INT.* The primary message that the *E/W* should be concentrating on is her memory of the crime. Any other sources of information that require her attention at the same time will detract from remembering the crime. This will occur whether the distracting source is external (listening to the *INT's* question) or internal (thinking about other information, such as, her telephone number). One principle of interviewing is to *minimize non-essential sources of distraction, especially when the memory task becomes difficult and requires full concentration.*

The *INT* is also subject to the limitation of conscious processing. There are several tasks that demand his limited mental resources. He must listen to the *E/W's* statement to determine the details of the crime. This task will be more or less demanding, depending on the complexity of the crime, the *E/W's* communication skills, rate of speech, accent, etc. The *INT* must write down the information on a notepad while listening to the *E/W.* He must also generate and keep in mind relevant questions to ask the *E/W* to draw out a more complete description. Although each of these tasks might be accomplished easily when done individually, they can be overwhelming when done simultaneously. It is precisely at times like this when a tape recorder becomes extremely helpful.

MENTAL REPRESENTATION

When we observe an event, we store information about that event in our memories. What is stored in memory is not the event itself, obviously, but some mental representation or code of the event. Our memories of the event therefore are very much determined by the types of mental coding system we use.

Three guiding principles determine how knowledge is coded or represented.

1. The memory code reflects the mental processes that were applied at the time the event was initially perceived.
2. Knowledge is represented in terms of its component features.
3. Each event or unit of knowledge is represented in many different codes.

Memory Codes Reflect Mental Processes

The mental code representing an event is not an exact replica of the event. Rather, it reflects the event as it has been interpreted in a specific psychological and environmental context (Koffka, 1935). Two people might perceive the same event; however, if their expectations or other thought processes differed at the time then their mental records,[1] and hence, their recollections, would also differ. In an extreme case, two people might observe a crime, and whereas one is horrified by it, the other does not even realize that a crime has been committed. Similarly, the same event would be represented differently if it were experienced in two different environmental contexts, e.g., at a football stadium and at home. The coded event, what is stored in the mind, reflects the actual event as colored by the observer's thought patterns, her emotional reactions, her physiological state, and the physical environment at the time the event occurred.

To make matters even more complex, the effects of these mental

---

1. We use the expressions, "mental records" and "mental codes" interchangeably.

and emotional processes are cumulative. The observer's thoughts and reflections about the event, even after it has occurred, also affect its representation. This is particularly troublesome when *E/Ws* are interviewed several times, because the thoughts evoked by the initial interview can alter the event's ultimate representation (Fisher & Chandler, 1991).

Because the memory code reflects, in addition to the event, the observer's thoughts and feelings, an *E/W's* recollections sometimes may be inaccurate, even though she is extremely confident (Deffenbacher, 1980).[2] Some of the characteristics she attributes to the objective event may actually reflect her own thoughts or emotions.

How do all of these factors (the *E/W's* thoughts, her emotions, her physiological state, and the environmental context) affect the *E/W's* ability to recall? Of primary interest for us, *memory of an event is greatly influenced by how many of the* E/W's *original thought patterns, emotional reactions, physiological state, and the physical environment can be recreated at the time of the interview.* The more similar her thought processes are at the interview to her thought processes during the event, the better her recollection will be.

Features of Memory

Many people believe incorrectly that an event either is represented in memory perfectly or that it is not represented at all. Psychologists suggest, however, that the mental representation of an event is a collection of individual features (Bower, 1967; Flexser & Tulving, 1978; Underwood, 1983). The knowledge of a person, for instance, is represented by a string of objective and subjective dimensions: height, weight, musculature, skin color, skin texture, friendliness, self-confidence, etc. According to this multi-feature view, each of the stored features may be accurate or inaccurate. The representation of a bank robber may be accurate in terms of his height and weight, but inaccurate, or even non-existent, in terms of body build and friendliness. Therefore, we may be able to recall some features of an event but not others. For instance, just because an *E/W* incorrectly recalls whether the assailant had a

---

2. Police often ask *E/Ws* at the end of an interview how confident they are about identifying the assailant from a picture. However, research indicates that there is little relationship between the *E/W's* confidence at this time and her ability later to recognize the assailant (Cutler & Penrod, 1989; Lindsay, Wells, & Rumpel, 1981). Investigators should therefore not refrain from showing a photoarray simply because the *E/W* indicated earlier that she was not confident.

beard does not necessarily imply that she will be inaccurate in recalling other facial features, e.g., whether the assailant had a scar.[3]

The same logic can be applied to remembering a name or a number sequence. An *E/W* who cannot recall a name that was spoken may be able to recall some features of the name: whether it was a typical or unusual name, English or French, long or short. She may even be able to indicate how many syllables it had and which syllable was stressed, although she cannot remember the exact name. This view, that partial information may be available even when the name is not, is at the heart of many specific memory retrieval techniques (see "Recalling Specific Information" in Chapter 8).

Multiple Representations

An event may be represented by several different memory codes. Each of these codes represents a different aspect of the event, so that some codes contain more useful information than others. *The* INT's *goal is to determine which memory code has the most useful information and then guide the* E/W *to activate that memory code.*

Precision of Knowledge

When an event is perceived, it is represented simultaneously at several different layers of precision, ranging from the very general to the very detailed (Fisher & Chandler, 1984, 1991). There may be many layers of representation, but to simplify the problem, let us describe only three. At the most general level of representation a bank robbery, for example, may be coded in the *E/W's* mind simply as "a bank robbery." When the *E/W* uses this very general representation to report what happened, she says only that she saw a bank robbery. Many detectives can identify with

---

3. A recent study (Fisher & Cutler, 1991) showed that the accuracy of recalling one feature of a perpetrator (e.g., hair color) is not predictive of the accuracy of recalling other features (e.g., clothing) or of recognizing the perpetrator in a lineup. Attorneys often try to convince jurors that, because one aspect of an *E/W's* testimony can be proven incorrect, the remainder of her testimony or her positive lineup identification should be invalidated. This ploy, which assumes that features are perceived and recalled interdependently, is not at all supported by our data, which suggests independent processing.

Another favorite argument raised by attorneys is that jurors should not believe the testimony of an *E/W* if she cannot recall some incidental feature of the courtroom scenario: "She can't even remember whether the bailiff is a man or a woman," argues the attorney to the jury, "so how can we trust her memory about an event that happened two years ago?" This argument is even weaker than the former, as it assumes not only that features are processed interdependently, but that this interdependence holds across different events (the crime and the courtroom).

the frustration of asking an *E/W,* "Tell me what happened," only to hear the simplistic, "I was robbed."

At an intermediate level of precision the event is represented and described as a set of actions: "Two guys came into the bank. One guy stood off to the side and the other waited on line. When he approached the teller, he pulled out a gun and demanded the money. The other guy yelled for everyone to lie on the floor. Finally, they both ran out of the bank and sped away in a car." This type of representation obviously has more specific information than the "bank robbery" statement, but it is far from ideal.

At the most detailed level of representation the bank robbery is coded as a string of sensory events containing the type of fine-grained, descriptive information that is essential for the investigation. "One robber was wearing a blue-green hat that was frayed in the front. I could see some hair sticking out from under his hat, on the left side. It was dark brown, with some red highlights just behind his ear. The back of his neck was tanned, and there was a two-inch diagonal scar on the side of his neck. The guy seemed nervous: his eyes darted around from side to side, and he spoke quickly and in a high-pitched voice. . . . "

In most cases, the investigator's goal is to activate the most detailed level of representation. Just because this detailed memory code exists, however, does not guarantee that it will be used, since the intermediate and general levels of representation are also available. Which level is activated depends on the *INT's* probing skills.

Detailed memory codes are difficult to activate because they are less accessible than are the general codes, and therefore the *INT* needs to be more skillful at guiding the retrieval process to locate them. Furthermore, reading out information from the detailed memory code requires a considerable amount of mental concentration. The *INT* may therefore have to provide greater motivation for the *E/W* to generate the necessary concentration. Finally, because of the intense concentration required, the read-out process is easily disrupted by external disturbances. When the *E/W* enters this state of heightened concentration, the *INT* must be especially careful to avoid interrupting her narration or disturbing her in any way.

How can the *INT* detect when the *E/W* is in this intense state of concentration? Frequently it is marked by characteristic eye fixations and speech patterns. The *E/W* may look away from the *INT's* face or close her eyes in order to reduce the amount of visual information she has to process. Also, her speech may become slower and more deliberate.[4] *It is imperative to avoid distracting the E/W when she shows these signs of intense concentration.*

Concept and Image Codes

Memory representations differ not only in terms of their precision but also in terms of their format. We shall refer to two types of memory representation: concept codes and image codes.[5]

Information in concept codes is stored as a listing of meaningful concepts, similar to a definition in a dictionary (Anderson, 1990). For example, the concept code describing an assailant might include the string of words or phrases: *nervous, clumsy, very tall, ugly, long scar,* etc.[6] When the *INT* asks for a description of the assailant, the *E/W* more or less opens her "mental dictionary" to "assailant" and reads out the list of attributes. These attributes are readily available and are easily communicated to the *INT.* There is a tradeoff, however, in that the concept code may be incomplete and imprecise (exactly how long was the scar, and where was it located?). If the *INT* needs more precise information, he will have to activate another type of mental code, the image code.

The image code is in the form of an image or mental picture. Unlike the concept code, the image code is in a form that resembles the object it represents, similar to a map, whose shape resembles the boundaries of the country it represents.[7] The image code of the assailant's face, for example, is shaped like the face. Coloring and texture are also represented on the image directly; the mental image has a specific color and texture which can be mentally "seen" and "touched." Auditory images also exist. The image code of a spoken message is an internalized "tape recording"

---

4. These behaviors are subtle and are not uniquely associated with intense memory retrieval. Therefore, they should be used with caution, more as a guide than as a hard-and-fast rule.

5. There is an ongoing debate within the psychological research community about whether images and abstract ideas are represented by the same format or by different formats (see, e.g., Kosslyn, 1981 and Pylyshyn, 1981). We adopt here the position of different formats only for ease of exposition.

6. To be more accurate, the concept code does not contain words and phrases but the ideas that these words and phrases refer to. Psychologists refer to these abstract ideas as propositions.

7. The physical entity of the mental code, the configuration of cells in the brain, does not resemble the object it represents. However, it *behaves as if* it had similar properties (second-order isomorphism; Shepard, 1975). For example, it takes longer to rotate a mental image through 90 degrees than through 45 degrees, just as it takes longer to rotate an actual object in space through 90 degrees than 45 degrees (Shepard & Metzler, 1971). The physical properties of the mental code are irrelevant for us. We are concerned only with the behavioral properties of the code.

of the message, where a loud sound is represented as a "loud" image. Because the image code is in the same form as the object it represents it contains more precise information than the concept code.[8] For example, the image code of a scar represents directly the length and the location of the scar, whereas the concept code may represent only that the scar was "long and on the left side." Once again there is a tradeoff. It is considerably more difficult to access the image code than the concept code. In addition, it is more difficult to describe verbally the contents of the image code than the concept code.

How does the *INT* know whether the *E/W* is describing an event from the concept code or from the image code? One cue to notice is whether the *E/W's* behavior mimics the form of the object being described. If the *E/W* is using the image code, her description of a room might start at some location and proceed in one direction (e.g., clockwise) as if she were actually walking through the room. If the same room were described from a concept code, the objects would be organized along a more meaningful or functional dimension. All of the appliances might be described first, and then the tables and chairs. Alternatively, the most expensive items might be described first, followed by the cheaper items. If the *E/W* were describing an assailant's voice from the image code, the *E/W's* voice pattern might change to mimic the assailant's. She might speak louder to reflect that the assailant was yelling or she might alter her speech to reflect the assailant's accent. If the *E/W* were describing the same assailant's voice from the concept code, she would indicate what the assailant said and then simply add, "he spoke in a loud voice," or " . . . with a southern accent." In one particularly dramatic case of describing an event from the image code, the *E/W* moved her hands along her sides to indicate exactly where the pockets of the robber's jacket were located.

Many events will be represented in both a concept code and an image code (Paivio, 1971), and both may be used during the interview. Which code is in use at any time depends on the *E/W's* perception of her task (Brooks, 1968; Tversky, 1969), which reflects how the investigator con-

---

8. In the concept code the object's characteristics are translated into a verbal (propositional) representation, whereas in the image code the characteristics are represented directly, without any intervening translation. In translating the information into the concept code, as in all other psychological transformation, errors are introduced. Furthermore, the accuracy of a verbal code depends on the *E/W's* language skills, so that *E/Ws* with poor language skills will have even-less-accurate concept codes.

ducts the interview. Ideally, the ***INT*** should encourage the ***E/W*** to use both codes, as each code contains some unique information.

In a recent interview of a woman who observed a suspect in a homicide case, the ***E/W*** remembered that the suspect had a gold earring in his left ear. She remembered this only after being probed about her image code of the suspect, not from an earlier probe of a concept code. Initially, she was asked a global question about the suspect's appearance ("Was he wearing any jewelry?"), which should have encouraged her to use the concept code (see "Probing Concept Codes" in Chapter 10). She indicated that she did not remember. Later in the interview, she indicated that she had a good side-view image of the suspect throwing his head back, as if to straighten his hair which had fallen in front of his eyes. This was our prompt to probe her about the image code she had of the left side of the suspect's face. When asked to focus on this image, she remembered seeing an earring in his left ear. As it turned out, this fact, along with other information uncovered, helped to identify the suspect and close the case.

MEMORY RETRIEVAL

Much of the forgetting we experience is caused by searching inappropriately for the stored mental record. That is, a record of the original experience exists in our minds; nevertheless, we fail to locate it.[9] To use a spatial analogy, we forget because we are looking in the wrong place in our minds. What can be done to make this search process more effective? There are three basic principles of memory retrieval enhancement: context recreation, focused concentration, and multiple retrieval attempts.

Context Recreation

No doubt all of us have experienced the following memory lapse. While watching television on the living room couch a pang of hunger

---

9. How do we know that a memory record exists, and that forgetting did not occur because there was no record of the event? Several psychological experiments have shown that many events that cannot be recollected when the rememberer is given one retrieval cue can be recollected when a different retrieval cue is provided (see Tulving, 1974). That recall was successful the second time means that the memory code must have existed all along and that the initial forgetting was caused by using an inappropriate retrieval cue (see also Chapter 2, Footnote 1).

arises and so we proceed absentmindedly to the kitchen to see what is available in the refrigerator. Having arrived in the kitchen, we suddenly forget why we went there in the first place. Bewildered and mildly embarrassed, we return to the living room to watch the rest of the television program. No sooner do we stretch out on the couch than we remember why we went to the kitchen in the first place. Why did we forget while in the kitchen but remember later when stretching out on the couch?

We said earlier that (a) one's physiological state (in this case, muscular feedback from stretching out on the couch) was a component of the mental record of the original event (getting a snack); and (b) recreating the original physiological state increases the likelihood of recalling the original event. By going back to the living room and stretching out on the couch, we recreated the original physiological state, which revived the thought pattern associated with that position. In practical terms, putting the *E/W* back in the same psychological, emotional, or physiological state as when the event occurred increases recollection (Tulving & Thomson, 1973). Recall is also enhanced by recreating the environmental context. To enhance recall in an investigative interview, therefore, *the* INT *should encourage the* E/W *to think back to the original event, recreating her thoughts, emotions, and physiological state at the time. The* INT *should also ask her to think about the immediate environment (room, weather, time of day, etc.) surrounding the event.*

Focused Concentration

Memory retrieval, like other mental acts, requires concentration, and any interference with this concentration is disruptive (Johnston, Greenberg, Fisher, & Martin, 1970). If the interview is conducted properly, the intensity of concentration on the *E/W's* face will be evident. She may close her eyes to improve concentration. If she keeps her eyes open, her pupils may dilate, and blinking will occur only infrequently (Geiselman, Woodward, & Beatty, 1982). On a global level, there will be a minimal amount of gross body movement and few, if any, characteristics of relaxed posture. As one of the *E/Ws* in our interviews exclaimed during a particularly intense session, "This is hard work!"

Frequently *E/Ws* will not attempt to search memory in a concentrated manner because the process is so mentally demanding. In those instances, the *INT* must encourage the *E/W* to make the necessary extra effort. The *INT* may also have to assist in the process by giving positive suggestions and reminding the *E/W* of the difficulty of the task. Because the concentration is so fragile, *the* INT *must also ensure that nothing occurs during the interview to interfere with the* E/W's *concentration, especially when retrieving from the most detailed level of representation.* This entails controlling the external environment and also the *INT's* interaction with the *E/W* to minimize any distractions.

Multiple Retrieval Attempts

One of the differences between good and poor rememberers is that those with good memories make more retrieval attempts than those with poor memories. People with poor memories think about an event for a few seconds, fail to bring up the memory, and then stop quickly. They terminate their retrieval efforts early because they believe "they have bad memories." By comparison, people with good memories make more retrieval attempts and do not stop trying to retrieve the event for a much longer time, perhaps because they know that "they have good memories." In fact, one of the reasons why good rememberers recall more is that they do not give up as quickly. In general, the more attempts the *E/W* makes to retrieve a particular episode the more information will be recalled (Roediger & Payne, 1982). *Witnesses should therefore be encouraged to conduct as many retrieval attempts as possible.*

A related idea based on the multiple-retrieval-attempts suggestion derives from the view stated earlier, that an event may be represented by several different memory codes. It follows from this that there may be many different retrieval paths that can activate a memory record (Anderson & Pichert, 1978). An event that goes unrecalled using one retrieval approach may be recalled if a different retrieval path is taken. For example, if an assailant made physical contact with the *E/W,* she might have both a visual and a tactile (touch) representation of the assailant's clothing. If she cannot recall the texture of the clothing by trying to visualize it, she might be able to recall it by thinking about what it felt like. In general, *the* E/W *should be encouraged to use a variety of different retrieval approaches.*

CHAPTER SUMMARY

1. Both the *INT* and *E/W* have limited mental resources. Therefore any internal or external sources that distract them from concentrating on their primary information sources will lower the quality of the interview.

2. The memory code reflects not only the objective event, but the psychological, physiological, and environmental contexts in which the event was experienced.

3. Events are represented as strings of features, each of which can be retrieved independently of the others.

4. Each event is represented in several, different memory codes.

5. Events are represented simultaneously at different levels of precision. The most detailed level is often the most valuable for the investigator; however, it is the most difficult code for the *E/W* to access and communicate.

6. Events are stored in both concept and image codes. The image code represents the event more accurately.

7. The three basic principles of memory retrieval enhancement are: recreating the context of the original event, inducing focused concentration, and encouraging the *E/W* to conduct multiple retrievals.

Chapter 8

PRACTICAL TECHNIQUES
TO FACILITATE MEMORY

Now that we have a general understanding of how information is represented in the mind and how it is retrieved, let us examine several concrete techniques that can be used to facilitate recovering these memories. Throughout this chapter, we proceed as if most or all of the *E/W's* experiences are stored somewhere in memory[1] and, despite her claims that she cannot remember, much of that information can be elicited by using the appropriate retrieval techniques. On her own, the *E/W* may not be able to recall certain details of the crime. With the *INT's* assistance, some of those details will become available.

The present chapter includes techniques to enhance memory in general and also techniques to assist in recalling specific information, e.g., names. The general-enhancement procedures rely on three of the principles described in the preceding chapter: (1) Recreating the context of the original environment, (2) Using focused concentration, and (3) Encouraging multiple retrieval attempts. Techniques to assist in recalling specific pieces of information rely primarily on the principle that events are not stored holistically, but as strings of individual attributes.

RECREATING THE CONTEXT OF THE ORIGINAL EVENT

The context in which an event occurs heavily influences how the event is stored in memory. The mental record of a bank robbery, for example, includes not only the robbery itself but also the physical and psychological environments in which it occurred. Thus, the lighting conditions and the observer's mental and emotional states at the time are important components of the memory record. Because context is such an important

---

1. It is impossible to confirm or refute this belief. In fact, Loftus and Loftus (1980) have raised cogent arguments that it is unlikely that all experienced events are stored in memory. Nevertheless, from a practical perspective, it is worthwhile to pursue this approach, as it leads to developing better retrieval techniques, which have been shown to improve the amount of information recalled.

determinant of the event's memory record, it also plays a vital role in determining which memory retrieval techniques are effective. The basic principle for investigative interviewing is that E/W *recall can be increased by recreating the event's context at the time of the interview.*[2]

The context of the original crime can be recreated either by explicitly requesting the E/W to think about the context or by asking specific questions that require her to think about it. For example, the *INT* can tell the *E/W* explicitly:

> Try to put yourself back into the same situation as when the crime was committed. Think about where you were standing at the time, what you were thinking about, what you were feeling, and what the room looked like.

If the *E/W* is told explicitly to recreate the context, she must be given enough time to do so before the *INT* probes for details. Generally, a few seconds (five–ten) should be adequate. The instructions should be presented slowly and deliberately, so the *E/W* can reconstruct the context while listening to the instructions. A common interviewing mistake is to rush through this phase, requesting the *E/W* to think about the context of the crime, and then immediately asking for a description of the event before the *E/W* has had adequate time to think about the context. After requesting the *E/W* to reconstruct the original context, the *INT* must wait until she has done so and only then start to probe about the crime. Typically, *E/Ws* indicate that they have thought about the context by nodding their heads, refocusing their eyes on the *INT,* or saying something like "OK."

If the *INT* wants to use the alternative method of context recreation, he can ask the *E/W* a series of questions, like, "Where were you standing at the time?" "What were your feelings like?" "What were you thinking about?" The questions should be asked one at a time, allowing the *E/W* to answer each. In the act of answering the questions, the *E/W* will recreate the original context. Both approaches, explicitly instructing the *E/W* to recreate the context and asking specific questions, are comparable so the *INT* can use either one or a combination of the two. For instance, the *INT* can explicitly instruct the *E/W* to recreate the lighting conditions but ask specific questions about her emotional state.

---

2. It is interesting to note that some police science manuals recommend asking such contextually-oriented questions, like: "Where were you standing at the time?" (e.g., Levie & Ballard, 1981; Weston & Wells, 1970). However, they suggest asking these questions at the end of the interview, when it is no longer valuable as a memory-enhancer. In order for context recreation to be helpful, it must be done toward the beginning of the interview, before the *E/W* attempts to remember.

If the *E/W* cannot remember some of the details of the original context, the *INT* can provide some of these cues for her, as long as the cues do not contain any leading information about the event. For example, he can draw a sketch of the crime scene, noting any permanent structures, like, buildings or traffic signs. Similarly, he may provide a photograph of the store or the intersection, as long as the photograph does not contain details uniquely associated with the crime.

Sometimes an *E/W* will indicate that, immediately after the crime occurred, she could remember a particular piece of information, but now, during the interview, she can no longer recall the information. For instance, she might indicate that she spoke about the crime with her husband at the dinner table the evening after it occurred, and at that time she could remember the insignia on the assailant's shirt. However, when she thinks about the crime now she can no longer remember the insignia. When this happens, the *INT* can recreate either the context of the original crime or the earlier episode in which the *E/W* successfully remembered. The *INT* might ask the *E/W* to place herself back at the dinner table where she discussed the crime with her husband and to recreate the mental thoughts she used to remember the crime. This is particularly valuable if the last successful recall (at the dinner table) occurred recently and if the *E/W* had some difficulty when she success-fully remembered the fact.[3] In order to use this strategy of recreating a recent successful recollection, the *INT* must know beforehand that the *E/W* had successfully recalled the fact earlier. Sometimes the *E/W* will mention this during the initial narrative description (see Chapter 11). If not, the *INT* should ask her explicitly whether she had ever successfully recalled the sought-for fact.

Because the memory record is more heavily influenced by the observer's mental thoughts than by the external environment, it is more valuable to encourage the *E/W* to recreate her mental thoughts than to recreate the physical environment. This is particularly important *if the* E/W *made a conscious effort to remember some aspect of the crime.*[4] *In such instances, the INT should encourage the* E/W *to recreate her thought processes of*

---

3. Difficult memory retrieval tasks are more likely to be done at a conscious level and therefore are more available for later recollection (Klatzky, 1980).

4. Crimes usually occur without warning, so *E/Ws* rarely make a conscious effort to memorize any details. For the most part, they respond instinctively with self-preservation being the primary instinct. When an alert, quick-thinking *E/W* is found, it is important to take advantage of her conscious attempt to remember.

how she tried to memorize the event. In one interview we conducted the *E/W* mentioned that, at the time of the crime, she had tried to memorize the license plate number of the get-away car. To capitalize on her insight, we asked her:

> Try to put yourself back in your car, when you noticed the get-away car leaving. You said that you tried to memorize the license plate, because you thought it might be important. What did you do to try to memorize the license plate?

This turned out to be a crucial instruction, because when the *E/W* had looked at the license plate she realized that the number was similar to her previous address. She then used that association to help memorize the license number. Once she remembered how she had tried to learn the number, she was able to recall two of the three digits. This is particularly noteworthy because this successful recall came more than one year after she had originally seen the car and after she had failed to recall the license plate at an earlier interview.

FOCUSED CONCENTRATION

We indicated in the preceding chapter that the *E/W* stores both general information about the crime ("there was a bank robbery") and also highly detailed information ("One guy had a small, jagged scar on his lower left cheek, a small mole over his right eye, . . . "). Not surprisingly, the detailed memory code is the one that contains most of the valuable information for the investigator. These detailed recollections are usually stored in the image code (as opposed to the concept code, see Chapter 7). The investigator's goal, therefore, is to extract as much information as possible from the detailed, image code.

Investigators may find some resistance here, even with a cooperative *E/W*, because retrieving from the detailed memory code requires intense concentration, often more than she is willing to put forth. Instead of intensifying her retrieval efforts, the *E/W* may resort to the simpler task of describing the crime at the more general level. That might solve the *E/W's* immediate problem of not expending mental effort; however, the resulting superficial description is of little investigative value. The *INT's* immediate task therefore is to motivate the *E/W* to develop the necessary focused concentration so she can describe the event at the most detailed level possible.

Many *E/Ws* do not appreciate how difficult it is to search through memory intensely for detailed facts. The *INT* should indicate that the task is not easy, but will require considerable concentration. The following statement serves as a model.

> I realize that this is a difficult task, to remember the details of the crime. All of the details are stored in your mind, but you will have to concentrate very hard to recall them. You have all of the information, so I'm going to expect you to do most of the work here. I understand that this might be difficult, but try to concentrate as hard as you can.

Maintaining Focused Concentration

Once the *E/W* develops the requisite focused concentration, it is essential that the *INT* does everything possible to help her maintain it. Unfortunately, through poor tactics, *INTs* sometimes unwittingly disrupt her concentration, either by their general actions or through poorly timed or poorly worded questions.

Most *INTs* never have the opportunity to observe themselves while conducting interviews, and often are unaware of their distracting mannerisms. Almost all of us have various nervous habits which we do not notice, but which are distracting to others, like, clicking pens, tapping fingers, etc. Because we do them unconsciously and repeatedly, they are not distracting to us and so we do little to eliminate them. Rest assured that they do distract the *E/W* from concentrating and, therefore, should be eliminated. To do that, the *INT* first needs to monitor his behavior. The *INT* can ask one of his co-workers to observe him while conducting an interview. Alternatively, he can videotape[5] himself conducting an interview and scrutinize the videotape objectively. As a personal note, we have listened to several of our own tape-recorded interviews and we are always astonished at the number of distracting mannerisms we display. Once the *INT* becomes aware of these sources of distraction, he should try to attend to these mannerisms consciously in his next few interviews in order to eliminate them from his repertoire.

Radios

One source of distraction *INTs* can eliminate very simply is the

---

5. Videotaping is more helpful than audiotaping, as some of the distracting actions are visual and are not noticeable from an audio tape. Obviously, though, an audio tape recording is better than nothing.

noise from their radios. In almost all of the interviews we examined, the *INTs* kept their radios on throughout the interview. Perhaps because detectives have their radios on most of their working day, they themselves do not find them distracting. Nevertheless, civilians generally do not listen to police broadcasts and are likely to find these signals distracting. The easiest way to eliminate this possible source of distraction is simply to *turn off the radio before conducting the interview.*

Eye Contact

A second, perhaps surprising, source of distraction comes from *INTs* making direct eye contact with *E/Ws*. Most people believe that direct eye contact is desirable because it helps to maintain rapport (see Chapter 3). This is true, and therefore is valuable especially at the beginning of the interview when first trying to establish rapport. However, at other times during the interview, especially when the *E/W* is trying to do mental tasks that require focused concentration, direct eye contact can be distracting.[6] The *INT* should look at the lower part of the *E/W's* face, so he does not appear to be rude, but not directly at her eyes.

Closed vs. Open-Ended Questions

Asking many closed questions forces the *E/W* to spend much of her mental capacity listening to the *INT's* questions instead of focusing inwardly on the source of her memory. If instead, the *INT* asks open-ended questions he can ask fewer questions, since each question elicits a more complete response. Obviously, the fewer questions the *INT* asks, the less likely he is to disrupt the *E/W's* concentration.

A related issue is that open-ended questions encourage the *E/W* to search through memory more intensely, thereby activating more precise levels of knowledge (see Chapter 7).[7] As a result, open-ended questions elicit more detailed descriptions than do closed questions.

---

6. We have been socialized to focus our attention on another person when he or she makes eye contact with us and we do not wish to be considered impolite by looking away. Therefore, when the *INT* makes direct eye contact with the *E/W,* he encourages her to focus on him as opposed to focusing internally on her memory of the event.

7. In answering an open-ended question, the *E/W's* memory search becomes more and more intense as she progresses deeper into the answer. The overt signs of focused concentration (deliberate, slow speech) are more likely to be found as the *E/W* progressively develops her answer. Therefore, questions that elicit longer, more elaborate, complete responses (open-ended questions) induce more focused concentration.

Interruptions

By far, the major source of distraction that *INTs* create is interrupting *E/Ws* in the middle of their narrative responses. Interruptions disrupt concentration because (a) they force the *E/W* to attend externally, on the *INT's* voice instead of inwardly, on her mental image, and (b) they prevent her from searching through memory intensely.[8]

Our analysis revealed that, more than anything else, the error of interrupting *E/Ws* discriminated between effective and ineffective interviewers (Fisher, Geiselman, & Raymond, 1987). Good interviewers were more patient and interrupted far less frequently than did poor interviewers. Because of its importance to effective interviewing and because of the frequency with which this rule is violated, *THE SINGLE MOST IMPORTANT SKILL* INTs *CAN LEARN IS NOT TO INTERRUPT THE* E/W *IN THE MIDDLE OF A NARRATIVE RESPONSE. THE* INT *SHOULD WAIT UNTIL THE* E/W *HAS COMPLETED HER NARRATION AND ONLY THEN, AFTER SHE HAS FINISHED, SHOULD HE ASK FOLLOW-UP QUESTIONS* (see also, Flanagan, 1981; Levie & Ballard, 1981; Prior & Silberstein, 1969; Rochester, N.Y.P.D., 1981; Wicks, 1974).

If interrupting is such a blatant, obvious mistake, why then do *INTs* interrupt so often? A compelling reason for interrupting is that the *E/W* has said something interesting and the *INT* wants to ask a follow-up question. He is concerned, however, that in further listening to the *E/W's* response and taking complete and accurate notes, he will forget his question. Given that these activities compete for limited mental resources, how can the *INT* (1) keep his question in mind while (2) listening to and (3) noting the *E/W's* answer? The solution is rather simple. Instead of keeping his question in memory, where it takes up precious resources, *the* INT *can write a note in his notepad as a reminder to ask the question later.* This maintains the question, but not at the expense of limited mental resources.

Suppose the *E/W* is giving a description of the assailant's car and, before completing the description, she switches over to describing the driver. The good detective naturally wants to extract as much informa-

---

8. In Footnote 7 we mentioned that the *E/W's* memory retrieval becomes more focused as she progresses further into the narration. The earlier part of the answer reflects a less focused memory retrieval than the later parts. Interrupting the *E/W* in mid-answer therefore leaves only the first part, which is the less focused. In order to get to the more focused, later part of the answer, the *E/W* must be allowed to complete her narration without interruption.

tion as possible about the car. Instead of interrupting the *E/W* in the middle of her narration to get more information about the car—and perhaps losing valuable information about the driver—he can simply write a note for himself as a reminder later to ask the *E/W* to complete her description of the car. Then, when the *E/W* has completed her narration, the *INT* can probe further about the car. He might say something like, "You just gave me a description of the assailant's car. You said it was a late-model, blue Ford. What else can you tell me about the car?"

Compare this approach to what happened in the following excerpt. The interview is of a woman who, while sitting in her car, was attacked by a stranger. The excerpt picks up in the middle of the interview, when the *INT* asks her for a description of the assailant.

> *INT:* Let's start at the top of him, if you can take yourself back to that moment when you first saw him and start to think about what was the first thing you saw. Start at the top of him and go down.
>
> *E/W:* The first thing I saw was the hat.
>
> *INT:* What kind of a hat was it?
>
> *E/W:* It was like a baseball hat.
>
> *INT:* But it was not a baseball hat.
>
> *E/W:* Right. It was made like a baseball hat. I saw the T-shirt.
>
> *INT:* What color was the hat?

Notice how his last question, about the hat, disrupts her train of thought about the T-shirt. As it turns out, the *E/W* volunteered little information about the T-shirt following this question. Obviously, we do not know how much information could have been elicited about the T-shirt had the *INT* not interrupted here. However, it is clear from the tape recording that the "hat" question interrupted her thinking about the T-shirt. Had the *INT* simply written a brief note in his notepad (*HAT ?*) as a reminder later to probe about the hat, he might have elicited more information about the T-shirt when it was most available.

The *INT's* notepad should contain information given by the *E/W* and also self-reminders to ask questions later. One system is simply to place a question mark (?) in the left margin as a reminder to probe for additional information. After these questions have been asked, the *INT* places a line through the question mark indicating that the question has been addressed. The *INT* checks periodically to see whether there are any question-marked notes that have not been probed.

When asking the E/W ***to return to an idea previously mentioned, the*** INT ***should try to repeat her words verbatim, or as closely as possible.*** He should try to duplicate the *E/W's* tone of voice, especially if there was unusual emphasis on a key word or phrase. In general, the *INT's* cue should be as similar as possible to the original version, as if he were replaying a tape-recorded message. The more similar his question is to the *E/W's* original statement the more effectively it will cue her to recover her mental thoughts from where she left off.

MULTIPLE RETRIEVAL ATTEMPTS

The core of this principle is that memory retrieval is a search process, and like all search processes, more searches lead to more finds. If a woman told you that she could not find a lost item after looking through her house for two minutes, certainly you would encourage her to continue looking. In a similar vein, the successful *INT* encourages the *E/W* to search through memory more thoroughly, especially if she has stopped the search process after only a few attempts. Additional search is valuable, however, only if new locations are examined. If the *E/W* examines the same places repeatedly, she will not locate anything new after the first search. Therefore, not only must the *E/W* be encouraged to search thoroughly, but also, she should be directed to explore new areas.

Increasing the Number of Retrieval Attempts

People often stop searching because they feel it requires too much effort. At such times, the motivational procedures suggested earlier can be used (see Chapters 3 and 4). Occasionally, however, the *E/W* will terminate her search prematurely, not because she is unmotivated, but because she believes the *INT* is unmotivated. This type of belief is conveyed by the *INT's* abrupt, hurried manner, as seen in the following behaviors:

- Opening the interview with a request for factual details, instead of a more personal introduction
- Indicating at the outset that the interview will take only a short time
- Constantly checking to note the time
- Leaving the radio on and interrupting frequently to listen to incoming calls
- Attending to issues related to other cases

- Fidgeting while sitting
- Standing during the interview (especially by an exit door) when it would be more appropriate to sit
- Speaking quickly
- Asking questions immediately after the *E/W* stops responding
- Interrupting in the middle of the *E/W's* response

We have suggested only a few of the more common errors that cause *E/Ws* to curtail their retrieval attempts. The serious investigator will no doubt think of many other behaviors that are equally harmful. Unless there is an emergency, and the *INT* must complete the interview quickly, these behaviors should be avoided.

On the positive side, the investigator can do things that encourage the *E/W* to conduct more memory searches than she might do on her own. The *E/W* will naturally pause somewhere in the middle of a narration, even if she has more information to convey. She may be looking for the word or phrase that best communicates her thought; she may be organizing the remainder of her narration; she may be searching through memory to generate more information. She may even stop to note the *INT's* reaction: Does he expect more information, or have I told him more than he really wants to know? If the *INT* asks an inappropriate question at this time, he may cut short a wealth of addi-tional information. He may be interrupting the mental processes needed to develop the remainder of the answer or he may be conveying subtly that he is satisfied with the *E/W's* answer and does not expect any more information. The patient *INT,* who remains silent while the *E/W* pauses, may find that his silence elicits more information than could any question.

Silence may serve as an effective cue to search through memory for more information, but only when the answer can be embellished. If the *E/W* has provided a complete answer to the *INT's* question, silence will not encourage additional memory search. If the *INT* asks, "How tall was the assailant?" and the *E/W* responds, "Five-foot-ten," silence will not generate any new information, because there is nothing that can be added to the answer. The *E/W* will just sit passively and wait for the *INT* to ask the next question. Silence might produce a more elaborate answer to a request like, "Tell me as much as you can about the assailant's face," or some other open-ended question, since, regardless of how the *E/W* responds, there is always more detail that could be provided. Silence, as a tool to induce more elaborate responses, will be most effective when it follows open-ended questions.

Another method to promote extensive retrieval is to encourage *E/Ws* to continue thinking about a fact that they could not recall earlier in the interview. Most people can monitor the contents of their memories very accurately. Even though an *E/W* may not be able to recall a certain fact right now, she can indicate how likely she will be to recover the fact later.[9] In the classic case, when a person is in a state of imminent recall, but cannot recall the information at the very moment—it is on the "tip of the tongue"—she will be more than likely to recall the information later (Brown & McNeil, 1966). The *INT* should therefore be sensitive to the *E/W's* intuition about the likelihood of recalling different facts and use that knowledge to decide which facts should be probed further. *If the* E/W *indicates that she cannot now recall a particular fact, but is confident that she knows the information, the* INT *should return to that fact later in the interview.*

Although the *E/W's* awareness of her own knowledge is generally accurate, there may be some ideas that she feels are not available, but which, in fact, can be brought to consciousness. This lack of awareness may occur because she is searching for the information incorrectly. Suppose, for example, that the *E/W* was attacked by several assailants. Later, during the interview, she is asked whether any names were mentioned. The *E/W* might say that she cannot remember any names, because the assailants never spoke to each other. Nevertheless, she may know the name of one of the assailants because it was engraved on a bracelet that the *E/W* noticed. She might have thought that the answer was to be found only in her memory for sounds and therefore never checked through visual memory.[10] One of the ways around this problem is to encourage the *E/W* to use a variety of different retrieval paths.

---

9. This seems to contradict an earlier claim, that *E/Ws* often cannot predict accurately whether they will be able to recognize the assailant's face if later shown a photoarray (see Chapter 7, Footnote 2). It appears that the ability to recognize faces obeys somewhat different rules of memory than does the ability to recall verbal labels (Fisher & Quigley, 1991; Wells & Hrcyiw, 1984), especially in terms of predicting performance on a later test (Cutler, Fisher, & Chicvara, 1989).

10. A detail from a complex event may be represented in several different memory codes. If the *E/W* monitors the wrong memory code, she may mistakenly believe that she cannot recall that detail (cf. "Principle of Detail" in Chapter 9).

VARIED RETRIEVAL

Eyewitnesses generally describe events in the order in which they occurred. They describe initially the first few actions and progress chronologically to the middle of the sequence and finally to the last few actions. One technique to encourage varied retrieval is to ask the *E/W*, after she has given the chronological ordering, to describe the events in backward order. She may begin with the last event, or some other prominent event in the sequence, and describe what happened just before that event, then what happened just before that. Often new details, especially actions, are remembered in the backward order that were not recalled in the forward order (Burns, 1981; Geiselman, Fisher, MacKinnon, & Holland, 1986).

It has been found that an action that is peripheral to the theme of a crime (e.g., smoking a cigarette while committing a bank robbery) is more likely to be recalled in a reverse-recall order than in a forward-recall order. This is important because peripheral actions are more likely than central actions (e.g., putting the money into a bag) to provide a basis for linking one crime with another.

Several investigators and prosecutors have mentioned to us that recalling in a backward order recall has also been effective when interrogating suspects. When recalling in an unexpected fashion, suspects often mistakenly say something that is incompatible with the original explanation they were planning to give.[11]

A second version of the varied-retrieval technique follows from the tendency for people to report events egocentrically, from their own perspective.[12] They will describe what happened from where they were standing at the time, or how the event affected them. To develop an alternative retrieval path, the *INT* might ask them also to describe the

---

11. When sequential events are rehearsed repeatedly in the same order, the contents of the memory become associated with the pattern in which they are rehearsed (Belmont & Butterfield, 1971). Requesting the information in a different order disrupts the rehearsal pattern and thereby provides access to other contents (see Geiselman, & Callot, 1990). This tactic can be generalized to requesting information in any unrehearsed format. We do not know of any hard data to support our claim, but at least theoretically, this procedure ought to be effective in cross-examination as a means to combat an opposing *E/W's* having rehearsed a testimony. Of course, one would need some insight into how the *E/W* rehearsed her testimony. We leave that up to practicing attorneys.

12. A noteworthy historical example of this principle was John Dean's testimony at the Watergate hearings. Dean's highly detailed report initially was interpreted by many as an indication of his excellent memory. Upon later analysis, it was found to be highly egocentric, overstating the importance of his role in the Watergate events (Neisser, 1981).

event from someone else's perspective. For example, suppose the *E/W* was a customer in a convenience store as it was being robbed. When asked to describe the robber, the *E/W* might rely on her image of the robber as she walked past him in the aisle. If the robber did not speak to the *E/W,* she might not describe the robber's voice. However, the *E/W* may have heard the robber speak when demanding money from the cashier. Had the *E/W* been asked to adopt the cashier's perspective and then describe the robber, she may have remembered that the robber had spoken and that he had a unique speech characteristic, e.g., a slight lisp. Care must be used when employing this technique, since the *E/W* may misinterpret the instructions of adopting someone else's perspective as an invitation to fabricate an answer. To combat this tendency, the *INT* *must remind the* E/W *to report only those events that she actually witnessed.* Also note that this technique can be used effectively only with adults, as young children have difficulty adopting another person's perspective (Flavell, 1986; Geiselman & Padilla, 1988).

Both of these varied-retrieval probes (change perspective and change order) are most helpful in complex cases, with many actions and many people involved. In simple cases, they provide less new information.

Finally, retrieval may be varied by probing different sensory modalities. Most people seem to have a preference for describing the visual characteristics of a scene rather than the auditory properties, and they are even less likely to use their knowledge of touch, smell, and taste (see Rock & Harris, 1967). Although *E/Ws* often do not voluntarily use these senses to describe events, valuable information may be uncovered if the *INT* directs attention to these other senses. Using vision alone, an *E/W* may not be able to describe the texture of the assailant's skin. However, if the *INT* encourages her to use her sense of touch, thinking about the sensation when the assailant grabbed her, she may realize that the assailant had very rough hands and had hairy arms. Based on the *E/W's* account of the crime, the *INT* should determine what is the most effective sense modality to probe. If the *E/W* indicates that the assailants spoke to one another or to her, then certainly the *INT* should request that the *E/W* think about the sounds of their voices. If the *E/W* came into physical contact with the assailant, the *INT* should probe for touch.

Since event details may be stored in both an image code and a concept code (see Chapter 7), the *INT* should probe along both dimensions to be complete. An *E/W* who cannot recall whether or not the assailant was wearing any jewelry may remember, when focusing on the mental image of the assailant's neck, that he was wearing a necklace. Conversely, an *E/W* who does not mention the necklace when describing her mental image of the assailant's neck may realize that he was wearing a necklace when asked to describe the general style of the assailant's clothing (e.g., whether conservative, loud, neat, disheveled).

RECALLING SPECIFIC INFORMATION

Whereas the preceding techniques were directed toward improving recollection in general, this last section describes techniques that are geared toward enhancing recollection of specific pieces of information. Typically, these are characteristics of either people (e.g., names, faces, voices, clothing, general appearance) or objects (vehicles, number sequences, weapons). Although this listing seems varied, in fact, all of the specific memory-enhancement procedures derive from two underlying principles. (1) Knowledge about an event is represented as a collection of attributes. (2) The various attributes about an event are associated, so that activating one attribute may stimulate other related attributes.

If an *E/W* cannot recall the assailant's name, she may still be able to recall specific attributes of the name, e.g., whether it was long or short. Because these attributes are related to one another, recalling one attribute may provide access to other attributes, and the combination of attributes may lead ultimately to the originally-unrecallable name. The operating principle underlying all of the specific memory-enhancement techniques is to *encourage the* E/W *to think about partial attributes of the concept.*

Every event can be described by an almost infinitely long list of attributes. For instance, if an *E/W* briefly glanced at the license plate of the get-away car, she might have noticed that,

1) the sequence was composed mainly of digits
2) the letters were consonants,
3) two digits occurred twice in succession,
4) the first digit had a circular shape,
5) the digits were similar to her father's telephone number,
6) she tried to remember the last three digits,
7) the name of the second digit had two syllables,
8) the characters were printed in orange on a black background,

These features fall into three categories: (1) properties of the to-be-remembered object that are unrelated to the context of the event (four is an even number), (2) characteristics of the object as it appeared in the specific context (the digits were printed in orange ink) and (3) meaningful or subjective interpretations of the event (the last three digits reminded the *E/W* of her father's telephone number). We shall refer to these three types of features as (1) event-free, (2) contextual, and (3) subjective. The interviewing procedures to facilitate recollection encourage the *E/W* to think about the to-be-remembered object along these three kinds of features.

Since the procedure is the same for all types of to-be-remembered information, we shall examine only two specific types, names and number-letter sequences. The suggestions provided are not intended to be exhaustive, and the reader should try to expand and adapt the suggestions to his or her specific investigative needs.

To facilitate recalling names, the *INT* should request the *E/W* to think about the following event-free properties.

(1) Frequency: Was it a common name or an unusual name?
(2) Ethnicity/nationality: Was the name characteristic of any ethnic or national group?
(3) Length: Was it a short name or a long name? How many syllables did it have?
(4) Stress pattern of syllables: Which syllable was stressed?
(5) Beginning letter: Think about the first letter by going through the alphabet, from *a* to *z*.

Contextual properties of names include:

(1) Speaker's voice: Think about the speaker's voice when he said the name.
(2) Visual pattern: Think about the handwriting in which the name was written.
(3) Local context: Think about where on the page the name was written, or where the speaker was standing at the time.
(4) Relation with other names: Were any other names mentioned?

Subjective properties of names include:

(1) Similarity to others: Did it remind you of anyone you know?
(2) Affiliation: Did the name remind you of an occupation or other group (political party, game, etc.)
(3) Pleasantness: Was the sound of the name pleasant or not?

To facilitate recalling number-letter sequences (as in license plates, telephone numbers, addresses, etc.) the **INT** should request the **E/W** to think about the following event-free properties:

(1) Length: How many characters were in the sequence? Was it long or short?

(2) Order: Were the digits in ascending or descending order? Were the letters in alphabetic order?

(3) Mixture: Was the sequence made up only of numbers, letters, or were they mixed?

(4) Repetition: Were any characters repeated (e.g., 6699)?

(5) Odd/even: Were the numbers mainly odd or even?

(6) Magnitude: Were the numbers large or small?

(7) Letter type: Were the letters mainly vowels or consonants?

(8) Pronounceability: Were the letter groups pronounceable (e.g., BAP) or not (e.g., BPA)?

(9) Meaningfulness: Did any of the letter groups form a word or a portion of a word (e.g., PRE)?

Contextual properties of number-letter sequences include:

(1) Presentation style: If the numbers were spoken, think about the speaker's voice. If written, think about the handwriting.

(2) Sensory pattern: If the numbers were written, think about whether they contained straight lines or curves. If spoken, were they one- or two-syllable numbers?

(3) Location: Where on the page were they located? Where was the speaker standing at the time?

Subjective properties of number-letter sequences include:

(1) Familiarity: Was the sequence, or some portion of it, similar to any others you know (e.g., your telephone number, address)?

(2) Difficulty remembering:[13] Did the sequence seem easy or difficult to remember?

---

13. If the *E/W* tried to remember the event afterward, the information may have been recoded into a different form. Typically, adults try to maintain information in memory by repeating it to themselves (Atkinson & Shiffrin, 1968). Even if the event initially was seen—so it was represented originally in a visual code—it would have been recoded into an auditory or articulatory form in the process of repeating it (Wickelgren, 1969). Note that in order for the *INT* to know whether to probe for the original (visual) code or the recoded (auditory) form, he must determine beforehand (a) whether the *E/W* intentionally tried to remember the event after it occurred, and (b) if so, in what form (code) did she try to maintain it in memory. Similar to the case where an *E/W* tries intentionally to learn the event for later memory (see this chapter, Footnote, 4), the *INT* must determine what mental operations the *E/W* used in order to probe memory successfully.

One important property of events that is important in many investigations, whether civil or criminal, is when the event occurred. Unfortunately, dating events turns out to be a relatively difficult task. If the *E/W* did not make a conscious effort to remember exactly when an event occurred, her recollection might be in error. The typical time-dating mistake is to claim that events occurred more recently than they actually did. An effective method to improve people's ability to date events is to provide them a landmark and ask whether the event occurred before or after the landmark (Loftus & Marburger, 1983). Thus, the *INT* might ask: "Did the event occur before or after your birthday?" Almost any prominent landmark will serve as an effective standard.

A second method to improve time-dating an event is to identify the context during which the event occurred. For events that occurred long in the past, the *INT* might ask the *E/W* to remember which house, or which city, she was living in at the time. For a more recent event, one requiring a finer discrimination, the *INT* might ask the *E/W* to think about which television show she was watching when the event occurred, assuming of course, that it is possible to determine when the television show was aired.

CHAPTER SUMMARY

1. Eyewitness recall can be improved by recreating the event's context (psychological, physiological, environmental) at the time of the interview. Context can be recreated either by asking the *E/W* specific questions about each aspect of the context, by instructing her to think about the context, or by providing a general, non-leading cue, e.g., a photograph of the location.

2. If the *E/W* intentionally tried to memorize the event, she should be encouraged to think about what mental procedures she used to remember the event.

3. Detailed memory requires intense concentration. Because this may be taxing for the *E/W*, the *INT* should motivate her to engage the necessary mental effort.

4. The *INT* should try to avoid distracting the *E/W* during states of intense concentration, either through his overt actions, asking many closed questions, or interrupting her response. Making self-reminder notes can assist the *INT* to overcome his need to interrupt.

5. The *INT* should encourage the *E/W* to search through memory

along many different retrieval routes. She may describe the event using different sensory modalities (e.g., visual, auditory), change the order of report (forward and backward), or change perspective (adopt someone else's view).

6. Recalling specific information (names, number sequences, etc.) is improved by encouraging the *E/W* to think about partial features. To recall digit sequences, she might think of the magnitude of the digits, whether they were constructed with straight lines or curves, where on the page they were located, etc.

7. Time-dating an event can be improved by comparing the event to some other prominent landmark in the *E/W's* life or by trying to reconstruct the context in which the event occurred.

Chapter 9

WITNESS-COMPATIBLE QUESTIONING

The rationale underlying this chapter is the intuitively obvious, but often ignored, principle that the *E/W* knows more about the event than does the *INT*. An effective interview should therefore be directed primarily by the *E/W's* knowledge, not by the *INT's* investigative needs.[1] Obviously, the *INT* must try to meet his investigative needs. To be successful, however, he should meet these needs in a format that is most compatible with the *E/W*. Experienced investigators, whose traditional approach is driven primarily by their own investigative needs, may have to overhaul their thinking to one that is more witness-oriented. Although uncomfortable initially, in the long run, this reorientation will yield more effective interviews.

To conduct a witness-oriented interview, the *INT* must keep in mind that (a) each *E/W* has a different area of expertise, and (b) each *E/W* has a somewhat different mental image of the crime. *Interviews, therefore, should be compatible with the individual* E/W's *expertise and her mental images of the event.*

INDIVIDUAL EYEWITNESS EXPERTISE

Whether it is because of innate ability or specific life experiences, each individual has different perceptual skills. Some are better able to discriminate colors, whereas others are better at spatial relationships. Similarly, some people are more prone to notice articles of clothing, whereas others observe body build. An interior decorator, for example, may provide discriminating information about how furniture is arranged, whereas someone who is interested in physical fitness may give a better description of the assailant's body build. To make best use of these

---

1. An analogous concept in business is the principle of client-centered marketing: gearing marketing tactics toward the consumer's needs rather than trying to force the seller's product on the consumer (Connor & Davidson, 1985).

individual differences, *E/Ws* should be encouraged to elaborate on those dimensions that they are most knowledgeable. Interviews that are not adapted to the *E/W's* unique skills, but which constrain everyone to answer the same set of questions, obviously can not take advantage of each person's specialty.

In order to take advantage of individual differences, the *INT* must identify each *E/W's* perceptual strengths and steer the interview in that direction. How does the *INT* determine the *E/W's* perceptual skills? Since he is not about to give her a formal personality test before the interview, knowledge about the *E/W* will have to come from listening carefully to any personal background information she reveals during the interview, and any subtleties that can be inferred from her manner of speech.

It has been suggested by some that there are stereotypical differences between men and women: men supposedly are interested in cars and other mechanical objects, whereas women are interested in clothing. Such stereotyping is more harmful than helpful, especially nowadays when men's and women's interests overlap. Rather than rely on any pre-established stereotypes, *INTs* should listen carefully to what the *E/W* actually reveals about himself or herself during the interview.

Two good sources of information about the *E/W's* skills are her job and her hobbies. Frequently, people acquire jobs because they are particularly skillful in some area. Conversely, they may develop special skills because of their experience on the job. Thus, a car mechanic can be expected to know more than the average person about cars. Similarly, an *E/W* who casually mentions that she has a gun collection can provide better-than-average information about weapons. Such information about the *E/W's* occupation, hobbies, and interests can be gathered by engaging her in general conversation at the beginning of the interview, when developing rapport. The *INT* should listen carefully to the *E/W's* wording when speaking. What dimensions does she use to describe objects? Does she focus on color, size, sound, mechanical properties, . . . ? Generally, people who are particularly discriminating along a dimension over-analyze things along that dimension. Painters, for example, notice the colors of objects more so than the average person, whereas dentists notice people's teeth and facial structure.

The *INT* should also attend to non-verbal messages, which provide additional insights into a person's interests. People who are particularly well-groomed notice other people's grooming habits; similarly, those who wear excessive jewelry are more observant of others' jewelry. These idiosyncrasies should be noted for later use because they provide insights into the *E/W's* unique skills.

Once the *E/W's* strengths have been determined, she should be given the opportunity to describe the crime in those terms. This can be accomplished either by explicitly asking her to describe the event along those dimensions (asking the hair stylist to focus on the assailant's hair) or by asking a non-directive question and encouraging the *E/W* to answer in her own manner ("Tell me in your own words as much as you can about the assailant."). This non-directive question, like the open-ended question discussed earlier, allows the *E/W* to describe the event in her own terms and does not constrain her to use unfamiliar language. The one tactic to avoid is to require everyone to answer questions in the same mold. Such uniformity might be desirable in scientific surveys, but is inappropriate for investigative interviews.[2]

INDIVIDUAL EYEWITNESS IMAGES

Not only do people differ along general perceptual abilities, they also differ in terms of their mental images of the specific event. Two *E/Ws* with identical perceptual abilities will still have different mental images of the crime if they were in different locations or had different thoughts or feelings at the time. The store clerk may have looked directly at the robber, whereas a bystander may have seen only a right-profile view of the robber as he was running out of the store. Both of these *E/Ws* have somewhat different pictures of the robber, and each can provide some information not available to the other. To elicit the maximum amount of information the interview should be tailored to tap into each *E/W's* unique mental images.

In violation of this rule, most police interviews are highly standardized (George, 1991). Often police ask the same series of questions to all *E/Ws* alike (Fisher, Geiselman, & Raymond, 1987). In more than half of the cases examined, the *INT* asked consecutive questions about the

---

2. Traditionally, scientific surveys attempt to standardize the question format, so that any differences in the observed responses will reflect differences among the respondents. By maintaining a uniform question format, instead of tailoring it to the individual respondent, it is assured that the survey instrument will be more compatible with some respondents' knowledge than with others', which defeats the goal of standardization. Survey scientists may wish to consider exchanging some of the surface uniformity (question form) for greater psychological uniformity.

assailant's age, height, and weight (or body build).[3] When asked why they use this "age-height-weight" order so often, many detectives answered that it was compatible with the crime report that they filled out. In fact, several detectives indicated that they used the checklist on the crime report to guide their questioning. When interview scripts become so standardized that they mirror a bureaucratic form more closely than the *E/W's* unique mental image of the crime, it is not surprising that much information is left uncovered. The first step in correcting this error is for the *INT* to reorient himself toward the *E/W* as the primary source of information.

We realize that it is important to examine all of the items covered on the crime-report checklist as they are investigatively and legally relevant. Our argument is not to omit these questions, but rather, to ask them in an order more compatible with the *E/W's* knowledge of the crime. Detectives may want to keep a copy of the checklist with them as a reminder of questions they may have forgotten to ask. *The checklist should serve only as a reminder to ensure completeness; it should not guide the sequence of the interview,* as suggested in some investigator's (Flanagan, 1981; Stone & DeLuca, 1980) and physician's manuals (Prior & Silberstein, 1969).

Interviewers who adopt a witness-oriented approach can expect that many of the obstacles to effective interviewing they currently face will cease to exist. New issues, however, will have to be addressed. How can the *INT* determine each person's mental image of the crime? How can these images be probed most effectively?

Determining the Eyewitness's Mental Images

In order to make the interview compatible with the *E/W's* knowledge of the crime it is first necessary to determine what are her mental images? The simplest way is *directly to ask the* E/W *what mental images she has of the crime,* specifically of the perpetrator. The *INT* can ask, "What are the different views you had of the robber?" "What is the best view you had of the robber?" or "Where was the robber standing (sitting)

---

3. In a recently conducted training seminar, one of the police participants volunteered to demonstrate a typical interview. Not surprisingly, he asked the "witness" these same three questions in the "age-height-weight" order. This occurred less than ten minutes after our opening remarks about the typical mistake of using this standardized order of interviewing. At the next training seminar, this time for state attorneys, the volunteer, an experienced attorney who had been conducting witness interviews more than thirty years, used the exact same "age-height-weight" order.

when you had the best view of him?" If the *INT* believes that the *E/W* has additional information, follow-up questions should be asked, like "Did you see him from any other angle, or from a different view?"

A more indirect, but often more illuminating, approach requires *listening carefully to the* E/W's *general narration of the crime at the beginning of the interview and trying to infer her mental images.* Success in this approach depends on the *INT's* listening skills and his ability to construct the event from the *E/W's* perspective. The *INT* must put himself in her place, "seeing" what she originally saw, "hearing" what she heard, and "feeling" what she felt.

The more direct approach, of asking explicitly where the *E/W* viewed the assailant, is particularly helpful in the early stages of learning the Cognitive Interview, before the *INT* has become skillful enough to infer the *E/W's* images indirectly. We recommend that *INTs* first learning to use the Cognitive Interview use the more direct approach (see Chapter 13 for the suggested order in which to learn interviewing skills). However, even veteran *INTs* who are adept at inferring the *E/W's* images by listening to her narration should use the direct-question format.

The *E/W* can help the *INT* to understand her perspective by drawing a simple sketch of the location indicating significant landmarks and exactly where she was situated. If the *INT* has adopted the *E/W's* perspective while listening to her narration, he should have a good idea which are the clearest views she had of the assailant. To illustrate, suppose the *E/W* provides the following narration.

> I saw the man come into the store and didn't pay much attention to him. There weren't very many people in the store at the time, since it was in the middle of the afternoon. Maybe there were two or three people in the store. I did notice that the man seemed to be taking a lot of time by the cigarette stand, which is surprising, since most people know which brand they want, so they just select their brand and then leave. The next thing I know, he's standing at the checkout counter and he pulls a gun on me. It looked like a cannon. He's holding the gun in his right hand, and then he yells at me to take all the money out of the register and give it to him. I was scared he was going to shoot me, so I just did what he said and emptied the register. He picked up the bills, put them in his pocket, and then ran out the door.

From this description, it appears that the *E/W* has at least four mental images of the robber: (1) a poor view of the robber as he entered the store, (2) a distant view of the robber near the cigarette stand, (3) a close-up view of the robber, with gun in hand, standing across the counter, and (4) an in-motion view of the robber running out of the door. In addition to these inferences from her narration, the *INT* might ask the *E/W* directly whether she has any views of the robber other than the four indicated. Once the *INT* has isolated the various mental images, he is now ready to mine their contents.

Before developing a global probing strategy, let us take a step back to examine the psychological processes associated with reading out information from mental images. With an understanding of the read-out process, the overall strategy will be more comprehensible.

Psychological Processes of Reading Out Information from Mental Images

In most cases, the *E/W* will have several mental images associated with the crime, as in the example just described. In addition, she will also have a concept code to represent the crime (see Chapter 6), and general knowledge unrelated to the crime, e.g., her telephone number. Prior to the first question, all of these mental codes are in a resting state, "on the back burner," so to speak. The information is stored somewhere in her mind, but the *E/W* is not consciously aware of it. It is something like the knowledge of one's birthday. It is always available, but until the relevant question is asked, the information is not in an active state of consciousness.

When a question is asked, the appropriate mental code is brought into consciousness and the respondent "reads out" the information. For example, if the *INT* asks the *E/W* to describe the robber's gun, she brings into consciousness the image of the robber, with gun in hand, standing across the counter. She then zeros in on the appropriate part of the image (the gun) to answer the question. If the next question pertains to the same image ("Describe his right hand") she continues to use the image. If the next question refers to a different image ("Did you notice any writing on the back of his jacket as he was running out the door?"), she abandons the current image (robber standing across the counter) and dredges up a different image that is more appropriate for the question (robber running out the door). Similarly, if the second question is about information stored in general knowledge ("Do you have an alarm system?), she abandons the first image and draws into consciousness the general-knowledge code containing the requested information (about the alarm system).

Each time a question is asked, the *E/W* checks to see if the question can be answered from the image currently in consciousness. If it can, she "reads out" the information from the appropriate part of the image. If the question cannot be answered from the image currently in consciousness, that image is abandoned in favor of a more appropriate source: either another image, a concept code, or general knowledge—or she says, "I don't know." The new code is then brought into consciousness, replacing the earlier code, and the process repeats.[4]

Two subtle principles of interviewing follow from this view, the Principle of Detail and the Principle of Momentum. The Principle of Detail suggests that, because the *E/W* checks first with the image presently in consciousness, a more informative image (one with more explicit detail) that is not currently in consciousness may not be examined. As a result, the *E/W* may possess more detailed information about an object than she provides in the interview. The Principle of Momentum suggests that once an image is brought into consciousness, it is more efficient to use that image to answer the next several questions than to bring up a different image for each question. Let us examine these principles more thoroughly to explore their practical implications.

Principle of Detail. An object may be represented in more than one mental image. In the scenario just described (page 121), the robber's face is represented both in the ***next-to-the-cigarette-stand*** image and in the ***across-the-counter*** image. Whether the ***cigarette-stand*** or the ***counter*** image is used to answer a question about the robber's face depends on which image currently is in consciousness. The current contents of consciousness, in turn, depends on the previous question. If the previous question was relevant to the ***cigarette-stand*** image ("How long was he standing there?"), then that image will be in consciousness and will be used to answer the face question. If the previous question was relevant to the ***across-the-counter*** image ("Describe the gun"), then the ***across-the-counter*** image will be in consciousness and used to answer the face question.

Which of these two images, ***cigarette-stand*** or ***across-the-counter,*** contains more detailed information about the face? Probably the ***across-the-counter*** image, since the *E/W* was closer and had a better view. Therefore, a

---

4. The model described parallels Kintsch and Van Dijk's (1978) model of text processing.

question about the robber's face will be better answered if it follows a question relevant to the ***counter*** image than if it follows a question relevant to the ***cigarette-stand*** image. The same question might elicit two different answers, one more detailed than the other, depending upon when in the interview it is asked.[5] One key to successful interviewing is to ***order the questions so that the most detailed image is used to answer any question.***

Let us apply the Principle of Detail to eliciting a physical description of the assailant. A close-up, frontal view usually generates the most detailed description of the assailant's face and hairline. This view is also most appropriate for upper-body clothing, like the shirt and jacket. Although excellent for some details, the frontal view may contain little information about the profile, for example, whether the assailant's chin was protruding, or whether he wore an earring. Such information might be better described from a side view, even if it was from further away than the close-up, frontal view. Thus, if the current question calls up the frontal view ("Did he have any gold teeth?"), the next question should be one that is best described by the same view (e.g., "What color were his eyes?"). If the next question is inappropriate for the frontal view (e.g., a question about the length of his sideburns), the *E/W* might respond, "About average; I really couldn't see them very well." If the sideburns question were asked while the profile image was in consciousness, a more detailed response might be generated ("Yes, I remember, he had long, curly sideburns, almost down to the bottom of his ear"), which might then trigger off another associated piece of information ("and he had a scar just under his left ear").

An interview with a victim of an armed robbery provides a particularly graphic demonstration. The *E/W* was in his car when he was approached by a gun-wielding man, who requested his wallet. From the *E/W's* narration, it is clear that he had two views of the robber: (a) a close-up view of the robber's upper body and face, when he stood at the side of the car (the bottom half of the robber could not be seen as he was standing behind the car door), and (b) a full-length view of the robber as he fled from the car. Following several questions that activated the *E/W's*

---

5. That the same object or event is represented in more than one mental code also helps to account for inconsistency across *E/W* testimony (see Chapter 5, Footnote 3). Which of these mental codes is activated depends on the *INT's* question (Fisher & Chandler, 1991). Radically different interviewing styles (e.g., prosecutor vs. defense) and contexts (the crime scene vs. the courtroom) promote activating different mental codes and, therefore, different *E/W* statements. That an *E/W* has several mental representations of an event does not necessarily imply that her recollection is inaccurate.

upper-body image (a), the **INT** probed about the robber's face and his clothing. When asked to describe the robber's pants, the **E/W** said that he could not see his pants, because his lower body was hidden by the car door. However, it is clear from the **E/W's** narration that he must have seen the robber's pants when he fled the scene. Had the **INT** asked the same question (about the robber's pants) after activating the view of the robber fleeing (image b) instead of the upper-body image (a), he might have elicited more information about the robber's pants, and also his shoes.

Principle of Momentum. Each act of drawing up an image code into consciousness requires some mental effort. Because **E/Ws** have only a finite amount of mental resources, every act of drawing up an image into consciousness increases the difficulty of the task and causes recollection to suffer.[6] The **E/W** may draw into consciousness a less detailed code (the concept code), or she may make less of an effort to read the information from the image code. In either case, her recall will be less valuable.

One key to successful interviewing is to present the questions in an order that minimizes the number of times the **E/W** must draw a mental image into consciousness. This is accomplished by *ordering the questions so that each question can be answered by the image currently held in consciousness.*

Compare the following two question sequences. The same three questions are asked in both sequences: two questions relevant to the *face-to-face* image and one relevant to the *running* image. (The questions refer to the sample narration presented earlier, in which the **E/W** has one view of the assailant face-to-face as he is holding the gun in his right hand, and a second view of the assailant's back as he is running away.) When the questions are asked in the correct order (both *face-to-face* questions are asked consecutively), the **E/W** must change images only once, between Questions # 2 and # 3.

Correct Question Order

Question Number	*INT's* Question	*E/W* Image Used
1.	Describe the gun.	Face-to-face
2.	Describe the assailant's right hand.	Face-to-face
3.	Describe the back of his jacket.	Running

---

6. Asking the identical questions in an order requiring more mental images to be drawn into consciousness can cause a decrement in memory of almost 20% (Fisher & Quigley, 1988).

When the incorrect order is used (the *running*-image question is asked between the two *face-to-face* questions) the *E/W* must change images twice, between Questions # 1 and # 2, and again between Questions # 2 and # 3.

Incorrect Question Order

Question Number	*INT's* Question	*E/W* Image Used
1.	Describe the gun.	Face-to-face
2.	Describe the back of his jacket.	Running
3.	Describe the assailant's right hand.	Face-to-face

When an image is brought into consciousness, the next several questions should be compatible with that image. Once the *INT* has determined which image the *E/W* is using, he should *exhaust the image of its contents before asking questions about a different image.*

A common mistake here is to interrupt probing an image with questions that refer either to another image or to general knowledge. The following excerpt, in which the *INT's* questions fluctuated between images relevant to the crime scene and general knowledge, exemplifies these errors. (Note also the excessive use of closed questions, Chapter 6.)

[The *E/W* is a young woman whose boyfriend was shot when an intruder came into her house. The excerpt starts in the middle of the *INT's* probing about the type of gun used.]

INT: What kind of gun did he have?

E/W: I don't know . . . it was small, I think a 22 [caliber].

INT: What color was it?

E/W: Silver.

INT: Was it a pistol or a revolver? Do you know the difference?

E/W: Pistol.

INT: Where did Pedro get shot?

E/W: It went through the neck . . . When he was laying down, it looked like the bullet went out from there.

INT: Did you ever hear Pedro mention this guy's name?

[This is a general-knowledge question that has little to do with the *E/W's* image of the crime. As such, it forces the *E/W* to give up her image of the scene to answer the question.]

E/W: No.
INT: Is Pedro married?
E/W: No.
INT: Where do you work?
E/W: Acme Import-Export Company.
INT: Where is that located?
E/W: 100 Main Street.
INT: When this guy left your house, how did he leave?

[Here, the *INT* returns to the crime scene, but by now, the intrusion of general-knowledge questions has forced the *E/W* to abandon her earlier image.]

E/W: Through the front door. As soon as he shot Pedro, he ran.
INT: At what point did he take the purse?
E/W: ... It must be when he ran, because when they were in the bathroom struggling, he didn't have it at that time.
INT: Did you see him when he ran out the front door?
E/W: Yes, I saw him, but I'm not sure he had the purse at that time.
INT: How much money did you have in the purse?

[This is another general-knowledge question that disrupts the *E/W*'s memory for the specific details of the crime.]

E/W: Around forty dollars.
INT: Did you have any jewelry?
E/W: No, but I had my credit cards and my license.
INT: What kind of credit cards did you have?
E/W: Visa, and the stores, ...
INT: How about your license. What name was on the license?
E/W: Anna Lopez.
INT: Do you know Pedro's home telephone number.
E/W: 949-8630.
INT: How did this person get into your house?

[We now return to the crime scene, causing the *E/W* to resurrect the crime-relevant image.]

E/W: Through the sliding glass door.
INT: Was the door unlocked?
E/W: No.
INT: OK, when did you get divorced from Mark?

[This is the third general-knowledge question to interrupt the flow of crime-relevant recollection within approximately four minutes. The interview continues with several general-knowledge questions about the *E/W*'s ex-husband.]

INT: When this person got out of your house, do you know which way he ran? Did he go toward the parking lot, or the other way, down the sidewalk?

[This question about the crime scene should have been asked immediately after the question about the assailant running out the front door. By this time in the interview, following so many disruptions to the image-readout process, the *E/W* no longer seems to be concerned with describing the event from a detailed image code, but reverts to a superficial action-oriented description most likely emanating from the concept code. Not surprisingly, the remainder of the interview elicited little relevant detail.]

Developing a Probing Strategy

In order to conduct a witness-compatible interview using the Principles of Detail and Momentum effectively, it is helpful to develop a global questioning strategy before actually probing the images. The core of such a probing strategy addresses three questions. Which images should be evoked? Which details should be extracted from each image? In what order should the images be probed?[7]

Of the various images the *E/W* has of the crime, only some contain facts relevant to the investigation. These images contain information about the assailants, weapons, vehicles, central actions, other witnesses, and the like, and should be evoked. Other images contain only incidental information (physical appearance of innocent bystanders, *E/W's* vehicle, etc.) and need not be examined. If they are probed during the interview, as an indirect method to collect additional information, they should be probed only after examining the more-informative images.

As in the earlier narrative (page 121), the *E/W* may have observed the assailant several times during the crime: when he entered the store, when he stood by the cigarette stand, when he drew his gun, and when he ran out of the door. Although some of these images contain more information than others, each image contains some unique information. Overall, the *face-to-face* image (when he drew his gun) may hold the most information about the assailant; however, the *running-out-the-door* image may

---

7. The material in the next section is the most difficult part of the Cognitive Interview to master. It should be learned only after all of the other basic skills have been perfected, as suggested in Chapter 13.

provide the best view of the assailant's back, and the *cigarette-stand* image may provide the best view of the left profile. All of the facts will fall into a pattern reflecting which image contains the most descriptive information for each fact (see Table I).

Table I
MENTAL REPRESENTATION OF A CRIME

	Mental Image			
Fact	*Enter-store*	*Cigarette-stand*	*Face-to-face*	*Run-out-door*
Left profile		X		
Right profile	X			
Front face			X	
Back				X
Hairline			X	
Right hand	X		XX	
Shoes	X			
Jacket insignia		X		
Shirt			X	
Belt buckle			X	
Gun			XX	X
Get-away car				X

Note: Some facts (e.g., Right hand, Gun) are represented in more than one image. The image with the clearest view of this fact is indicated by a double-X (XX).

As portrayed in this table, the assailant's right profile and his shoes are best represented in the *entered-the-store* image; the left profile and the insignia on his jacket are best represented in the *cigarette-stand* image, the assailant's face (from the front), hairline, right hand, shirt and belt buckle are best represented in the *face-to-face* image; and the assailant's back and the get-away car are best represented in the *running-out-the-door* image. Some facts are represented in more than one image. The gun, for instance, is most clearly represented (XX) in the *face-to-face* image, but it is also represented (X) in the *running-out-the-door* image.

After the **INT** has clustered the various facts around their respective images, he can then probe each fact when the most appropriate image has been evoked. In the preceding example, the **INT** should plan to ask about the assailant's right profile and his shoes after evoking the *enter-the-store* image. The left profile and jacket insignia are probed together in the *cigarette-stand* image, and so on.

In addition to the Principles of Detail and Momentum, the *INT* should consider other criteria in deciding which images to probe first, second, third, etc.

Eyewitnesses become mentally fatigued in trying to recall detailed information. Therefore, the *INT* should *first activate and probe the image with the most relevant information and then progress to the less-important images.* Refer to the mental representation in Table I. If the most relevant information is the assailant's face, probing should start with the *face-to-face* image. If the investigator already has a good description of the assailant's face, so that the most important piece of information still remaining is the get-away car, he should start with the *running-out-the-door* image. After each image is exhausted, the next-most-valuable image is activated and probed. This process continues until all of the images have been exhausted.

If a question is repeated within a short time span, the *E/W* is likely to give the same answer on both occasions. The first time a question is asked about the assailant's face, the *E/W* may indicate that it was clean-shaven with some pock marks on the left cheek. If shortly after she is asked again about the assailant's face, she will give the same answer. She may even say, "I just told you, he was clean-shaven and had some pock marks on the left cheek." In the same manner, if the *E/W* cannot provide any information the first time a question is asked, she will likely not respond if the question is repeated shortly thereafter. She might even say with some annoyance, "I just told you, I don't know."[8]

In order to generate new information from a repeated question several other mental activities must intervene (see Madigan, 1969). If an object is represented in two separate images, the two images should not be probed consecutively. Instead, the *INT* should evoke and probe a different image between the two. In the above example, if the *E/W* observed the gun in both the *face-to-face* and the *running-out-the-door* images, the *INT* should not probe these two images consecutively for information about the gun. He could probe the *face-to-face* image followed by the

---

8. When identical questions are presented in close proximity, the *E/W* will not search through her memory of the event to answer the second question. Rather, she will remember the answer she recently gave to the first question and simply repeat it (see Raaijmakers & Shiffrin, 1980, in Chapter 9, Footnote 4).

cigarette-stand image or the **enter-the-store** image and then, after these intervening images, probe the **running-out-the-door** image.

Interviewers always run the risk that *E/Ws* will lose their composure when faced with a stressful image, thereby jeopardizing the rest of the interview. To minimize the chances of that happening, **INTs** should probe anxiety-provoking images later in the interview, after they have tapped the other more innocuous images (see Chapter 4). For similar reasons, if the *E/W* is particularly anxious and has little confidence in her ability to recall information, the **INT** should start with the image that is easiest to describe, even if it is not highly informative.

CHAPTER SUMMARY

1. Interviews should be directed to the individual *E/W's* perceptual strengths and mental image of the event.

2. Interviewers should look for cues indicating the *E/W's* perceptual strengths and either ask specific questions directed toward these dimensions or ask more non-directive questions, encouraging the *E/W* to respond in her own style.

3. Interviewers can determine the *E/W's* mental record of the event by asking her directly about her mental image or by inferring it from actively listening to her narration of the event.

4. A strategy for probing the *E/W's* mental images should be developed according to the Principles of Detail and Momentum. Questions should be ordered so that (a) the most detailed image is used to answer each question (Principle of Detail), and (b) each question can be answered by the image currently held in consciousness (Principle of Momentum).

6. The most informative image should be probed first, proceeding to less-informative images. The question order should also reflect the *E/W's* anxiety, confidence, and whether or not she has recently answered a similar question.

Chapter 10

PROBING IMAGE AND
CONCEPT MEMORY CODES

Once the *INT* has developed an efficient strategy for probing the *E/W's* memory codes, he still must go through the mechanics of extracting the information. This stage is the heart of any investigative interview so it is essential that it be conducted systematically and efficiently.

Before beginning to probe specific images, the *INT* ought to take a few moments to think about his plan of attack. What are the *E/W's* images? In what order should they be probed? Which details should be extracted from each image? Although the *INT* should try to follow his plan of attack, he should regard it as only tentative. If any new information arises during the probing phase that suggests a change in strategy, he should be flexible enough to alter his plan accordingly. For example, a response to a probe of one image may suggest another particularly valuable image that the *INT* had not been aware of. If that happens, the *INT* should note the new image and probe it immediately after exhausting the current image.

PROBING IMAGE CODES

Preliminary Activities

To probe mental images most effectively, competing sensory signals should be minimized. The interview room should be set up with as few distracting sights and sounds as possible (see Chapter 5). To block out the remaining signals, *the* E/W *should be encouraged to close her eyes and concentrate on her mental image.* The *INT* might suggest:

> This is a very difficult task and will require a lot of concentration. You'll probably find it easier to concentrate if you close your eyes.

To clarify these instructions and also to lower the *E/W's* resistance to closing her eyes, the *INT* can set an example by closing his eyes. Some

E/Ws will be reluctant to close their eyes, especially if proper rapport has not yet been established by the *INT.* In that case, the *INT* can suggest that the *E/W* keep her eyes open, but focus on a solid visual field, like a blank wall.

Activating the Image

Activating a specific mental image begins by recreating the psychological and environmental context. The context here is very specific in that it refers to a particular moment during the event, for example, when the assailant yelled at the *E/W* to open the safe. In trying to activate this mental image, *the* INT *should recreate as faithfully as possible the* E/W's *earlier description of the scene, preserving her original wording and non-verbal expression.* If the *E/W* had said earlier that the assailant "pulled out a gun from his pocket and screamed, 'open the safe, or I'll shoot,'" then the *INT* should restate the *E/W's* message in exactly those words, if possible. If the *E/W's* voice rose in intensity to mimic the assailant's screaming, then the *INT* should do the same in recreating the context, although at a more moderate level so as not to disrupt the *E/W's* concentration.

Following this context recreation, *the* INT *should ask the* E/W *to generate in her mind a detailed image of the scene, elaborating and sharpening the image as much as possible.* This takes several seconds if done properly, and *it is imperative that the* INT *keep quiet while the* E/W *is "developing" the image.* Witnesses who claim to have an image instantaneously should be encouraged to think about the image further to elaborate on the details. The more time the *INT* allows for this mental focusing, the more detailed the image and later description will be.

A typical mistake here is to start probing the image immediately after instructing the *E/W* to develop it in her mind. Similarly, *INTs* sometimes err by fusing together the image-development and description stages by saying something like, "I'd like you to develop the image in your mind and then describe it to me." The *INT* must demonstrate patience here and *allow the* E/W *several seconds to concentrate exclusively on developing the image before describing it.* In order to assist the *E/W* to develop the image thoroughly and minimize the disruptive effects of describing it prematurely, the *INT* can suggest:

Don't say anything yet. Just take some time and try to develop the image first, so that it is sharp and clear in your mind.

Then, after waiting several seconds for the *E/W* to develop the mental image properly, he can request a description.

Probing the Image

After the *E/W* has activated and developed the mental image, she is now ready to describe its contents. With the *E/W* thus primed to provide a detailed description, the *INT's* next question is crucial toward conducting an effective interview. The following guidelines should therefore be followed closely.

(1) The question must be delivered slowly, deliberately, and softly, so that the *E/W* can maintain the image without being distracted.

(2) The question should be framed around information relevant to the investigation.

(3) The question must be open-ended, enabling the *E/W* to supply an extensive answer.

(4) The question should contain an explicit request that the *E/W* provide elaborate detail.

The following excerpt illustrates the general procedure.

INT: Sue, try to close your eyes. You'll be able to concentrate better.

E/W: I'd prefer to keep my eyes open.

INT: OK, then focus on the middle of the wall, over there (pointing).

E/W: All right.

INT: Now, conjure up in your mind's eye the image you have of the robber when he was standing across the counter. Take your time and develop that image until it is very sharp. Don't say anything yet; just try to develop the image as sharply as possible.

[Pause several seconds to allow the *E/W* to develop the image]

E/W: OK, I've got it.

INT: (softly, deliberately, and slowly): Now, focus in on the robber's face.

[Pause to allow the *E/W* to focus specifically on one area of the image].

INT: Now, tell me everything you can about his face. Include every detail that you see. Any detail you can provide could be helpful, so don't leave anything out.

[Note how the question is framed ("Focus in on the robber's face") and how it requests an extensive answer ("tell me everything you can ... include every detail")]

In response to this framed, open-ended request for extensive, detailed information, the *E/W* should provide either a narration or a listing of attributes. As this response is the primary source of information, it is imperative not to interrupt here. Similarly, to squeeze out the last ounce of information at this time, the *INT* should wait for several seconds after the end of the *E/W's* narration before he continues the probing.

Follow-Up Probing for Incomplete Narrations

On most occasions, the *E/W* will provide many details; however, the narration certainly will not be complete. She may, for instance, describe several details about the assailant's eyes, scars, beard, and mouth, but not say anything at all about his hair. Or, she may provide some, but not all, of the facts about specific features (eyes, hair, mouth, etc.). For instance, she may describe the assailant's hair color, but not hair length. In any case, the report will be incomplete in some respect and will require further probing of the image. This re-probing for missing information should be done immediately, while the relevant image is still active, before moving on to the next mental image (see "Principle of Momentum" in Chapter 9).

If the omitted details can be organized around a specific feature, especially one that is highly informative, like hair, then the *INT* should re-probe the *E/W's* image by focusing specifically on the omitted feature. The procedure for doing this is the same as before, namely, asking an open-ended, framed, question. The *INT* might suggest:

> I'd like you to focus specifically on the assailant's hair. Take your time and, again with your eyes closed, try to imagine what his hair looked like.[1]

After pausing for a few seconds to allow the *E/W* to re-activate and develop the image, the *INT* once again asks explicitly for a complete, detailed description: "Now, tell me as much as you can about his hair."

If the *E/W's* narrative response touched on all of the relevant features,

---

1. If the *E/W* does not do so on her own, the *INT* should request again that the *E/W* close her eyes and image the scene again. This generates more information than simply asking the *E/W* once, at the beginning, to close her eyes and create a mental image (George, 1991).

but simply was incomplete (e.g., she described the color and texture of the assailant's hair, but not the length or style), then the follow-up probing should take the form of specific, closed questions. The *INT* can preface these questions by saying:

> I'd like to go back to some of the things you mentioned before and ask you some more specific questions. You said that he had straight, brown hair. What was the length of his hair? (After the *E/W* responds about hair length, the *INT* asks another closed question about hair texture.)

Only those direct questions that are relevant to the currently-activated image should be asked now. All other questions, even those pertaining to the same object but which are incompatible with the currently-activated image, must be held in abeyance until the relevant image has been activated (see "Principle of Detail" in Chapter 9).

These follow-up questions should be ordered to start at one end of the image and proceed in a single direction, e.g., top-to-bottom, with a minimum of "jumping around." Thus, a questioning sequence of the assailant's clothing that follows a top-to-bottom order, such as, shirt-belt-pants-socks-shoes, is preferable to one that jumps around, e.g., belt-shoes-shirt-socks-pants (see also Prior & Silberstein, 1969; Stone & DeLuca, 1980). Following a simple, one-directional order facilitates the *E/W*'s memory search task and also simplifies the *INT*'s task of keeping track of which items have already been probed and which still remain to be probed.

If the answer to a specific question reveals an important, previously-unprobed source of information (e.g., the assailant was wearing distinctive jewelry), the *INT* should re-probe this specific source following the general procedure as outlined above, i.e., recreate the context, activate the image, probe the image with an open-ended question followed by specific probes.

Probing the Remaining Images

The same general procedure is also used to probe the remaining images. When switching from one mental image to another, the *INT* should make it clear that there is a break in the sequence. After having exhausted one of the images, he may say:

> Now let's examine another image. You mentioned earlier that you also saw the assailant when he ran out the door. Let's try to explore this new image the same way we did the earlier ones.

Before proceeding to activate and read out the new image, the *E/W* should be reminded to treat this new image independently of the earlier ones. That is, she should describe the newly-activated image as it currently appears to her and not simply repeat the answers that she gave earlier in the interview (cf. "Multiple Interviews with Eyewitnesses" in Chapter 5). The *INT* should request that the *E/W* respond to each image separately, whether it contradicts or is inconsistent with an earlier statement.

Re-Probing Earlier-Activated Images

Although it is preferable to exhaust each image of its contents before proceeding to the next image, at times, it will be necessary to re-probe an image examined earlier in the interview. After re-activating the earlier image, the *INT* should direct the *E/W's* attention specifically to the desired piece of information. Thus, whereas the original probing of the image was to elicit as much (relevant) information as possible, the re-probing is directed only at the missing piece of information. Of course, if the *E/W* volunteers new, relevant information, the *INT* should pursue it, but that is not the primary goal of re-probing.

PROBING CONCEPT CODES

After having probed all of the relevant image codes, most of the available sensory information will have been elicited. There still remains, however, the kind of global, undetailed information that resides in the concept codes. Here one finds such information as global, physical characteristics (height, weight, etc.), personality traits (he seemed uneducated), abstract ideas, like explanations (he dropped the bag because he was in a rush), and subjective impressions (he looked like my Uncle Harry).

Generally *E/Ws* can describe events from concept codes even without prodding, as these codes are easily accessed. The *INT* can simply ask the *E/W* to indicate in her own words, "What happened?" or "What did the assailant look like?" To elicit additional conceptual information, especially about action sequences, the *INT* can use the varied-retrieval strategies indicated in Chapter 8: encouraging the *E/W* to change the order of retrieval, from forward to backward, or to adopt someone else's perspective. She might, for instance, take the perspective of the assailant and indicate the reasons why the assailant did what he did. If there were many assailants, and one in particular seemed to be in charge, the *E/W* might take the leader's perspective and think about the general plan to coordinate the group's activities.

The *INT* may also want to elicit a subjective impression of the assailant's physical appearance. He might ask, "Did he remind you of anyone you know?" Or, the *INT* may say to the *E/W:*

> Describe any general impressions you had of the assailant, like whether he fit into any stereotype, for example, a typical athlete, car mechanic, high-school student, . . .

In eliciting descriptions of clothing, the *INT* can request information about the general style of the assailant's clothing, whether it was neat or sloppy, whether it was drab or colorful, etc. If the *E/W* volunteers any subjective impressions, these should be followed up by probes to convert them to objective descriptions (see "Recalling Specific Information" in Chapter 8).

The following sample interview illustrates some of the major concepts developed on probing image and concept codes. In the example here, the interview begins after the *E/W's* narrative description of the crime. From this narration, the *INT* inferred that the *E/W* had two clear views of the assailant, (a) a close-up, frontal view when he pointed a gun at her, and (b) a distant, left-profile view as he was entering the get-away car.

INT: Joan, I realize that this is a difficult task, and that you're upset, but it is important to concentrate as much as you can. Try to close your eyes, as you'll be able to concentrate better.

[*INT* closes his eyes as a model.]

> You said before that you got a clear view of him when he pointed the gun at you, that it was the first time you've ever seen a real gun. Take your time now and try to develop in your mind a clear picture of what he looked like. Don't say anything yet; just try to develop a clear picture of him.

E/W (immediately): OK, he was real big, maybe 250 pounds.
INT: Wait, don't say anything yet. First, try to develop as clear an image in your mind as possible. Just think about what he looked like.
E/W: (after several seconds): OK, I can see him.
INT: Good, now try to focus specifically on his face. Again, don't say anything. Just develop the image of his face.

E/W: (after several seconds): OK

INT: Now, tell me everything you can about his face. Don't leave out any detail. Just tell me whatever you think of.

E/W: It was kind of roundish, like he was overweight. He had a bad complexion, with pimples. Small eyes, I'm not sure what color though. He had short, brown hair. That's about all.

[*INT* pauses to allow for further elaboration]

E/W: Yes, also his ears were kind of big. They stuck out on the side.

INT: Let's go back to his hair. You said it was short and brown. Can you describe the hairline?

E/W: It was receding a bit, especially up here [points], off to the side.

INT: And what was the length of his hair?

E/W: Short, almost like a crew cut.

INT: You mentioned that he had pimples. Where were they?

E/W: Over here [pointing].

INT: What else can you tell me about his complexion?

E/W: He just looked like a typical teenager, with acne, especially on his forehead. He had some pock marks on his left cheek. He wasn't the handsomest kid I've ever seen.

[Following additional probing of the assailant's face, the *INT* switches to the gun, which was also available in this image.]

INT: You said that he was pointing a gun at you at this point. Try to focus your image again, this time on his holding the gun. Don't say anything yet; just concentrate on his holding the gun.

E/W: OK.

INT: Now, try to describe the gun. Tell me as much as you can about it.

[The *E/W* knows little about guns and provides only minimal description, even after the *INT* asks direct, closed questions.]

INT: Try to concentrate on his hand as he was holding the gun.

[The *INT* waits until she has developed the image]

In which hand was he holding the gun?

E/W: The right hand.

INT: Tell me everything you can about his right hand, as he was holding the gun.

E/W: He had large hands, like he was very strong. They were pretty hairy, especially on his forearms.

INT: Were there any markings on his arms, like scars or tattoos?

E/W: No.

INT: Did you observe any jewelry on his wrist?

E/W: Yes, he had a watch. It had a silver band, I think.

INT: Can you tell me anything else about the watch?

E/W: No, I didn't get a real good view of it.

INT: Were his arms covered by any clothing, or were they bare?

E/W: He was wearing a short-sleeve shirt, so his forearms were bare, but his upper arms were partially covered by the sleeve of his shirt.

[The *INT* proceeds to probe about the shirt, using this last comment as the guide. He then probes for other clothing in a top-to-bottom order. After having covered all of the information relevant to this image, he proceeds to the second image, of the assailant entering the get-away car.]

INT: Let's switch now to the car. You mentioned before that you saw him as he was getting into the car. You said that it was parked next to the mailbox. Try to develop the image now of the car as it was parked next to the mailbox. Don't say anything yet; just work on developing a clear picture of the assailant getting into the car.

[The *INT* waits for the *E/W* to develop the image.]

Which parts of the car did you notice?

E/W: The right side and the back.

INT: Try to put yourself back in the same state of mind as when you originally saw the back of the car. Think about what you were thinking about at the time. [pause]

Now, try to develop in your mind the image of the back of the car. Just work on sharpening the image in your mind. [pause] Now tell me everything you can about the back of the car. Don't leave out any details that you can think of.

E/W: I tried to look at the license plate, but I just got a glimpse of it and didn't see it very clearly. The car was reddish-brown. It looked like it wasn't very new, since there were some scratch marks, or the paint was peeling off. The rear lights were oval-shaped; I think the top part was red and the bottom part white.

INT: What else can you remember?

E/W: The back windshield wrapped around the side of the car.

INT: Can you remember anything else about the windshield?

E/W: No, that's about all.

INT: OK, let's go back to when you got a glimpse of the license plate. Where was it located?

E/W: In the middle of the car, just above the bumper.

INT: Can you remember any of the digits or letters on the license plate?

E/W: No, I looked at it, but not for long enough to make out any of the numbers or letters.

INT: I can understand that it is difficult to make out the numbers or letters when you only see them for a split second. Even if you can't remember any of the numbers or letters, try to think about what the plate looked like. Was it a local plate, from Florida, or was it from out of state?

E/W: I'm pretty sure it was a Florida plate.

INT: Was it made up of mostly numbers, mostly letters, or a mixture of the two?

E/W: There were numbers and letters, mixed together.

[The *INT* continues to probe about the license plate, using the specific procedures mentioned in Chapter 8.]

INT: You said that the license plate was just above the bumper. Try to focus on the rear bumper, just below the license plate. [pause]. Now, try to tell me as much as you can about the bumper of the car.

E/W: It was that black hard rubber, and it went all around the back of the car.

INT: Were there any decals or stickers on the bumper?

E/W: There were some stickers on the bumper, on the right side, but I didn't notice what was on the stickers.

[The *INT* continues to probe for distinctive features of the car, first covering the back of the car, then the right side. Because the *E/W* did not indicate in her description the make and model of the car, the *INT* concludes this section with related, closed questions about the car.]

INT: You said that you saw the assailant getting into the right side of the car. Did he get into the front or the back?

E/W: He got into the front door.

INT: Try to picture in your mind the assailant getting into the front door on the right side of the car. [pause] Focus in on him as he is entering the car. [pause] I want you to describe him from this image. Don't worry if you say something different from what you told me before. Just describe him from this image.

[The process of eliciting a person description continues here, using the same general procedure as earlier, except that here, more emphasis is placed on features not available from the earlier image (left profile, the assailant's back, etc.) In her description, the *E/W* mentions that the assailant was wearing a hat, a fact not mentioned earlier when probing the frontal image. After completing the probing of this "entering-the-car" image, the *INT* returns to the earlier image to probe for more details about the assailant's hat.]

INT: Let's go back to that earlier image, of the man when he was pointing the gun at you. Concentrate on the upper part of his face and his head. [pause] Was he wearing a hat or not at this point? [This is not a leading question, as the *E/W* mentioned the existence of the hat.]

E/W: Yes, I guess I forgot to tell you before.

INT: That's fine. Try to focus in on the hat, and just think of what it looked like. [pause] Now, tell me whatever details you can about the hat. Just describe what it looks like from this image, and don't worry about anything you said earlier.

[After the *E/W* provides additional information about the hat, the *INT* begins to probe for information from concept codes]

INT: When you looked at the assailant, what was your general impression of him? About how old was he?

E/W: About 18 or 19

INT: Can you describe his general appearance?

E/W: He was very big, actually fat. Maybe 250 pounds. He was tall, but not extremely.

INT: Compare him to me. Was he taller or shorter than me, or was he about the same size?

E/W: Maybe an inch or two taller than you.

INT: I'm 5-foot-11. About how tall was he, then?

E/W: About 6 feet, maybe 6-foot-1.

INT: What else can you tell me about his general physical appearance? Did he remind you of anyone you know?

E/W: Not really, maybe a little bit like my cousin, because of his hair.

INT: What about his hair reminded you of your cousin?

E/W: It was combed the same way, with the part way off to the left side. It looked really weird.

[The interview continues, with the *INT* probing for additional information in concept codes.]

CHAPTER SUMMARY

1. To facilitate the *E/W's* activating an image code, the *INT* should promote concentration by minimizing unnecessary distractions in the interview room. He should also instruct the *E/W* of the necessity to concentrate intensely and encourage her to close her eyes.

2. In activating the *E/W's* image, the *INT* should refer to it by using the same words she used earlier when describing the image.

3. The *INT* should instruct the *E/W* to develop the image clearly in her mind before describing it verbally.

4. When probing the image code, the *INT* should ask an open-ended question framed around a relevant component of the image. The *INT* should explicitly request for a detailed, elaborate response. The *INT's* question should be presented slowly and deliberately.

5. Follow-up questions should be asked about relevant information not included in the *E/W's* narrative response.

6. The *INT* should introduce a clear break when switching from one image to another.

7. Probing concept codes can be improved by asking the *E/W* to adopt someone else's perspective or by asking her to report the event in various temporal orders.

Chapter 11

SEQUENCE OF THE COGNITIVE INTERVIEW

Having covered all of the specific interviewing techniques, we are still left with an important ingredient, namely, to coordinate these skills into a smooth-functioning operation. Just like a football coach, who must coordinate the movements of many different players and have a strategy of which plays to select at the beginning, middle, and end of the game, an effective interviewer must coordinate the various questioning skills and have an overall strategy of which information to elicit in the beginning, middle, and end of the interview. Without such a coordinated approach, the interview will proceed inefficiently. The present chapter describes the subgoals of each part of the interview, from beginning to end, so that the *INT* can make efficient use of the probing skills developed thus far.

The general goal of the interview is (a) to guide the *E/W* to those memory codes that are richest in relevant information and (b) to facilitate communication when these codes have been activated. In order to determine which of the *E/W's* memory codes contain the richest information, the *INT* must first be familiar with the *E/W's* overall representation of the event. Only then can he make an educated decision as to which image contains the most valuable information. Having guided the *E/W* to the richest of these memory codes, the *INT* still must develop in the *E/W* the proper emotions and attitudes to retrieve and describe the event in detail.

The Cognitive Interview is divided into five sections, each of which makes a unique contribution to attaining the ultimate goal. The sections are: Introduction, Open-ended Narration, Probing Memory Codes, Review, and Closing the Interview. The introduction establishes the appropriate psychological states and interpersonal dynamics required to promote effective memory and communication during the remainder of the interview. The open-ended narration permits the *INT* to infer the *E/W's* overall representation of the event and to develop an efficient strategy for probing the various memory codes. The probing stage is the primary information-gathering phase during which the *INT* guides the *E/W* to the richest sources of knowledge and thoroughly exhausts them of their contents. In the review stage, the *INT* reviews the information he has recorded to check on its accuracy and provides the *E/W* with an additional opportunity to recall. Finally, when closing the interview, the *INT* concludes any official police business, offers a suggestion to extend the functional life of the interview, and tries to leave the *E/W* with a positive, last impression.

A step-by-step guide of the Cognitive Interview is provided as a handy reference in Appendix A.

INTRODUCTION

Because first impressions are lasting and can affect the tone of the entire interview, it is especially important that the *INT* complete this phase successfully. Unfortunately, many *INTs* waste this unique opportunity. They either rush through the introduction in order to start collecting detailed information immediately or they spend the time collecting background information to fill out forms required by a bureaucracy. In so doing, they close off later opportunities to collect in-depth information. Conducting a successful interview requires that the *INT* approach the introduction as an investment, where a small expenditure of time can lead to a large payoff later.

The success of every phase of the interview depends on the *E/W's* general psychological state and her social interaction with the *INT*. Therefore, the *INT's* primary goals during the introduction are to develop in the *E/W* the appropriate psychological mood and to promote effective social dynamics between the *E/W* and the *INT*. Having accomplished these primary goals, the *INT's* secondary goals are to convey the general guidelines to maximize later memory and communication.

Controlling the Eyewitness's Anxiety

Successful recall depends heavily on the *E/W's* ability to control her fears and anxiety, especially if she is a victim and the interview is conducted shortly after the crime. In such cases, it is essential that the *INT* spend time at the very outset of the interview to calm the *E/W* and to build up her confidence. Failure to do so often results in spending the remainder of the interview very inefficiently.

Because the *E/W's* anxiety can be a barrier to conducting a successful interview, it is worthwhile to alter the standard sequence of activities to calm a particularly anxious *E/W.* In such cases, the beginning of the interview might be reserved exclusively for non-threatening questions not directly related to the crime. Background, personal information (address, telephone, etc.), which should normally be asked toward the end of the interview, is more functional at the beginning of the interview with an anxious *E/W,* because answering such questions has a calming effect.

The second general goal of the introduction is to develop the social dynamics required to promote effective communication between the *E/W* and the *INT.* This entails developing a sense of rapport between the two and establishing the expectation that the *E/W* should play a central role in the interview.

Developing Rapport

Developing rapport is an essential ingredient in all interviews. However, it is particularly important when interviewing children and victims who have suffered physical or psychological abuse. As a byproduct of the rapport-building stage, in which the *INT* and *E/W* share their common experiences, the *INT* will learn about the *E/W's* personal background, her interests and her skills. In the process, some of the *E/W's* perceptual strengths should become evident thereby allowing the *INT* later to guide the interview toward those areas of expertise.

Establishing the Centrality of the Eyewitness's Role

Eyewitnesses may be reluctant to speak during the interview because they perceive the *INT* as controlling the interview. They wait for him to ask the proper questions and they generate answers only when asked direct questions. To discourage this type of passive responding and encourage a more active, voluntary style of communication, the *INT* should convey to the *E/W* that she is expected to be active and play the central role in the interview.

Maximizing Memory and Communication

Once the psychological and interpersonal aims have been met, the *INT* can concentrate on conveying general guidelines to maximize memory retrieval and communication. The *INT* should not assume that the *E/W* will volunteer information relevant to the investigation without being expressly told to do so. Rather, he should explicitly indicate his need for detailed information. This is especially true for interviews with children, who are unlikely to provided detailed descriptions without encouragement.

The *INT* should remind the *E/W* here not to edit any of her thoughts, but to say anything that comes to mind. This includes thoughts that seem trivial, out of sequence, or even contradictory to what she said at a previous interview. Care should be exercised here so that the *E/W* does not interpret these instructions as license to fabricate answers.

The final goal of the Introduction, promoting more focused concentration, can be met by explaining to the *E/W* that detailed memory search is a difficult task and that effective recall requires intense concentration. During these instructions the *INT* should convey his expectations that the *E/W* will concentrate thoroughly in retrieving from memory. These instructions must be supplemented by the *INT's* actions indicating that he is prepared to take the time necessary to promote such concentration.

OPEN-ENDED NARRATION

In the next phase of the interview the *E/W* describes in narrative style her general recollections of the event. The primary function of the open-ended narration is for the *INT* to infer the *E/W's* mental record of the event. With this knowledge, the *INT* can tailor the remainder of the interview to be compatible with the *E/W's* unique mental record. During this narrative phase, the *INT* should be attending more closely to *how* the knowledge is stored than to *what* (specific details) is stored. When did the *E/W* see the suspect? Which mental images provide the clearest view of important details?

Interviewers sometimes find it difficult to ignore specific facts mentioned by the *E/W* during this narrative phase and get bogged down trying to record all of the details. In the process, they lose sight of the *E/W's* overall picture of the crime and they conduct the remainder of the interview ineffectively. Remember, the goal of this narrative phase is to develop a strategy for the remainder of the interview, not to collect specific details (see also Stone & DeLuca, 1980). Excessive attention to one or two details at this point may sacrifice many facts that might have been uncovered later in the interview.

The narrative phase of the interview is comparable to planning a vacation. Before deciding exactly which cities and attractions to attend (which mental images to probe) experienced travelers first find out what each place has to offer. Certainly they would not drive to a location before determining what are the attractions. For all they know, they may wind up in an uninteresting place only to find out later that had they gone to a nearby location they could have seen many spectacular sites. Unless they were obsessively spontaneous—which might be fun, but probably inefficient—they would first speak to friends or travel agents to find out what is available in various places and then decide which places meet their interests. In the same way, before "visiting" one of the *E/W's* mental images and probing for details, the *INT* should first determine what can be found at the various mental images. Which images best meet his investigative needs? Having determined this, he can selectively probe the most appropriate images and in the most efficient order. Attending to details at the very outset, before knowing what are the various options, may well ruin the investigator's "trip."

Recreating the General Context

Before requesting the *E/W's* narration, the *INT* should recreate the general context associated with the event. At this point in the interview, the context is global. It refers to the *E/W's* general state of mind just prior to the event and the general physical environment surrounding the entire event. The *INT* might ask the *E/W* to describe why she was going to the bank and what were her general plans for the day.

Requesting the Narration

After the *INT* has recreated the general context, he is now ready to elicit the narration. He might say:

Tell me in your own words whatever you can remember about the crime from that point on. Tell me everything you can, in as much detail as possible.

Uninformative Descriptions

The resulting narration is generally focused on the event's actions, without much attention to detailed descriptions of the assailants. Many of the *E/W's* fears and anxieties, along with her sense of outrage with the unfairness of the experience, also punctuate the narration. Although many of these details are not particularly relevant for the investigation, the *INT* should still allow the *E/W* to describe these feelings, at least initially, and defer focusing on more relevant details until later in the interview. Obviously this requires the *INT* to use his better judgment as to how much irrelevant information is acceptable before interrupting and refocusing the *E/W's* description. It is preferable to err on the side of being too lenient here, even if it wastes some time, than to be too controlling and thereby force the *E/W* into a Dragnet ("just-the-facts") style of responding. Tight control, when applied early in the interview, may save some time, however, it will take its toll later and prevent access to other relevant information. Unless it has gone very far astray, the *INT* should not interrupt the narration.

If the narration does stray markedly from the target, the *INT* should not reprimand the *E/W,* but should suggest gently that she focus more closely on the crime. Similarly, when the *E/W* describes her feelings and concerns, the *INT* should simply acknowledge them and encourage her to continue with the narration.

Anxious Witnesses

If the *E/W* becomes extremely anxious during the narration, the anxiety must be treated first before returning to the narration. Forcing a highly anxious *E/W* to respond will generate errors or incomplete responses. Even worse, it may convert a cooperative *E/W* into a reluctant or uncooperative *E/W* for the remainder of the investigation.

Re-Probing Factual Details

Although most *E/Ws* will provide an action-oriented narration and will not focus on a detailed, physical description of the assailant, some *E/Ws* will generate detailed, informative answers. As this is the type of description *INTs* are seeking, they often interrupt in the middle of the narration to record the details and probe further. Interrupting here is an error as it may disrupt the *E/W's* narration and cause it to be incomplete. As a result, the *INT* may draw an incorrect inference of the *E/W's* overall representation of the crime, which will lead to inefficient probing later in the interview. The net result of this simple interruption is that it can cause the loss of many facts later in the interview. Rather than interrupt the *E/W's* narration, the *INT* should make a simple note to remind himself later in the interview to re-probe a fact mentioned earlier.

Determining the Eyewitness's Representation

The easiest way to determine the *E/W's* mental representation of the event is simply to ask her directly which views she had of the assailant or other important objects. The more indirect method is to infer the *E/W's* mental representation by listening attentively to her narration, adopting her perspective, and seeing the event in the same way as she initially experienced it. During the narration, the *INT* should pay particular attention to any indications that the *E/W* had a clear view of the suspects, important objects, or relevant actions.[1] The *E/W* may indicate her viewing perspective by using phrases like, "I saw him out of the corner of my eye," or "I first noticed him when I turned around." Sometimes the *E/W* will indicate the physical context isolating the scene, as in "He was standing near the door," or "He was walking toward the safe."

Indications that the *E/W* has a particularly clear mental image, that she is drawing from the image code, are often marked by a change in her form of responding. She may speak more deliberately or alter her voice quality to mimic the assailant's speech. She may change her eye fixations by deflecting her gaze away from the *INT* by defocusing her eyes to search internally. The level of description may become more detailed, again reflecting a change from the concept code to the image code.

Notating the Eyewitness's Images

When the various signs of the *E/W's* image codes occur, the *INT* should note them so he can probe the images later for additional

---

1. The clear "view" refers to any of the senses, not only visual. The *E/W* may have a clear sound image, in which she can hear internally the sound of the assailant's voice, or a clear tactile image in which she can feel internally the assailant's skin.

information. At this stage the *INT's* notes should be sketchy (see Stone & DeLuca, 1980), with just enough detail so that later he can re-create the scene and remind the *E/W* of key words and phrases she used earlier. The *INT* is not so much interested in notating the details of the narration as the mental images the *E/W* is drawing from.

Most of the *INT's* knowledge about the *E/W's* mental images of the crime comes from listening carefully to her narration. Sometimes, however, a valuable mental image is not included in the narration. The *E/W* may simply have forgotten to describe it. She may have been concentrating on other mental images, or she may have thought about the image at an inappropriate time and felt awkward introducing it abruptly. Whatever the reason, after the narration the *INT* should explicitly ask the *E/W* whether she has any mental images of the crime, especially of the assailant, that she has not yet described. To be on the safe side, especially for those who are not yet expert in the Cognitive Interview, *INTs* should ask the *E/W:* "What is the best view you had of the assailant?"

Developing a Probing Strategy

After having listened to the *E/W's* narration, the *INT* should know which people, objects, and actions are represented in each image. Based on this knowledge, the *INT* can develop a tentative probing strategy to tap these mental records efficiently. The goals of the probing strategy, in line with the Principles of Detail and Momentum, are (a) to bring to conscious awareness those images containing the best view of relevant information and then (b) probe these images until all of their information has been exhausted. The most informative images are probed first, progressing to the images with less valuable information. The probing strategy also takes into account (a) the degree of arousal of each image, (b) whether it contains information also represented in other images, and (c) the *E/W's* momentary confidence.

A note of caution is sounded here. Although the *INT* should try to follow a well-thought-out, systematic plan to probe the *E/W's* memory codes, he should be flexible in using this plan. If unexpected information arises during the interview that suggests alteration, he should modify his earlier plan accordingly.

PROBING MEMORY CODES

The general goal of this stage is to guide the *E/W* to the various information-rich memory codes, activate the codes, and extract and notate as much information as possible.

Activating Mental Images

The *INT* should preface this part of the interview by indicating that he will be probing for a more detailed description of some of the things that the *E/W* mentioned earlier, in the open-ended narration. It is helpful now to remind the *E/W* that the description task is very difficult and requires intense concentration. To facilitate this concentration, and also to block out distracting signals, the *INT* should encourage the *E/W* to close her eyes.

The procedure to evoke a specific mental image begins by recreating the psychological and environmental context associated with the specific event, e.g., when the assailant first took out his gun. The *INT's* directions should reflect as accurately as possibly the *E/W's* earlier reference to the moment, duplicating her words and non-verbal actions as faithfully as possible.

Once the *INT* has directed the *E/W* to the appropriate image, he should (a) encourage her to develop the image in her mind as sharply as possible, and (b) describe it in detail. These two components, developing and describing the image, should be separated to ensure that the *E/W* develops a sharp image.

Guided General Narration

The form of the *E/W's* description should be that of a guided narration. To ensure that the resulting narration is extensive, yet focused on relevant information, the *INT* should (a) frame the question to direct the *E/W* to a specific part of the image (b) ask an open-ended question, and (c) request the *E/W* to give a detailed, extensive description.

The resulting narration will be the primary source of information during the interview (George, 1991). It is therefore imperative not to interrupt the *E/W's* response. To encourage a complete response, the *INT* should allow for a short period of silence after the *E/W* stops speaking before continuing the probing.

Follow-Up Probing

Some of the information from the activated image will not be included in the *E/W's* guided narration, and the *INT* will have to probe more assertively, either with closed questions or with open-ended questions that have limited scope (e.g., "Describe his mouth"). In line with the Principle of Momentum, all follow-up probes should be directed to information relevant to the activated image.

Probing the Remaining Images

The same general procedure, of recreating the specific context followed by guided narration and specific probes, is also used in probing the remaining images. When switching from one mental image to another, the *INT* should make it clear that there is a break in the sequence and that a new image will be drawn upon. To discourage the *E/W* from simply repeating her earlier answers when describing the second image, the *INT* should explicitly instruct her to treat the two images independently, describing the new image as it currently appears, even if the resulting description contradicts what she said earlier. Any contradictions that do arise should be resolved, but later in the interview.

Re-Probing Images Activated Earlier

Interviewers should try to exhaust each image of its entire contents when it is probed initially. Obviously, this is impossible, and sometimes it is necessary to re-probe an image examined earlier. Usually this occurs if new information about the image's contents arises after the image has been probed initially. For example, after having already probed the left-profile image, the *INT* may learn that the assailant had an earring in his left ear. Another possibility is that in the initial probing of an image, the *E/W* felt that an important piece of information was on the "tip of her tongue" but she could not retrieve it then. When re-probing an image, the *INT* should isolate and probe only for the targeted information.

Probing Concept Codes

The concept codes, which contain less detailed, but easily accessed, information should normally be probed after all of the relevant image codes have been probed. If the *E/W* is extremely anxious, and it is important to lower her anxiety before proceeding, the concept codes should be probed first.

Probing concept codes usually does not elicit much detailed information directly. However, access to detailed information may come through an indirect route. Subjective comments, for example, may be converted to objective information. Responses to probes of the concept codes may also lead to detailed information by alerting the *INT* to image codes not available earlier in the interview. The *INT* should activate these newly-determined image codes in the same fashion as other image codes.

REVIEWING THE INTERVIEW

In the final review, the *INT* repeats to the *E/W* all of the relevant information, either from his notes or from memory. The purpose of the review is (a) to allow the *INT* to check the accuracy of his notes, and (b) to provide an additional opportunity for the *E/W* to search through memory to uncover new information. If she does remember any additional information during the review, she should interrupt him and tell him immediately. To assist her in listening actively and interrupting with corrections or additions, the *INT* must speak slowly, with pauses after each segment of the review.

If the *E/W* does volunteer new information, the *INT* should immediately follow up this new lead to probe for additional details. If there is an as-yet-untapped image associated with the new information, the *INT* should probe in the same manner as previous searches through images.

CLOSING THE INTERVIEW

In reviewing our collection of police interviews, we observed that many *INTs* terminated the session on a flat note. They had asked all of their questions and had nothing left to say. The ending seemed generally unplanned, reflecting more a lack of questions than anything positive and systematic. Because the end of the interview leaves a final, lasting impression, its potential should be used to greater advantage and should follow purposeful guidelines. We suggest three specific goals for the end of the interview: (a) collecting background information, (b) extending the functional life of the interview, and (c) creating a positive, lasting impression.

Collecting Background Information

In any investigation, it is necessary to collect some background information about *E/Ws,* potential suspects, other bystanders, etc. Often this information is not directly relevant to the crime; yet, it is important for the investigation to proceed smoothly. For example, the *INT* may need to find out the *E/W's* telephone number, place of business, addresses of potential suspects, etc. This type of information is impersonal, somewhat like a census interview. As such, it does little to help in developing rapport between the *INT* and the *E/W.* If anything, it tends to alienate the *INT* from the *E/W,* because it is so impersonal. Therefore, in the normal course of events, it is best to defer this rapport-suppressing section to the end of the interview, after the detailed information has been gathered. In addition, because this background information is easily accessed and requires little communication skill, *E/Ws* should be able to give the correct answers even at the end of the interview when they may be mentally exhausted from the more difficult memory searches completed earlier.

The only time we recommend conducting this phase early in the interview is if the *E/W* is highly anxious and is unable to answer difficult, sensitive questions related to the crime. In such cases, the *INT* can make good strategic use of these background questions to help calm the *E/W.*

Extending the Functional Life of the Interview

Witnesses will continue to think about the crime long after the interview is over. In so doing they will recall information not mentioned in the interview. The investigator's job is to facilitate the *E/W's* reporting this information after the interview has been terminated. This is accomplished by the *INT* conveying his expectation that the *E/W* will think of new information and that she will call at such time.

Creating a Positive, Last Impression

In terminating the interview, the *INT* should attempt to leave a positive, last impression by expressing his thanks for the *E/W's* participation and by showing concern for her as an individual, especially for an *E/W* who is a victim. It is appropriate if only for humanitarian reasons. Creating a positive last impression can also be self-serving by facilitating later investigations with the *E/W* or other members of the community.

To finalize the process, the *INT* should contact the *E/W* a few days after the formal interview to check on her personal health and to make one last effort to determine whether she has thought of any new information.

CHAPTER SUMMARY

1. The goals of the Introduction are to (a) develop the appropriate psychological mood in the *E/W*, (b) promote effective social dynamics between the *INT* and the *E/W*, and (c) convey general guidelines to maximize memory and communication. These are accomplished by controlling the *E/W's* anxiety, developing rapport, establishing the centrality of the *E/W's* role in the interview, and promoting focused concentration.

2. The Open-ended narration allows the *INT* to infer the *E/W's* mental representation of the event. The *INT* guides the *E/W* to recreate the general context of the event, and then encourages a narrative response to an open-ended question. Based on the *E/W's* narration, a tentative probing strategy is developed to elicit detailed information.

3. Image codes are probed first, followed by concept codes. The *INT* activates the relevant image code, and then guides a narrative response with a framed, open-ended question, directed to a relevant portion of the image. Incomplete responses are followed up by direct, closed questions or constrained open-ended questions. Responses to probes of concept codes are less precise, but may lead indirectly to unlocking more precise information.

4. The *INT* reviews with the *E/W* relevant information gathered during the interview to (a) check on the accuracy of his notes, and (b) provide her an additional opportunity to recall. In reviewing the facts, the *INT* encourages the *E/W* to interrupt if he makes a mistake or if she thinks of additional information.

5. In closing the interview, background information is collected. The *INT* tries to extend the functional life of the interview by encouraging the *E/W* to call him with additional information she remembers after the interview is terminated. Finally, he tries to end the interview by leaving the *E/W* with a positive, last impression. Some time after the interview, he should contact the *E/W* to inquire about her health and elicit any new information.

Chapter 12

SAMPLE INTERVIEWS WITH ANALYSIS

Two sample interviews are presented in this chapter to illustrate the concepts that have appeared throughout the book. The two interviews reflect very different *E/Ws*. The first interview is with a relatively calm, bystander *E/W* with good verbal skills—in many ways the ideal *E/W*. The second interview is more problematic—and, unfortunately, more typical—as the *E/W* is a highly anxious victim with poor verbal skills.

For the sake of economy, the sample interviews are not complete. Many details required in a formal police investigation have been omitted, along with many of the non-essential interactions between the *E/W* and the *INT*. Although the interview here obviously was created for the purpose of instruction, most of the details have been culled from real interviews gathered in our field study.

We encourage readers to go through this section actively, looking for errors in the *INT's* approach and to think about what questions they would have asked and how they would have phrased the questions. We have intentionally built in a few errors. Try to understand why these are errors and how the questions should be altered.

On the left side of the page is the sample interview; on the right side are our comments about relevant principles of interviewing. The principles are indicated by name only to avoid being unnecessarily repetitive. The interested reader can refer back to the appropriate section of the book for a more thorough explanation.

INTERVIEW ONE: BYSTANDER EYEWITNESS TO A JEWELRY STORE ROBBERY

Background: Two days before the interview, the *E/W*, Jane Wilson, was browsing through the Midtown Diamond Exchange when two armed men entered and demanded of the cashier the contents of the register. The *E/W* was in the rear of the store and, although frightened, she did

159

not panic. The *E/W* has good verbal skills, and at the time of the interview, she is relatively calm.

Interview	*Comments*
INT: Are you Jane Wilson? I am Detective Jeremy Zukerman from the Metropolitan Police Department. We spoke briefly on the phone yesterday about the jewelry store robbery and I'd like to get a more thorough description of what happened.	
E/W: Come in.	
INT: You sounded upset on the phone yesterday. How are you feeling now?	Show concern
E/W: Better. That was really frightening, especially when they started yelling and I saw the gun. I've never seen a gun before, except on t.v., and it really shook me up.	
INT: That's a natural response. After all, the robber did have a gun and it was a dangerous situation. I remember being in a similar situation many years ago, before I became a police officer. I was shopping in a store and there was hold-up. I remember being frightened when it happened.	Validate *E/W*'s feelings Convey understanding and similar feelings
E/W: The whole neighborhood is changing. It's gotten to the point where I'm afraid to go out at night. There's so much crime. I'd like to see all of these guys behind bars where they belong, so we can walk in the streets again in safety.	
INT: That's what we would like to do, to make this a safe area again. If you can give us enough information, that would help us in trying to catch them and take them off the streets.	Identify *E/W*'s concern and indicate how cooperation is in *E/W*'s interest
In order to catch these people, I need you to give me as many details as possible, so don't leave anything out. The more details you can give me, the easier it will be for us to find them and prosecute them.	Explain need for detailed response

E/W: OK, where would you like to start?

INT: From what you told me on the phone yesterday, it sounded like you got a pretty good look at the robbers and that you remember a lot about what happened. So, I expect that it will take a while for us to go through the interview.

Establish the expectation that *E/W* will recall much and that the session will take time for thorough recall

Where's a good place to talk so that we won't be distracted?

Minimize distractions

E/W: Let's go into the living room. I'll shut off the t.v.

INT: (referring to photograph): Are those your children? I've got three kids at home, two girls and a boy.

Personalize the interview; Establish rapport

Jane, it's important to keep in mind that you have all of the information. I am trying to find out what happened from you, so I expect you to do most of the talking. Don't wait for me to ask questions. Whenever something comes to mind, tell me, even if it seems trivial or contradicts something you said earlier. Don't omit anything.

E/W to take active role

Do not edit responses

If you don't know a specific fact, that's OK. Just say that you don't know. Don't make up something, though, just to give me an answer. I realize that this is a difficult task, to remember all of the details of the crime. So try to concentrate as much as possible.

Avoid fabrication

Promote concentration

Before we start, I'd like you to tell me a little bit about where you were in the store and what you were thinking about just before the robbery took place.

Recreate original context

E/W: I wanted to buy a watch for my husband's birthday. In the past few years, I bought a few pieces of jewelry in the store. They're very reasonable, and they have good-quality merchandise. I must have been standing toward the back of the store when they started yelling.

INT: If you can, try to draw a simple sketch of the store. Indicate where you were standing, and where the robbers and the cashier were.

Sketch of scene to understand *E/W*'s perspective

(*E/W* draws sketch)

INT: What were the lighting conditions in the store?

Recreate context

E/W: It was pretty bright. It's a jewelry store and they want everything to sparkle, I guess.

INT: Jane, try to put yourself back in the same location as when you first noticed the robbers and tell me in your own words everything you can remember about what happened, until the end of the robbery. Try to be as detailed as possible

Request open-ended narration

Request detailed description

E/W: Well, I didn't notice anything unusual at first, just some people in the store looking at the jewelry. Then, all of a sudden, I heard yelling. At first I thought someone was sick or hurt, but then I saw these two men yelling at the owner, something about putting money into a bag. One of the men turned around and yelled to the customers, DOWN ON THE FLOOR. I really got scared then because he had a gun. I don't know anything about guns, but it was really big, much bigger than toy guns I've seen. I fell to the floor, and was scared because the man with the gun looked crazy. He seemed very nervous; he kept on looking around at his partner and told him to hurry up and "let's get outta here." I didn't get a very good view of the other man, who took the money. I mainly concentrated on the man pointing the gun at us. After a while, the man in the front yelled to the man pointing the gun at us, "let's go" or something like that, and then they both ran out of the store. By that time, I was really shaking. I guess the owner of the store called the police. They came in a few minutes. One of the police officers asked me a few questions about what happened and then took my name and telephone.

The *INT* takes only brief notes here, to remind himself of the *E/W*'s views of the event for later probing:
a) 2 robbers (R) yell at owner: $ into bag
b) R1 yells at customer "DOWN ON FLOOR" (Notes change in voice)
c) *E/W* scared, R1 big gun
d) *E/W* falls to floor, scared
e) R1: crazy, nervous

f) R2 to R1: "let's go"
g) Rs run out

He said he'd get back to me in a while. And then I went home and called my husband about what happened. — *E/W* speaks to husband

INT: Are there any other views that you had of the robbers? — Final request to elicit clear image

E/W: No, those were the only times I saw them.

[Before continuing the interview, the *INT* plans his probing strategy for the next phase. The *E/W* has four views of R1, (a) initially, when he is yelling at the owner, (b) while he turns around and yells at the customers, (c) after the *E/W* falls to the floor, and (d) when R1 and R2 run out of the store. Images (b) and (c) are close, frontal views and will provide the best views of R1's face. Because the *E/W* focused on the weapon in image (b), she may also provide here additional information about R1's hands while holding the weapon. View (c), from the floor, may provide extra information about R1's shoes and pants. View (d) may provide information about the backs of the robbers and also how they ran. In addition, she has some subjective impressions of R1 (nervous) and a clear voice image of his saying DOWN ON THE FLOOR. The *E/W* has only two, probably undetailed, views of R2, (a) initially, when he is yelling at the owner, and (d) when R1 and R2 are running out of the store. She also heard him speak to R1 ("let's go").

The *INT* plans to probe about R1 first, as he is the better viewed, and will start with the images that contain the best information of R1's face, clothing, and the weapon. These images are in views (b) and (c). After exhausting these frontal views of their contents, he will proceed to view (d) and probe about R1's back and how they ran. Finally, he will activate image (a) to elicit any new information not contained in the other images. R2 will be probed second, starting with frontal information from image (a), yelling at the owner, and proceeding to image (d), running out of the store. Voice information will also be probed by focusing on the *E/W*'s image of R2 saying "let's go." Any new information that may arise during the remainder of the interview will be incorporated to be compatible with the *E/W*'s mental representation.]

INT: I'd like to go back to the images you mentioned before and ask you to describe the robbers again, but this time in more detail. I realize this is going to be difficult and take lots of concentration. But remember, the more details you can give me, the more likely we are to catch these people. — Request more detailed description

Encourage focused retrieval

Convey need for detail

Let's go back to when the man with the gun turned around and yelled at you, DOWN ON THE FLOOR.

Recreate specific context using *E/W*'s original words and intonation

Try to focus in on just this one robber, the one who was yelling at you.

Probe about one assailant at a time

You may find it easier to concentrate if you close your eyes. (*INT* closes his eyes) Try to develop a mental picture as thoroughly as possible, when the man first turns around. Don't say anything yet. Just develop the image as clearly as you can.

Close eyes
INT models
Develop detailed image. Delay description until after image is fully developed

(Few-seconds pause allowing *E/W* to develop the image)

Pause to allow *E/W* to develop image

Concentrate on his face and head. (Pause) Now, try to describe his head and face in as much detail as you can. Don't leave anything out.

Framed question
Open-ended question
Explicit request for detail

E/W: He had an oval-shaped face, with puffy cheeks. Dark complexion. He had a high forehead. He had dark hair, either brown or black; it was combed almost straight back, with a slight part on the left side. There was something strange about his mouth, like it was crooked. . . .

INT takes detailed notes here

INT: (silent pause)

Short pause after *INT* stops responding

E/W: . . . Maybe it was his mustache. It wasn't even; it seemed like it was thicker on the left side than the right. . . . That's about all I can remember.

INT: Keep that image in mind. Try to focus in around his eyes. Tell me whatever you can about his eyes, eyebrows, or the upper part of in his face.

Refocus on important details
Distinctive features upper face

E/W: They seemed strange . . . real big pupils, like when people look crazy. I don't remember the color of his eyes. Probably dark, but I'm not sure. He had some wrinkles around his eyes. Also, he was perspiring. You could see the light bouncing off the sweat on his forehead.

INT: Was he wearing glasses or not?

Image-compatible question; Follow-up direct question

E/W: No.

INT: Let's go back to his hair again. You mentioned that it was dark and combed straight back. What else can you tell me about his hair?

Open-ended follow-up question

E/W: It was straight, maybe a bit wavy, but definitely not curly.

INT: Can you describe the length of his hair?

Neutrally worded question (noun form: "length")

E/W: It covered a little bit of his ears, so it wasn't real short. But it wasn't very long.

INT: You mentioned that he had puffy cheeks. Concentrate on his cheeks again. . . . (pause) . . . Now, try to describe his face.

Refocus on portion of image not yet described

E/W: There was nothing outstanding. No scars or any noticeable marks on his face.

INT: Was he clean-shaven or did he have facial hair?

Follow-up direct question

E/W: He was clean-shaven.

INT notes contradiction (*E/W* said "mustache" before) but does not probe immediately

INT: How dark was his skin?

ERROR: Biased question ("dark")

E/W: He was somewhat dark, like he'd been out in the sun, but not very dark.

INT: Overall, what was the most distinctive feature of his face?

Most distinctive feature

E/W: I guess his eyes, that he had this really crazy look, with large pupils.

INT: Let's take a different approach now. You seemed to indicate before that the man yelled

Clear break when changing images

at you, DOWN ON THE FLOOR. I'd like you to think now about when he yelled that order to you. Concentrate on his voice only and the sounds of those words. (pauses to develop auditory image) Try to describe the sound of his voice. Tell me everything you can about the sound of his voice or anything else related to the way he spoke.

Pause before requesting description
Request for detailed description

E/W: It was surprisingly high-pitched, like he was nervous. I think he also had a slight accent, but I'm not sure what kind. It didn't sound like regular English, . . . like he learned English only a few years ago.

E/W: Can you remember what about his speech made it seem not like regular English?

Convert subjective impressions into objective

INT: I'm not positive, but now that I think about it, he said "down on floor," without the word "the."

E/W: Let's switch again to another image. After he yelled at you to get down on the floor, you fell to the floor. What were your thoughts at the time?

Clear break when changing images
Recreate context

E/W: I was scared because he had that gun and he seemed crazy.

INT: Try to think about the position you were in and what your thoughts were after you fell to the floor and saw the man with the gun. (pause) Can you describe that to me?

Recreate context

ERROR: *complex wording*

E/W: I was lying on the floor, looking up at the robber. I remember that the floor was very hard; it was also cold. I guess I was scared at first, but then when I realized that all they wanted was to take the money, I relaxed a bit. But the sight of the gun still scared me.

INT: I'd like you now to concentrate on the gun the man was holding. Again, close your eyes and try to focus on the gun. Take your time, close your eyes, and develop the image of the

Close eyes

gun. Now try to describe the gun in as much detail as you can.

E/W: I don't know a lot about guns. It was black. I don't know what else to tell you.

INT: Here are sketches of two different types of guns. (shows sketches of typical revolver and automatic) Did the gun look more like this one (points to automatic) or this one (points to revolver)?

E/W: It looked more like this one (automatic).

INT: Look at my gun, since it's the same type. (shows *E/W* his gun) How did the robber's gun compare to mine?

E/W: This part (points to barrel) was longer. And the handle had a different shape. I'm afraid I can't describe it very well.

INT: That's OK. If you can, try to draw a picture of what the handle looked like.

E/W: (draws picture of gun handle)

INT: Let's go back to that picture of the man holding the gun. Try to get it clear in your mind again. (pauses for her to create image) Now, try to focus on how he was holding the gun.

E/W: He was holding the gun in his right hand, like this (demonstrates). I remember his hand because I concentrated on the gun. He had very long finger-nails. His hands looked pretty big, like he was very strong. And he had a scar on the outside of his thumb.

INT: Show me on your hand where the scar was.

E/W: (points to where scar was)

INT: When you were lying on the floor and looking at him, did you see his shoes?

E/W: Yes

INT: What kind were they?

E/W: They were running shoes.

ERROR: No pause between imaging and describing

Recognition better than recall, especially for non-experts

Relative judgments better than absolute judgments

Use non-verbal response format

Framed question

Non-verbal description

ERROR: Abrupt shift of images

ERROR: closed question before open-ended

INT: You don't know what brand they were, do you?	*ERROR:* negative wording
E/W: No.	
INT: What color were they?	*ERROR:* too many closed questions
E/W: Gray.	
INT: Now, let's go to his pants. Did you notice them?	
E/W: Yes.	
INT: Try to concentrate on your image of the pants, looking up at him from the floor (pauses to allow *E/W* to develop image) Tell me everything you can about his pants. Remember, tell me every detail you can think of.	Open-ended question Request for detail
E/W: They were blue jeans, . . . dark blue, not the faded ones. They looked kind of old since the pocket was torn over here (points to front-left pocket). He had a brown leather belt with a large buckle, like a cowboy belt.	
INT: In what way was it like a cowboy belt?	Convert subjective descriptions
E/W: I think there was an engraving of a horse on the belt.	
INT: OK, let's go to the shirt now. What color was it?	*ERROR:* starts description with closed question
E/W: White.	
INT: Was it short-sleeved?	*ERROR:* leading question
E/W: Yes.	
INT: Were there any markings on it?	*ERROR:* too many closed questions
E/W: No.	
INT: Did you see his face when you were lying on the floor?	
E/W: Yes	
INT: Try to concentrate on his neck and the under side of his chin. Just focus in on this area, from the top of his shirt to his chin.	Image-compatible probing (with view from the floor)

(pauses to allow *E/W* to develop image) Try to describe in detail what you see.

E/W: His shirt was open at the neck. I noticed that he had a thin, gold chain around his neck. I couldn't see if there was a pendant or not, because the bottom of the chain was inside his shirt. . . . He had some chest hairs that you could see at the top of his shirt. He had pretty hairy arms too, especially around his forearms.

INT flexibility: *INT* notes additional image (arms) to probe after exhausting current image

INT: Did you notice his face when you were lying on the floor?

E/W: I was focusing on the gun most of the time, so I didn't look very carefully. I think I took a quick glance at him when he said something to us, but I don't remember much.

INT: You just mentioned that he had pretty hairy forearms. When did you notice his arms?

Use *E/W*'s words to activate images.

E/W: When he was holding the gun. I was looking at his right arm, since he held the gun in his right hand.

INT: Try to concentrate on his right arm as he was holding the gun. Just focus in on his arm. (pauses to allow *E/W* to develop image) Tell me whatever you can about his right arm.

E/W: As I said, it was pretty hairy. He was pretty muscular, like he worked out with weights. He had large biceps too. And he had some kind of a mark on his upper arm. It could have been a tattoo or a birth mark. I'm not sure, but there was some kind of unusual mark there.

INT: Can you describe this mark in any more detail?

Follow-up probe

E/W: No, I just noticed it briefly, and I didn't get a very clear look. But there was something there, about here (points to her arm) on his arm.

[The *INT* continues to probe images (d) and (a) for additional information about the two robbers in the same fashion as just described. Images (a) and (d) are probed with less intensity, as they contain only limited information (image d, while running out the store) or were not carefully observed (image a, when the *E/W* did not fully realize what was happening). The interview continues by probing for information that the *E/W* may have conveyed to her husband when she spoke with him on the phone after the robbery.]

INT: Jane, you mentioned earlier that, after the robbery, you spoke to your husband about what happened. Did you talk about it in much detail or just about your general reactions to being in a robbery?

E/W: My husband is the curious type, so he wanted me to give him a complete description of what happened. I guess he was playing amateur detective and wanted to find out who committed the crime.

INT: How well were you able to describe what happened when you spoke to your husband?

E/W: Well, it was right after the robbery, so it was easier to remember some of the details then. In fact, I told my husband the name of one of the robbers—the other robber called him—but now I can't remember what it was. I should have written it down.

INT: Let's go back to when you were speaking to your husband. Where were you at the time?

Recreate context of earlier successful recollection

E/W: I was home. I was speaking on the telephone in the kitchen.

INT: Try to think back to when you spoke to your husband on the phone and to reconstruct the conversation.

E/W: I told him what happened. Naturally, he asked me if I was OK, and then he asked me whether I had spoken to the police. I said, "No," but told him that I thought I remembered what the men looked like and I remembered one of their names. But I can't remember his name now.

INT: Try to think back to the moment in the conversation with your husband when you thought of the robber's name. Take your time, and think back to how you remembered his name.

Recreate mental operations of earlier recall

E/W: Let's see, I remember that my husband made a joke about it, because we have a nephew with a similar name, Robbie, but that wasn't exactly the name. It was a foreign name, a little longer than Robbie. . . . Roberto. That's it, the man called him "Roberto."

Recalling partial features

INT: Which guy was Roberto, the one who held the gun to you or the guy at the front of the store?

E/W: The guy who held the gun to us.

INT: Is there anything else you can remember when you spoke to your husband that is not clear now?

E/W: No, just the name.

[The *INT* is now ready to start probing some of the non-image codes.]

INT: Was one of the robbers the leader or did the two seem to be working together as equals?

E/W: The man who stayed at the cashier and got the money seemed to be in charge. He gave Roberto orders about what to do next. The man in charge also seemed to be more intelligent.

INT: What about him made him appear more intelligent?

Convert subjective impressions

E/W: I'm not sure. I think he spoke more distinctly than Roberto, or he spoke without an accent. He was also dressed better. He was wearing regular pants, not jeans. And he was more clean-cut. He had glasses too. You know how sometimes wearing glasses makes people think you're smarter.

INT: Jane, I'd like you to try to put yourself into the role of the leader and think about what happened from his perspective. That is, try to imagine what he was thinking about and how he must have thought about the robbery. I realize that is a difficult task to do, so try to concentrate. Don't make up anything. Tell me only those things you actually saw, but take the robber's perspective.

Varied retrieval (change perspective)

Warning against fabrication

E/W: OK. Well, after we came into the store I took out my gun and started to yell at the owner to give me the money. I put an empty bag on the counter and told him to fill it. I told Roberto to watch the other customers in the store to make sure none of them interfered. The owner was very scared and he just put the money on the counter, not in the bag. So I put it into the bag. There were a few watches or pieces of jewelry also on the counter, so I took them too, since they were so convenient. I think I dropped one of the pieces, but I was in too much of a rush to stop to pick it up. As soon as I had all of the money, I yelled to Roberto, "Get in the truck." Roberto left first. Then I backed out of the door, waving my gun and yelling to the customers, "Don't anybody try to be a hero." And then I ran out.

[A few new pieces of information come to light here: the presence of a bag for carrying the money, pieces of jewelry taken in addition to the watch, a frontal view of the robber in charge and his gun, and a truck as the get-away vehicle. Each of these sources will be probed to extract additional information, similar to the way the images were probed earlier.]

INT: So far, you've given me lots of details about the robbers and what happened. I'd like you now to describe the robbers in more general terms, like height and weight or body build. Also, if you have any general impression about them, or if they reminded you of anyone, tell me. Let's start with the man who held the gun to you, Roberto.

E/W: He was short, about 5-foot-7 and kind of barrel-chested. He looked like a boxer, maybe because he had a flat nose and I think he hadn't shaved in a while. He wasn't exactly the kind of guy you'd expect to find in an art gallery.

INT: About how old was he?

Follow-up direct question

E/W: I guess in his mid-twenties.

[The *INT* continues to probe for other general traits before probing about R2.]

INT: OK, let's go to the other robber. Try to describe him.

E/W: He was a bit older, maybe around 30. He seemed more refined.

INT: About how tall was he compared to me? Was he taller, shorter, or about the same height?

Relative judgment; provide standard

E/W: Just about your height, maybe an inch shorter.

INT: I'm 5-foot-11. So how tall would you say he was?

E/W: About 5-foot-10 or so.

INT: Did you have any general impressions of him? Did he look like anyone you know?

E/W: Not really; he looked a little like the cartoon character, Bart Simpson, because his hair stood up funny, but other than that, there was nothing unusual.

INT: Jane, you've given me a lot of information and I'd like to make sure that I have it all written down correctly. Let me go over my notes with you as a final check. Try to think about the robbery as I am reading my notes to you. If, at any time, I say something that seems incorrect, or if you think of something new

Review to check accuracy of notes and encourage additional retrieval

that you haven't told me, make sure you stop
me immediately to tell me.

[*INT* reads his notes slowly]   Review notes slowly

INT: I'm going to need some information about
you for our official records. It's just some-   Save official
thing that is required by the police depart-   background informa-
ment whenever we take a statement. Jane, what   tion for end
is your full name?

E/W: Jane Ellen Wilson.

INT: And your address?

E/W: 222 Alpine Road.

INT: Jane, you've been very helpful in the
investigation. Thank you for your time. I hope   Thank *E/W* for
this hasn't been too much of an ordeal for you.   participating
You will probably find that in the next few
days, you will continue to think about what
happened during the robbery. That's natural.
When you do, you'll also probably think of   Extend life of
some new information that we haven't covered   interview
today. Write down the information and give
me a call. Here's my card. Thank you again
for being so cooperative.

[A few days after the interview, the *INT* telephones the *E/W* to follow
up the formal interview to inquire about her health and to ask whether
she has thought of any new information.]

INTERVIEW TWO: VICTIM OF SHOOTING

Background: The victim, Carla Thompson, is a 45-year-old woman who
was shot in the leg while standing in front of a store. Apparently, the shot
was fired from a passing car and was intended to hit another person
standing near the victim. The interview takes place in the hospital,
where the victim is being treated. Ms. Thompson has poor verbal skills
and is still highly anxious one day after the shooting.

The reader will note that the following interview does not generate
nearly as much information as did the first. That is mainly due to factors
outside of the *INT's* control. The event occurred very quickly with little
opportunity to observe the criminal. More important, the *E/W* is not
nearly as calm and does not have as good verbal skills to describe the

event as did the first *E/W*. However, these factors are outside of the *INT's* control. His job is simply to get the most out of each *E/W,* whatever the natural limits might be.

Comments

INT: Carla, I am Detective Mark Blake from the County Sheriff's Office. My partner, Bob Locker, spoke with you yesterday about the shooting, and I would like to talk to you today to get some more information.

E/W: Where were the police yesterday? Why do you let such crazy people roam the street? I was minding my own business, and then, out of nowhere, somebody shoots me. For no reason. I wasn't bothering anyone. I could have been killed out there. What is this city coming to? Now, here I am in the hospital. I have to go to work tomorrow to pick up my paycheck and I can't even move. I don't think I'm going to be much help. I really didn't see much. It all happened so fast.

INT: How are you feeling now? Are you in pain?

Inquire about *E/W's* health

E/W: I can hardly move my leg. And every time I go to sit up it hurts even more.

INT: Can I do anything to help you?

Show concern

E/W: No, there's nothing you can do. If that idiot hadn't shot me, I wouldn't be here now.

INT: It really is unfair. There are some crazy people out there, and innocent people often wind up suffering because of them.

Validate *E/W's* feelings

My wife was hit by a car once. The car went through a red light and hit my wife as she was crossing the street. She wasn't doing anything, just crossing the street, and she wound up with a broken leg.

Indicate similar experience in your life

E/W: I knew I shouldn't have gone outside last night. My sister, Alisha, keeps on telling me that it's not safe outside at night and that I shouldn't go out, especially at night. But you have to go buy food. You can't sit home all the time. Maybe I should have listened to my sister. I'd be safe at home now instead of being scared out of my wits. Who knows, this is a crazy world nowadays.

[Sensing that the *E/W* is highly anxious and must vent her feelings, the *INT* allows her more liberty at the outset to talk about these feelings before starting to collect facts relevant to the crime.]

INT: Carla, I can understand your feelings of frustration. You can't blame yourself, however, for going shopping.

> Convey idea that *E/W*'s behavior is acceptable

E/W: What am I supposed to do, stay home all day? I don't understand it. I was just standing there and before I know it, I have a bullet in my leg and I'm in the hospital. Is that fair? I work hard. I don't bother anyone. And then this crazy idiot shoots me.

INT: That really is unfair.

> Validate *E/W*'s feelings

E/W: I don't even own a gun, because I'm afraid of them. My cousin keeps a gun in the house, and I don't feel safe there. I'm always afraid it's going to go off.

INT: You're right. Guns can be dangerous.

E/W: I keep hearing the sound of the gun, and every time I hear it, I become frightened. I can't remember anything other than the sound of the gun and the pain in my leg.

INT: It must have been very scary.
Carla, we would like to try to catch the person who shot you so we can make the streets safer for innocent people like you. I'd like to ask you some questions about what happened earlier today. Do you feel up to answering some questions?

> Confirm *E/W*'s feelings
> *INT* working to meet *E/W*'s needs

E/W: Officer, I don't remember much about what happened. The other police officer spoke to me earlier and I told him everything I knew. I'm not going to be able to tell you anything new.

INT: That's fine. Don't worry about what you told the first officer. Just tell me as much as you can about what happened.

Request independent response in multiple interviews

[Because the *E/W* has given many signs of fear and seems unable to concentrate intensely at the beginning of the interview, the *INT* begins the interview by collecting background information, in part, just to relax the *E/W*.]

INT: First, I need to get some background information. We have to do this in all police investigations, so please bear with me for a few minutes.

Excuse impersonal nature of background information

Carla, what is your full name?

E/W: Carla Maye Thompson

INT: And what is your address?

E/W: 7400 Hillside Avenue

INT: Good. Now I'd like to try to go back to what happened yesterday to see what you can remember.

E/W: I really don't think I'll be able to remember much.

INT: That's OK, just do the best you can. Anything you can tell me will be valuable, so just relax and take your time. We're not in any rush. I understand that you're upset now. That's only natural after a crime like this. If you want to take a break at any time, because you're feeling anxious, just tell me and we'll stop.

Not rushed
Anxiety is natural after crime
E/W to control anxiety

[With a more composed *E/W*, the *INT* might make suggestions here to promote more intense concentration, e.g., "everything is stored in your mind, so I expect you to concentrate." With the present *E/W*, who is highly anxious, the *INT* skips those instructions so as not to create any additional, unnecessary anxiety. Instead, he opts for the alternative approach, to encourage her to relax, but to try to be as informative as possible. Later in the interview, after the *E/W* is more relaxed, the *INT* may encourage her to concentrate with greater intensity.]

INT: Carla, when you think about today's events, many thoughts may come to your mind. Say whatever comes to mind, whether you con- | Do not edit anything sider it trivial, or out of order, or even if it | from report disagrees with something you said earlier. Just tell me whatever comes to your mind without holding anything back.

Try to think back to before the shooting took | Recreate general place. Can you remember where you were and | context what you were thinking about?

E/W: I was just standing in front of the super-market. I don't remember thinking about anything in particular.

[The *E/W* seems unlikely to generate a detailed description of the context from a general request. Therefore, the *INT* changes strategy to recreating the context by asking questions about specific dimensions.]

INT: Where were you going at the time?
E/W: I was just coming home. I was standing by the stop-light waiting for it to change to green.
INT: Were there any other people near you?
E/W: Just one other person. He was also waiting to cross the street.
INT: Can you remember the traffic conditions at the time?
E/W: It was around noon, before rush hour, so traffic was pretty light.
INT: OK, Carla, now what I'd like you to do is to tell me in your own words what happened | Request for open-from the time the shooting occurred until you | ended narration couldn't see the car any more.
E/W: I told you, I don't remember very much. I was just standing by the light. A car drove up and someone shot me. I still can't figure out why. The policeman said that they might have been aiming at the man standing next to me. Just my luck. They want to shoot somebody

else and they shoot me instead. That's the story of my life. I have the worst luck. My car breaks down every three months. My husband just lost his job. I just got out of the hospital. I don't know what to do.

[To prevent the *E/W* from rambling on about irrelevant personal matters, the *INT* interrupts here, although without being critical, to steer her back on target. Also, since the *E/W* did not reveal much in her narration, the *INT* must probe more forcefully to find out what are her mental images.]

INT: That does sound discouraging. Let's go back to what you said about the shooting.

INT comments on *E/W*'s feelings as bridge back to relevant details.

Where did you see the man who shot you?

ERROR: leading question; *E/W* did not yet indicate suspect was male.

E/W: I heard him yell something and I turned to look at him.

INT: Where was the car at that time?

Reconstruct specific context

E/W: Just before the intersection. The car slowed down and the man yelled something.

INT: And then . . .

Encourage more elaborate response

E/W: I heard the shots. I think there were two shots.

INT: What happened after the two shots?

Encourage more detail

E/W: I fell down and was in terrible pain. I didn't know what was going on at first, because there was no warning.

INT: Did you see the car after the shots?

Probe for other relevant images

E/W: Yes, it made a left turn at the corner and went up Cook's Lane. It was going pretty fast at the time and I was very surprised, so I didn't get a very good look at the car.

INT: What is the best view you had of the car?

E/W: Probably when the man yelled, just before he shot.

Isolate and probe best image first

[The *E/W* plans to probe the two relevant images, first of the car as it approached the *E/W* and then when the car left and turned at the intersection. He will probe the first image for details about the front and the right side of the car, the shooter, the gun, and other people in the car. He will probe the second image for details about the rear and the left side of the car, the driver, and any other passengers who might have been viewed from the left side.]

INT: OK, Carla, I'd like you to concentrate on this image of the car. It may be easier to concentrate if you close your eyes.

Close eyes

E/W: I don't want to close my eyes. I get real scared.

INT: That is scary sometimes. In that case, try to look straight ahead at the wall in front of you.
Try to think about when the car pulled up in front of you and the man yelled. Just try to picture that image in your mind. Don't say anything yet.

Look at blank field as alternative to closing eyes
Recreate specific context

Encourage developing image before description

(The *E/W* responds immediately)

E/W: It was a new car. I don't know much about cars.

INT: Wait before you start to describe the car. Take your time and think about the image of the car first. Just concentrate on the image of the car for a few seconds. Don't say anything for a while.

Request the *E/W* to develop image thoroughly before describing
Discourage immediate description; encourage image development

(Waits for the *E/W* to concentrate on the image)
Now, just tell me where on the car you are focusing.

E/W: The side.

INT: OK, now try to describe the side of the car in as much detail as possible. Don't leave out anything. Tell me every detail you can about the side of the car, even if it seems unimportant.

Explicit request for detail

Framed question

E/W: Well, it was blue. It looked pretty new, maybe two or three years old. I don't know what kind of car it was. I just know my own car is a Dodge. That's it.

INT: You said it looked new. What about it made it look new?

Convert subjective to objective

E/W: It was pretty shiny and didn't have any scratches in it.

INT: You said it was blue. Can you tell me what shade of blue it was? Here are some patches of blue (takes out book of color patches). Which of these matches closest with the color of the car?

Recognition easier than recall; use non-verbal response format

E/W: This one here (points to color patch).

INT: Was it exactly like this patch or a little different?

Relative judgment better than absolute

E/W: It was a little darker, I think, and maybe a bit greener.

INT: Try to visualize the front of the car. (pauses to encourage developing images) Now try to describe whatever you see.

E/W: I just saw it quickly. It was kind of square-shaped. And there was a design, like an emblem, in the front.

INT: Can you draw a picture of the design?

Use non-verbal format

E/W: I'm not very good at drawing.

INT: That's OK, just draw it as well as you can.

E/W: (draws simple sketch of design)

INT: OK, now try to think about the front windshield and describe it to me. Was it tinted or clear? Were there any markings, like stickers, or a crack on it?

ERROR: no pause to develop image

ERROR: complex question (multiple questions)

E/W: It was clear, I think.

INT: Did you see a license plate in the front of the car?

E/W: No.

INT: Did you see the license plate in the rear of the car?

ERROR: question is incompatible with currently activated image

E/W: No, it was going too fast.

INT: Carla, try now to focus in on the man who shot you. Where was he sitting in the car?

Recreate context

E/W: In the front seat, on the passenger's side.

INT: And which part of him did you see?

E/W: Only the very top, his chest and a little of his face.

INT: Think for a while about what he looked like when you saw him. You said that he yelled something and then you looked up. You see his face and chest. Try to focus in on that picture. Take your time and develop that image. (pauses to develop image) Tell me whatever you can.

Reconstruct specific context

E/W: I didn't really see much of him, because it was dark inside the car. All I could see is that he was wearing a light-colored shirt or jacket. That's all.

INT: You mentioned that you also saw his face. What can you remember about his face? Was he white or black?

ERROR: ask open-ended question first

E/W: He was white. That's about all I can tell you. It was dark and it happened so quickly.

INT: You don't remember if he had a beard?

ERRORS: negative wording and leading question

E/W: No.

INT: What kind of gun was he holding, a revolver or an automatic?

ERRORS: did not develop image; technical language for civilian

E/W: I don't know.

INT: You said that, after the shots were fired, the car made a left turn on to Cook's Lane. What were you thinking about at the time?

ERROR: impose clear break when changing images

Recreate context

E/W: I was scared, and my leg hurt. I looked at the car because I was mad and I wanted to know who shot me.

INT: Try to think about that moment, when you see the car turning and you are trying to see who shot you. Try to see the car in your mind as it is turning. Don't say anything; just try to imagine the car from this view. (pauses to develop image). Now, try to tell me any detail you can about the left side of the car as it is turning?

Recreate specific context

Request image development before description

Explicit request for detail

E/W: It was a small car, with a square shape . . .

INT: Mm-hm. What else?

Encourage more detailed description

E/W: It had two round lights in the back . . .

INT: (silent pause)

Pause after *E/W* stops talking

E/W: . . . and something shiny on the back, maybe the name of the car. I didn't see it that well because it was too far away.

INT: Try to draw a sketch of what the back of the car looked like. First draw the general shape of the back and then try to fit in any details you can remember. Try to be as complete as possible, including lights, where the license plate is located and anything else you can remember.

Non-verbal response format

Request for detail

E/W: (draws sketch of car)

INT: Let me show you a book that has pictures of different cars. Go through this book and tell me if you see a picture that looks like the car you saw.

Recognition superior to recall

E/W: (examines book of car pictures)

INT: When the car made the left turn on to Cook's Lane, did you see the driver or anyone else in the car?

Image-compatible question

E/W: I just got a glimpse of the driver, but I couldn't see anyone else in the car.

[The *INT* probes this image for any information about the driver in the same way as earlier images were probed. Following this, he probes for information in the concept codes. Because the *E/W* recalls having heard the assailant's voice, failure to probe for voice information is an error here.]

INT: Carla, let's go back to the man who was holding the gun. I realize that you didn't get a good look at him, but did you get any overall impressions of him? About how old was he?

E/W: I didn't really see him well enough to say, but I'd guess early twenties.

INT: Do you know about how heavy he was?   **ERROR:** Use noun form (weight)

E/W: No, I didn't see him very well, and he was sitting in the car.

INT: What about the driver, can you describe him at all?

E/W: No, I barely saw him.

INT: OK, Carla, thanks for your help. If you remember anything else, please call me.   **ERRORS:** no review of notes; abrupt ending, showing little concern; implies *E/W* will not recall new information

Chapter 13

TRAINING PROGRAM
TO LEARN COGNITIVE INTERVIEWING

We conclude this manual with a set of suggestions about learning to use the Cognitive Interview. We have included this section because the Cognitive Interview is a skilled act, and as such, it is not enough simply to memorize its principles. Being able to answer questions on a written test or being able to conduct the interview in a controlled classroom environment is not enough. In order for the Cognitive Interview to be of value in a real-world investigation, the *INT* must be able to perform the various techniques properly when the situation arises. That means applying the techniques automatically, without having to think consciously during the interview about what to do next.

Like any other skilled act, learning requires extensive practice. And just as one would not expect to learn to ride a bicycle or shoot a basketball without hours of practice, one should not expect to learn to conduct the Cognitive Interview without extensive practice. This book should serve as a guide for practicing, not as a substitute for practicing.

Our experience with American and Israeli investigators has been similar to that reported by George (1991) in training British police. That is, after having heard a brief lecture about the use of a particular interviewing technique, investigators often felt that they understood the logic of the procedure, and therefore, they did not have to practice. When required to conduct an actual interview, however, many realized that, although they understood the technique, they could not implement it as easily as they expected. Only after repeated practice did they both understand and have the ability to *use* the techniques skillfully.

According to George (1991), much of the success of the Cognitive Interview comes from the practice exercises in the training program. Many of the techniques comprising the Cognitive Interview—especially those concerned with the dynamics of interviewing (Chapter 3)—are also taught in Conversation Management. Nevertheless, training in the Cognitive Interview still produced far better results in George's field study. One important difference between the two programs is that more practice exercises are built into the Cognitive Interview training than in Conversation Management. Thus, whereas trainees may come out of Conversation Management understanding and knowing how to conduct an interview *in principle,* those trained in the Cognitive Interview know these skills *in practice.* We strongly recommend, therefore, that readers follow the training program as outlined below.

THIRTEEN BASIC SKILLS

Many specific skills have been described in this book. Thirteen, however, stand out as the most important and form the core of the training program.

1. Establishing rapport
2. Listening actively
3. Telling the *E/W* to actively generate information and not wait passively for the *INT* to ask questions
4. Asking open-ended questions
5. Pausing after the *E/W's* response before asking follow-up questions
6. Not interrupting
7. Explicitly requesting detailed descriptions
8. Encouraging the *E/W* to concentrate intensely
9. Encouraging the *E/W* to use imagery
10. Recreating the original context
11. Adopting the *E/W's* perspective
12. Asking eyewitness-compatible questions
13. Following the sequence of the Cognitive Interview

We strongly recommend that the learner use a building-block approach, progressing to the next set of skills only after having mastered thoroughly the skills learned earlier. Those who try to complete more than one phase at a time or progress to the next phase without having perfected all of the preceding skills will find that there are too many skills to think about at one time.

We suggest grouping the thirteen basic skills according to the following program:

> Phase A: (1) Establish rapport
>   (2) Active listening

Phase B:	(3)	Tell the *E/W* to actively generate information
	(4)	Ask open-ended questions
	(5)	Pause after the *E/W's* response
	(6)	Do not interrupt
Phase C:	(7)	Explicitly request detailed descriptions
Phase D:	(8)	Encourage the *E/W* to concentrate
	(9)	Encourage the *E/W* to use imagery
	(10)	Recreate the original context
Phase E:	(11)	Adopt the *E/W's* perspective
	(12)	Ask eyewitness-compatible questions
Phase F:	(13)	Sequence of the Cognitive Interview

Naturally, we recommend that *INTs* learn the entire Cognitive Interview, including Phases A–F plus all of the additional techniques indicated in this book. However, almost all of the techniques can be implemented individually, so that *INTs* can use whichever techniques they feel comfortable with, even before they have mastered the entire Cognitive Interview. Thus, *INTs* might adjust their current style of interviewing and begin to use only the technique of asking primarily open-ended questions even before they have learned the entire program. For best results, *INTs* should try to stick with the ordering of skills indicated here, incorporating the skills in Phase A before those in Phase B, etc.

Interviewers will likely find that after having completed Phases A and B, they will notice a dramatic jump in the amount of information being collected. In fact, most of the advantage of conducting a Cognitive Interview will be derived from using only those few skills listed in Phases A and B. After having learned these skills, *INTs* will find that conducting the Cognitive Interview is not as difficult as anticipated, primarily because the *E/W* will be doing most of the talking and the *INT* will simply be listening to an outpouring of information.

The skills in Phases C and D are relatively easy to learn, as they entail conveying specific directions to the *E/W,* and they do not require the *INT* to make difficult decisions. Nevertheless, *INTs* should allow themselves a few practice sessions to feel comfortable with these skills before implementing them in actual case interviews. Furthermore, they should not progress to the next set of skills, Phase E, until they have conducted several interviews incorporating these skills.

The next major hurdle is Phase E, as it requires reorienting the focus of the interview toward the *E/W* and understanding how the information is represented in her mind. Interviewers can expect that several sessions of practice will be required to learn this skill and to be able to use it automatically, as required during an interview.

Phase F is the most difficult to learn, and should not be attempted until having thoroughly mastered all of the preceding skills to the point where they seem natural. It is easiest to learn this phase in two stages, first learning the global sequence of the interview (Introduction, Open-ended narration, Probing Memory Codes, Review, Close), and then the strategy for probing image codes described in Chapter 9.

The global strategy will be the easier stage to learn, as it follows a logical sequence. The strategy for probing image codes will be the most difficult skill of the entire Cognitive Interview to learn, especially in complex cases when *E/Ws* may have many different images of several people. We advise the *INT* to start implementing this strategy initially by asking the *E/W* to tell him which is the best image she has of each assailant and then requesting a description of each assailant only from the best view. Once the *INT* is comfortable with this, he can progress gradually to probing multiple images and inferring the *E/W's* images.

Only after having mastered these thirteen basic skills should *INTs* begin to try to apply some of the other, secondary skills mentioned throughout the book. At this point, the reader should be at a level equal to or better than the best *INTs* in our field studies (See Appendix B, Footnote 2).

PRACTICE SCHEDULE

Although there will be individual differences in the amount of time required to progress through the various phases, most learners can expect that it will require several practice sessions to complete each phase.

Each phase of practice will progress most efficiently if it is divided into several short sessions rather than one long session. Ideally, each practice session will focus on only one or two skills, with most of the session devoted to practical exercises. Trying to pack in many skills into one long session, without ample time to practice, is not nearly as efficient as using several short sessions each devoted to practicing one or two specific techniques. Certainly we would not consider teaching someone to drive a car by explaining in one or two long sessions all of the required procedures. In the same manner that we teach new drivers to practice making only left turns, right turns, or parallel parking, teaching investigators to conduct effective interviews requires organizing each session around one or two related skills and then devoting most of the session to practicing.

Since a police investigation has the potential for major legal implications, investigators should not apply the various skills of the Cognitive Interview in a real case until they have practiced these skills thoroughly in a controlled, "safe" environment. We recommend that *INTs* practice initially by interviewing friends, family, or other police officers. Friends, family, neighbors, and other non-police personnel are the best practice *E/Ws* as they resemble typical, unknowledgeable civilian *E/Ws*. Police *E/Ws* may provide more accurate responses because they are better observers or they know what information is relevant for police investigations. Precisely because they are not naive, however, they do not provide enough of a challenge for *INTs* to practice the skills required to interview civilians.

When learning the Cognitive Interview, it is not necessary for the *E/W* to describe a real crime. Almost any event is sufficient, since the mental processes that govern memory and communication follow the same principles whether the event being described is a crime or not. Thus, interviewing a volunteer *E/W* to elicit a description of someone she met in the supermarket earlier provides excellent practice for developing interviewing skills. Similarly, investigators can practice eliciting descriptions of actions by interviewing someone about a play in a football game. If investigators wish to practice interviewing about more typical criminal events, they can ask *E/Ws* to view a film of a crime and then probe for details of the crime scene. Many police departments possess such films for recruit training.

For these practice exercises to be valuable, the *E/W* must describe an event that she actually observed or participated in. She should not fabricate or make up an event, even a crime scenario. The mental processes of describing an event that was actually observed are different than those of describing a made-up event that never occurred. It will provide better practice for the *INT* if the *E/W* describes an innocuous event that has nothing to do with a crime, but which she actually observed, than for her to fabricate a crime scene.

EXPECTED ERRORS

In our experiences of conducting training workshops and examining field police interviews, seven errors occurred most frequently and were the most difficult for investigators to overcome. We therefore recommend that those learning the Cognitive Interview pay particular attention to monitor these behaviors. Similarly, those responsible for developing training programs should ensure that extra practice be given to eradicating these errors.

1. The *INT* asks too many closed questions and not enough open-ended questions.
2. The *INT* interrupts too often.
3. The *INT* does not pause long enough after the *E/W* terminates her response before asking the next question.
4. After asking the *E/W* to develop a mental image, the *INT* does not wait long enough before requesting a description of the image.
5. The *INT* asks questions that are not compatible with the *E/W's* mental record.
6. The *INT* does not establish good rapport in the beginning of the interview.
7. The *INT* starts probing for detailed information before determining the *E/W's* overall mental representation.

FEEDBACK

It is essential that *INTs* receive feedback about their performance, as it is difficult for *INTs* to monitor themselves during an interview. Oftentimes in our workshops, *INTs* did not realize they had made mistakes until it was pointed out to them by someone else. Many of our investigators claimed that they rarely interrupted *E/Ws* in the middle of a response, and remained unconvinced until they heard actual tape recordings of their interviews. Most were surprised to hear that they made the same errors as the investigators in our studies. These feedback sessions are sometimes humbling experiences, but they are indispensable as learning devices.

There are many ways to receive feedback after an interview. The easiest is to tape (or video) record the interview. Then the *INT* can simply play it back and critique himself at his convenience. Less private, but more helpful, is to have a peer or supervisor evaluate the interview after it is concluded. Group critique sessions, where learners critique each other, are often the most efficient. They provide feedback for the individual *INT;* in addition, they force all of the group members to listen critically to notice others' mistakes. A secondary advantage of the group-critique format is that learners are less defensive and are more receptive to criticism, since they realize that, at some time, everyone in the group will be criticized. When conducting such feedback sessions—regardless of who is providing the feedback—it is important that the criticism be offered constructively so the learner does not feel threatened.

Another valuable learning procedure is to ask the *E/W* to evaluate the interview. Oftentimes, the *E/W* herself can provide valuable insights about how the *INT's* conduct affected her thought processes. Perhaps she might have responded slightly differently had the *INT* asked a different question, or kept quiet. Because the *E/W* does have valuable insights, it is worthwhile for each interviewer-in-training to play the role of the *E/W* so he can appreciate how the *E/W's* mental thoughts reflect the *INT's* actions.

We expect that, after having monitored their own interviews and those of other investigators, many investigators will have developed new techniques that we have not mentioned here. We encourage investigators to incorporate these techniques into their own interview styles and to share them with their colleagues.

Appendix A

REFERENCE GUIDE TO CONDUCTING THE COGNITIVE INTERVIEW

I. Introduction
   A. Control *E/W's* anxiety.
   B. Develop rapport.
   C. Tell *E/W* to actively volunteer information, not passively wait for *INT* to ask questions.
   D. Explicitly request detailed information.
   E. Tell *E/W* not to edit her thoughts.
   F. Tell *E/W* not to fabricate or make up answers.
   G. Convey that *INT* expects *E/W* to concentrate intensely.

II. Open-Ended Narration
   A. Recreate the general context.
   B. Request narrative description.
   C. Do not interrupt.
   D. Long pause after *E/W* stops speaking before asking next question.
   E. Identify *E/W's* images.
      1. Ask *E/W* to indicate clearest image.
      2. Ask or infer other images.
   F. Sketchy notes to indicate *E/W's* images.
   G. Develop a tentative probing strategy (Principles of Detail and Momentum).

III. Probing Memory Codes
   A. Re-emphasize importance of *E/W* concentration.
   B. Recreate context of specific event.
   C. Ask *E/W* to close her eyes.
   D. Ask open-ended, framed question.
   E. Request detailed description.
   F. Do not interrupt *E/W's* narration.
   G. Take detailed notes.

H. Long pause after *E/W* stops speaking before asking follow-up questions.

I. Exhaust image for information not included in narration.

J. Probe remaining images.

K. Re-probe images activated earlier.

L. Probe concept codes.

IV. Review

A. Review for *E/W* from *INT's* memory or notes.

B. Speak slowly and deliberately.

C. Ask *E/W* to interrupt immediately if she remembers new information or if errors in *INT's* review.

D. If new leads develop, probe relevant information.

V. Close

A. Collect background information.

B. Remind *E/W* to call when she thinks of new information.

C. Create a positive, last impression.

Appendix B

SUMMARY OF RESEARCH

The following is intended only as a summary of the research. For a more in-depth description, readers should consult the original articles, which generally appear in applied psychology and police science journals. Most of the research described was supported by grants from the National Institute of Justice.

In the first two major studies of the Cognitive Interview, (Geiselman, Fisher, MacKinnon, & Holland, 1985, 1986) 200 adults watched a 4-minute filmed simulation of a violent crime. These films are used by the Los Angeles Police Department for firearms training and are very realistic. The "eyewitnesses" then returned to the laboratory two days later and were interviewed by experienced law enforcement officers. In the first experiment, the *INTs* conducted either a standard police interview, a hypnotically-induced interview, or the Cognitive Interview. The Cognitive Interview in these early studies consisted of only four basic instructions which were given to the *E/W* at the start of the interview: (1) Try to recreate the psychological (e.g., thoughts) and environmental (e.g., lighting) conditions of the original event, (2) Do not edit anything from the report; say whatever comes to your mind when you think of it, even if it seems trivial or out of place, (3) Describe the event both from your (*E/W's*) perspective and that of another prominent person at the crime, and (4) Change the order of reporting; after describing the sequence in the natural, chronological order, try to describe the events in reverse order.

The interview sessions, which lasted approximately 20–30 minutes, were tape recorded and transcribed. A team of research assistants scored the transcriptions for the number of correct and incorrect statements given by each *E/W*. In the first experiment, with university students as the *E/Ws*, this simplified version of the Cognitive Interview and hypnosis interviews were equally effective in eliciting correct information and both were approximately 30%–35% more effective than the standard police interview. The Cognitive Interview elicited 41 facts per *E/W*, hypnosis 38 facts, and the standard interview 29 facts. Approximately the same percentage of facts were incorrect (15%) in all three interviews. In the second experiment, with nonstudents as the *E/Ws,* the Cognitive Interview was compared to only a standard police interview. The results were similar to the first experiment. The Cognitive Interview elicited approximately 20% more correct information than did the standard interview without generating any more errors.

In recent years an increasing number of children have been asked to testify about civil and criminal events, especially about events in which they were alleged to be victims. We therefore conducted follow-up studies to examine the effectiveness of the Cognitive Interview with young children (Geiselman & Padilla, 1988; Geiselman, Saywitz, & Bornstein, in press).

Volunteer *E/Ws* between the ages of 7 and 12 were shown one of the earlier-mentioned films and were interviewed three days later about what they had seen. In Geiselman & Padilla (1988), the Cognitive Interview enhanced recall of correct information by approximately 20% compared to the standard interview technique (37 vs. 31 facts). Again, the amount of incorrect information was the same for the Cognitive and standard methods. In Geiselman, Saywitz, & Bornstein (in press), the Cognitive Interview was especially effective with children when they received practice using the techniques prior to the target interview. With practice, the Cognitive Interview yielded a 45% increase in correct recall over standard procedures.

One possible reservation is that the Cognitive Interview makes *E/Ws* overly suggestible. That is, perhaps the *E/Ws* were simply picking up subtle cues about the correct answers from the *INT's* questions. If such were the case, any leading or misleading questions could unduly alter the *E/W's* memory, as has been found with hypnosis (Putnam, 1979).

This issue was examined in the next experiment (Geiselman, Fisher, Cohen, Holland, & Surtes, 1986). The *E/Ws* observed an event—an actor, wearing a green backpack, interrupted a meeting attended by the *E/Ws* —after which they were asked either neutral, leading, or misleading questions. One third of the *E/Ws* were asked neutral questions (What did the intruder who was wearing the backpack say to the instructor?), one third were asked leading questions (What did the intruder who was wearing a *green* backpack say to the instructor?), and one third were asked misleading questions (What did the intruder who was wearing a *blue* backpack say to the instructor?). Later, all of the *E/Ws* were asked to recall the color of the backpack. The (mis)leading question generally altered the *E/W's* recollections. Those receiving leading questions were most likely to recall correctly the color of the backpack, whereas those receiving misleading questions were least likely to recall the color of the backpack. However, *E/Ws* who received the Cognitive Interview were less affected by the (mis)leading information than those who received the standard interview. The Cognitive Interview, therefore, made *E/Ws* less, not more, suggestible to the effects of (mis)leading questions.

In all of the studies conducted, the Cognitive Interview led to better recall than did the standard interview. Nevertheless, not all of the relevant information was recalled, so there was still considerable room for improvement. One method of improving the procedure was to examine carefully the techniques that discriminated between good and poor *INTs,* building into the Cognitive Interview those techniques used by good *INTs* and deleting those techniques used by poor *INTs*.

We were also concerned about whether our previous findings reflected the isolated world of the laboratory, or whether they accurately reflected the real world of criminal investigations, with real victims and witnesses of crime. We therefore continued our research by examining tape-recorded field interviews of real victims and witnesses, graciously provided by the Metro-Dade Police Department. Our analysis of these tape recordings generated additional insights into improving the Cognitive Interview (Fisher, Geiselman, & Raymond, 1987).

After a final set of revisions, which led to the current version, we conducted a laboratory test to compare the original and current versions of the Cognitive Interview (Fisher, Geiselman, Raymond, Jurkevich, & Warhaftig, 1987). The procedure was similar to the previously-described studies in which *E/Ws* viewed a film of a simulated crime followed by a two-day interval before the interview; the only change in procedure is that the *INTs* were research assistants who were trained to use the original and revised versions of the Cognitive Interview. The revised Cognitive Interview elicited between 45%–50% more correct information than did the original version. In comparison to the earliest studies, the revised Cognitive Interview elicited 96% more information than did the standard police interview, and 65% more than hypnosis, again without increasing the error rate.

A second laboratory test of the revised Cognitive Interview was conducted with children as the *E/Ws* (Fisher & McCauley, 1991). Two important differences between children's and adults' cognition are (a) children rely more heavily on sensory information than do adults, who rely more on meaning, and (b) children are less able or willing to verbalize detailed, elaborate responses than are adults. We therefore modified the Cognitive Interview for children by encouraging them first to think about their mental images of the event and then to act their ideas out before describing them. Second, we primed children to generate elaborate responses by practicing giving detailed descriptions of a well-known activity (brushing their teeth). In the experiment, 8-year old children interacted with an adult by playing a Simon-says game in which they did a series of simple actions (sitting down, touching their toes, etc.). Two weeks later, the children were interviewed in the standard fashion or with the Cognitive Interview as modified for children. Almost twice (84% more) as many correct facts were elicited in the Cognitive than the standard interview, again with no differences in the number of incorrect facts.

Having demonstrated repeatedly in the laboratory that the Cognitive Interview can elicit more information than a standard police interview, we entered the last, and ultimately the most important, phase of our research program by testing the procedure in the field (Fisher, Geiselman, & Amador, 1989). Does the Cognitive Interview elicit more information when police detectives interview real victims and witnesses of crime? Sixteen experienced detectives from the Robbery Division of the Metro-Dade Police Department[1] tape recorded their interviews with victims and witnesses of crime (typically commercial robbery or purse-snatching). These tape recordings were then transcribed and scored by a panel of judges for the amount of information elicited (number of crime-relevant facts).

Following several of these interviews, the detectives were divided into two equivalent groups based on the preliminary interviews. One group of seven detectives received training to use the Cognitive Interview; the other group of nine detectives did not receive this additional training. The training entailed four one-hour sessions describing effective and ineffective interviewing techniques.[2] Following the in-class sessions, the trained group practiced the technique, after which they tape-recorded

---

1. We would like to thank Chief John Farrell, Lt. Ken Russ, and Sgt. Jim Wander, and the participating detectives for their assistance in the study.

2. The training provided in this field study (begun almost five years ago) was not as effective as that offered in the present training program, and it was not nearly as thorough as that described in this book. The result from the field study, therefore, is a low estimate of the value of the current version of training in the Cognitive Interview.

another field interview, and received feedback on their performance. After training, all of the detectives again tape recorded their next several interviews with victims and witnesses. These tapes were transcribed and scored blind for the amount of information per interview.

The results were clear. After training on the cognitive interview, the detectives elicited 46% more information than before training (40 vs. 27 facts). Of the seven trained detectives, six improved dramatically (between 34%–115% more information). The one detective who did not improve is the one detective who did not change his interviewing style from before training. In a comparable analysis, those detectives who were trained on the Cognitive Interview collected 63% more information than the untrained detectives (40 vs. 24 facts). It is impossible to evaluate the accuracy of the collected information, as this was a field study. However, the corroboration rates (percentage of collected information corroborated by other *E/Ws* to the crime) were extremely high in both the untrained (93%) and trained (94%) interviews.[3]

The one task in which the Cognitive Interview has not been effective as a memory-enhancer is in recognizing people from lineups or photo-arrays. In four separate studies, *E/Ws* either observed a videotape of a crime or they observed someone interrupt a classroom lecture (McCauley, Chin, Fisher, & Brock, 1991). Several days later, the *E/Ws* attempted to describe the target person (criminal or intruder) or identify him from a 4- or 5-person photoarray or lineup. Half of the *E/Ws* were given the Cognitive Interview and half were not. Although the Cognitive Interview groups provided better descriptions of the target person, there were no differences in recognizing him in photoarrays or lineups. We suspect that face-recognition and person-recognition tasks are done with only minimal conscious control. Therefore, little can be done to improve performance by providing instructions to alter the *E/W's* memory-retrieval operations. A more fruitful approach would be to improve the quality of the target person's image, for example, by using videotapes instead of photoarrays (Cutler & Fisher, 1990).

Virtually all of the initial research on the Cognitive Interview was

---

3. Note that the corroboration rate is extremely high in comparison with the accuracy rates reported in typical laboratory studies (80%–85%). Similarly high accuracy rates were reported in field studies by Yuille and Cutshall (1986) and Yuille and Kim (1987). Although not definitive, it is interesting that the accuracy-corroboration rates in the three field studies of eyewitness memory are considerably higher than their laboratory counterparts. If this difference between laboratory and field studies continues to appear, one may question the validity of describing in court the accuracy rates found in the laboratory as evidence of the general unreliability of eyewitness testimony in field cases (cf. McCloskey & Egeth, 1983).

conducted in our laboratories, either at the University of California, Los Angeles or at Florida International University. Naturally, all of these studies were conducted with American *E/Ws*. Recently other researchers have conducted independent studies in other laboratories using non-American *E/Ws* (see Memon, 1991, for a review of the research). Aschermann, Mantwill, and Kohnken (1991), for example, developed a German version of the Cognitive Interview and tested it in a laboratory study with adult, German *E/Ws*. Similar to the results we found with the original version (Geiselman, Fisher, MacKinnon & Holland, 1985), the German version of the Cognitive Interview elicited 38% more information than did a standard interview.

A second study, again with German *E/Ws,* was conducted by Kohnken, Thuerer, and Zoberbier (1991), and once again the Cognitive Interview was found superior to standard training. Witnesses receiving the Cognitive Interview recalled 52% more facts than did those receiving the standard interview. In addition to measuring the number of facts recalled by the *E/W,* the authors also measured the number of facts contained in the *INT's* written report describing the information gathered during the interview. Here, too, the Cognitive Interview contained more information (42% advantage). In both of the German studies described, the same amount of incorrect information was elicited by the Cognitive and standard interviews.

Detective Sergeant Richard George of the City of London Police Department recently conducted a very thorough and impressive field study with British victims and witnesses of crime. Thirty-two experienced police officers representing different types of investigation (uniformed officer, detective, traffic) and different police departments were assigned randomly to one of four training conditions: Cognitive Interview (CI), Conversation Management (CM: see Chapter 1), both CI and CM, or no additional training. Following training, each police officer tape recorded three interviews with victims or witnesses of a crime. The tapes were then transcribed and scored for amount and type of information (Does it answer a Who, What, Where, How, or Why question?).

The questioning style changed dramatically, from before training to after training, but only in the CI group. The changes involved primarily asking fewer closed questions and more open-ended questions, and injecting more pauses. In keeping with the shift from asking closed question to asking open-ended questions, *INTs* in the CI group also asked far fewer questions after training (15 questions per interview) than before training (52 questions per interview). Interestingly, the total amount of time per interview was about the same for all of the groups (approximately 16 minutes).

Similar to the results in Fisher, Geiselman, and Amador's (1989) field study, George's study showed that the Cognitive Interview elicited more information than did the standard police interview, whether comparing trained to untrained *INTs* (14% advantage) or comparing the trained detectives after versus before training (55% advantage). This advantage held for all types of information (who, what, when, where, how, and why). By comparison, neither the Conversation Management nor the combination of Cognitive Interview plus Conversation Management groups elicited more information than the untrained group.

As in any field study, it is impossible to examine the accuracy of any elicited fact. George (1991) therefore conducted a follow-up laboratory experiment. College students observed a planned altercation between two intruders and the professor. One week later the student-witnesses were interviewed by experienced police officers who received additional training either in the Cognitive Interview, the Cognitive Interview combined with Conversation Management, or no additional training. As in the field study, the Cognitive Interview elicited more (36%) information than did the standard interview, although now, the combination of CI and CM was as effective as CI alone. As in all of the laboratory studies we have conducted, the number of errors per interview was approximately the same across the different interviewing conditions.

The consistency of the findings across researchers and eyewitness populations suggests that the results are not the product of anything unique to our test procedures. Rather, they reflect a basic advantage of the Cognitive Interview techniques.

Because the Cognitive Interview is based on general principles of cognition and is not specific to crime, we conducted one last study to see whether the technique, when modified appropriately, could be used to facilitate other types of investigation. One such area is public health, in which investigators often interview people showing signs of food poisoning to determine the source of the illness, i.e., where was the unhealthful food eaten? In the past, public health researchers claimed that little could be done to improve the recollection of respondents (Decker, Booth, Dewey, Fricker, Hutcheson, & Schaffner, 1986).

To study this problem, Fisher and Quigley (1991) invited students to eat (healthful) foods from a table containing 34 different foods (soft beverages, cheeses, crackers, vegetables, etc.). The students were videotaped as they selected the foods. Four to fourteen days later the students returned to the laboratory and attempted to recall the foods eaten earlier. Half of the students were given a modified Cognitive Interview geared to the activities associated with selecting and eating foods and half were interviewed in the standard fashion, with no explicit memory-enhancement instructions. Those in Cognitive Interview group recalled twice as many foods selected as those in the No-Instruction group (12.2 vs. 5.9), without generating any more errors. Even when provided a menu of foods as a guide, the Cognitive Interview group recognized more of the foods (83%) than did the No-Instruction group (75%).

Based on its effectiveness in both criminal and non-criminal investigations, we suspect that the Cognitive Interview can be applied in a wide variety of investigations, especially when demands are made on the respondent's memory and communication skills. We encourage other researchers to examine novel uses of the Cognitive Interview and to inform us of their results.

BIBLIOGRAPHY

Alagna, F. J., Whitcher, S. J., Fisher, J. D., & Wicas, E. A. (1979). Evaluative reaction to interpersonal touch in a counseling interview. *Journal of Counseling Psychology, 26,* 465–472.

Anderson, J. R. (1990). *Cognitive psychology and its implications.* New York: W. H. Freeman.

Anderson, R. C., & Pichert, J. W. (1978). Recall of previously unrecallable information following a shift in perspective. *Journal of Verbal Learning and Verbal Behavior, 17,* 1–12.

Aschermann, E., Mantwill, M., & Kohnken, G. (1991). An independent replication of the cognitive interview. *Applied Cognitive Psychology, 5,* 489–495.

Atkinson, R. C., & Shiffrin, R. M. (1968). Human memory: A proposed system and its control processes. In K. W. Spence (Ed.), *The psychology of learning and motivation: Advances in research and theory.* Vol. 2. New York: Academic Press.

Baddeley, A. D. (1986). *Working memory.* Oxford: Oxford University Press.

Bailey, F. L. & Rothblatt, H. B. (1971). *Successful techniques for criminal trials.* Rochester: The Lawyers Co-operative Publishing & Bancroft-Whitney.

Bartlett, F. C. (1932). *Remembering.* Cambridge: Cambridge University Press.

Belmont, J. M., & Butterfield, E. C. (1971). Learning strategies as a determinant of learning deficiencies. *Cognitive Psychology, 2,* 411–420.

Bower, G. H. (1967). A multicomponent theory of the memory trace. In K. W. Spence & J. T. Spence (Eds.), *The psychology of learning and motivation* (Vol. 1). New York: Academic Press.

Broadbent, D. E. (1957). A mechanical model for human attention and immediate memory. *Psychological Review, 64,* 205–215.

Brooks, L. (1968). Spatial and verbal components of the act of recall. *Canadian Journal of Psychology, 22,* 349–368.

Brown, C., & Geiselman, R. E. (1991). Eyewitness testimony of mentally retarded: Effect of the cognitive interview. *Journal of Police and Criminal Psychology, 6,* 14–22.

Brown, R., & MacNeill, D. (1966). The "tip-of-the-tongue" phenomenon. *Journal of Verbal Learning and Verbal Behavior, 5,* 325–337.

Burns, M. J. (1981). The mental retracing of prior activities: Evidence for reminiscence in ordered retrieval. (Doctoral Dissertation, University of California, Los Angeles, 1981.) *Dissertation Abstracts International, 42,* 2108B.

Cady, H. M. (1924). On the psychology of testimony. *American Journal of Psychology, 35,* 110–112.

Cahill, D., & Mingay, D. J. (1986). Leading questions and the police interview. *Policing,* Autumn, 212–224.

Chelune, G. J. (1979). *Self-disclosure.* San Francisco: Freeman.

Chi, M. T. H., & Ceci, S. J. (1986). Content knowledge and the reorganization of memory. *Advances in Child Development and Behavior, 20,* 1–37.

Connor, R. A., & Davidson, J. P. (1985). *Marketing your consulting and professional services.* New York: Wiley.

Cutler, B. L., & Fisher, R. P. (1990). Live lineups, videotaped lineups, and photoarrays. *Forensic Reports, 3,* 439–448.

Cutler, B. L., Fisher, R. P., & Chicvara, C. L. (1989). Person identification from live versus videotaped police lineups. *Forensic Reports, 2,* 93–106.

Cutler, B. L., & Penrod, S. D. (1989). Forensically relevant moderators of the relation between eyewitness identification accuracy and confidence. *Journal of Applied Psychology, 74,* 650–652.

Decker, M. D., Booth, A. L., Dewey, M. J., Fricker, R. S., Hutcheson, R. H., & Schaffner, W. (1986). Validity of food consumption histories in foodborne outbreak investigations. *American Journal of Epidemiology, 124,* 859–862.

Deffenbacher, K. A. (1980). Eyewitness accuracy and confidence: Can we infer anything about their relationship? *Law and Human Behavior, 4,* 243–260.

Deffenbacher, K. A. (1988). Eyewitness research: The next ten years. In M. Gruneberg, P. Morris, & R. Sykes (Eds.), *Practical aspects of memory: Current research and issues.* New York: Wiley.

Dent, H. R. (1982). The effect of interviewing strategies on the results of interviews with child witnesses. In A. Trankell (Ed.), *Reconstructing the past.* Netherlands: K. H. Aver Publishing.

Dillon, J. T. (1982). The effect of questions in education and other enterprises. *Journal of Curriculum Studies. 14,* 127–152.

Eich, E. (1977). State-dependent retrieval of information in human episodic memory. In J. Birnbaum and E. Parker (Eds.), *Alcohol and human memory.* Hillsdale, NJ: Erlbaum.

Ellis, H. D. (1984). Practical aspects of face memory. In G. Wells & E. Loftus (Eds.), *Eyewitness testimony: Psychological perspectives.* Cambridge: Cambridge University Press.

Festinger, L. (1957). *A theory of cognitive dissonance.* Stanford, CA: Stanford University Press.

Festinger, L., & Carlsmith, J. M. (1959). Cognitive consequences of forced compliance. *Journal of Abnormal and Social Psychology, 58,* 203–210.

Fisher, R. P., & Chandler, C. C. (1984). Dissociations between temporally-cued and theme-cued recall. *Bulletin of the Psychonomic Society. 22,* 395–397.

Fisher, R. P., & Chandler, C. C. (1991). Independence between recalling interevent relations and specific events. *Journal of Experimental Psychology: Learning, Memory, and Cognition, 17,* 722–733.

Fisher, R. P., & Cutler, B. L. (1991). *The relation between consistency and accuracy of eyewitness testimony.* Unpublished manuscript. Florida International University, Miami.

Fisher, R. P., Geiselman, R. E., & Amador, M. (1989). Field test of the cognitive interview: Enhancing the recollection of actual victims and witnesses of crime. *Journal of Applied Psychology, 74,* 722–727.

Fisher, R. P., Geiselman, R. E., & Raymond, D. S. (1987). Critical analysis of police interview techniques. *Journal of Police Science and Administration, 15,* 177–185.

Fisher, R. P., Geiselman, R. E., Raymond, D. S., Jurkevich, L. M., & Warhaftig, M. L. (1987). Enhancing enhanced eyewitness memory: Refining the cognitive interview. *Journal of Police Science and Administration, 15,* 291–297.

Fisher, R. P., & McCauley, M. R. (1991). *Improving the accuracy of children's eyewitness memory with the cognitive interview.* Unpublished manuscript. Florida International University, Miami.

Fisher, R. P., & McCauley, M. R. (in press). Improving eyewitness memory with the cognitive interview. To appear in D. Ross, J. Read, & M. Toglia (Eds). *Eyewitness memory: Current trends and developments.* New York: Springer-Verlag.

Fisher, R. P., & Quigley, K. L. (1988). *The effect of question sequence on eyewitness recall.* Unpublished manuscript. Florida International University, Miami.

Fisher, R. P., & Quigley, K. L. (1991). Applying cognitive theory in public health investigations: Enhancing food recall. To appear in J. Tanur (Ed.) *Questions about Questions.* New York: Sage.

Flanagan, E. J. (1981). Interviewing and interrogation techniques. In E. J. Grau (Ed.) *Criminal and civil investigation handbook.* New York: McGraw-Hill.

Flavell, J. H. (1986). The development of children's knowledge about the appearance-reality distinction. *American Psychologist, 41,* 418–425.

Flexser, A. J., & Tulving, E. (1978). Retrieval independence in recognition and recall. *Psychological Review, 85,* 153–172.

Geiselman, R. E., & Callot, R. (1990). Reverse versus forward recall of script-based texts. *Applied Cognitive Psychology, 4,* 141–144.

Geiselman, R. E., Fisher, R. P., Cohen, G., Holland, H., & Surtes, L. (1986). Eyewitness responses to leading and misleading questions under the cognitive interview. *Journal of Police Science and Administration, 14,* 31–39.

Geiselman, R. E., Fisher, R. P., Firstenberg, I., Hutton, L. A., Sullivan, S. J., Avetissian, I. V., & Prosk, A. L. (1984). Enhancement of eyewitness memory: An empirical evaluation of the cognitive interview. *Journal of Police Science and Administration, 12,* 74–80.

Geiselman, R. E., Fisher, R. P., MacKinnon, D. P., & Holland, H. L. (1985). Eyewitness memory enhancement in the police interview: Cognitive retrieval mnemonics versus hypnosis. *Journal of Applied Psychology, 70,* 401–412.

Geiselman, R. E., Fisher, R. P., MacKinnon, D. P., & Holland, H. L. (1986). Enhancement of eyewitness memory with the cognitive interview. *American Journal of Psychology, 99,* 385–401.

Geiselman, R. E., & Padilla, J. (1988). Interviewing child witnesses with the cognitive interview. *Journal of Police Science and Administration, 16,* 236–242.

Geiselman, R. E., Saywitz, K. J., & Bornstein, G. K. (in press). Effects of cognitive questioning techniques on children's recall performance. To appear in G. Goodman & B. Bottoms (Eds.) *Understanding and improving children's testimony: Developmental, clinical, and legal issues.* New York: Guilford Publications.

Geiselman, R. E., Woodward, J. A., & Beatty, J. (1982). Individual differences in verbal memory performance: A test of the alternative information processing models. *Journal of Experimental Psychology: General, 11,* 109–134.

George, R. (1991). *A field and experimental evaluation of three methods of interviewing witnesses/victims of crime.* Unpublished manuscript. Polytechnic of East London. London.

Goodman, G. S., Bottoms, B., Schwartz-Kenney, B. M., & Rudy, L. (1991). Children's testimony for a stressful event: Improving children's reports. *Journal of Narrative and Life History, 1,* 69–99.

Greenspoon, J. (1955). The reinforcing effect of two spoken sounds on the frequency of two responses. *American Journal of Psychology, 68,* 409–416.

Greenwald, A. G. (1970). Sensory feedback mechanisms in performance control: With special reference to the ideo-motor mechanism. *Psychological Review, 77,* 73–99.

Haber, R. N. (1969). *Information-processing approaches to visual perception.* New York: Holt, Rinehart, & Winston.

Harris, R. (1973). *The police academy.* New York: Wiley.

Hilgard, E. R., & Loftus, E. F. (1979). Effective interrogation of the eyewitness. *International Journal of Clinical and Experimental Hypnosis, 27,* 342–357.

James, W. (1890). *The principles of psychology.* New York: Holt.

Johnson, N. F. (1972). Organization and the concept of a memory code. In A. Melton & E. Martin (Eds.), *Coding processes in human memory.* Washington, D.C.: V. H. Winston.

Johnston, W. A., Greenberg, S. N., Fisher, R. P., & Martin, D. W. (1979). Divided attention: A vehicle for monitoring memory processes. *Journal of Experimental Psychology, 83,* 164–171.

Kahneman, D. (1973). *Attention and effort.* Englewood Cliffs, NJ: Prentice-Hall.

Kintsch, W. (1970). *Learning, memory, and conceptual processes.* New York: Wiley.

Kintsch, W., & Van Dijk, T. A. (1978). Toward a model of text comprehension and production. *Psychological Review, 85,* 363–394.

Klatzky, R. L. (1980). *Human memory: Structures and processes.* San Francisco: Freeman.

Koffka, K. (1935). *Principles of Gestalt psychology.* New York: Harcourt, Brace.

Kohnken, G., Finger, M., & Nitschke, N. (1991). *Statement validity analysis and the cognitive interview with child witnesses.* Unpublished manuscript. University of Kiel, Kiel.

Kohnken, G., Thuerer, C. & Zoberbier, D. (1991). *The cognitive interview: Are the interviewers' memories enhanced, too?* Unpublished manuscript. University of Kiel, Kiel.

Kosslyn, S. (1981). The medium and the message in mental imagery: A theory. *Psychological Review, 88,* 46–66.

LaBerge, D. L., & Samuels, S. J. (1974). Toward a theory of automatic information processing in reading. *Cognitive Psychology, 6,* 292–323.

Landauer, T. K. (1986). How much do people remember? Some estimates of the quantity of learned information in long-term memory. *Cognitive Science, 10,* 477–493.

Latts, M. G., & Geiselman, R. E. (1991). Interviewing survivors of rape. *Journal of Police and Criminal Psychology, 7,* 8–17.

Leibowitz, H. W., & Guzy, L. (1990). *Can the accuracy of eyewitness testimony be improved by the use of non-verbal techniques?* Paper presented at the American Psychology-Law Society, Williamsburg.

Leonard, V. A. (1971). *Criminal investigation and identification.* Springfield, IL: Charles C Thomas.

Levie, R. C., & Ballard, L. E. (1981). Taking notes during the investigation. In E. J. Grau (Ed.) *Criminal and civil investigation handbook.* New York: McGraw-Hill.

Lindsay, R. C. L., Wells, G. L., & Rumpel, C. M. (1981). Can people detect eyewitness-identification accuracy within and across situations? *Journal of Applied Psychology, 66,* 79–89.

Lipton, J. P. (1977). On the psychology of eyewitness testimony. *Journal of Applied Psychology, 62,* 90–93.

Loftus, E. F. (1979). *Eyewitness testimony.* Cambridge, MA: Harvard University Press.

Loftus, E. F., & Loftus, G. R. (1980). On the permanence of stored information in the human brain. *American Psychologist, 35,* 409–420.

Loftus, E. F., Manber, M., & Keating, J. F. (1983). Recollection of naturalistic events: Context enhancement versus negative cueing. *Human Learning, 2,* 83–92.

Loftus, E. F., & Marburger, W. (1983). Since the eruption of Mt. St. Helens, has anyone beaten you up? Improving the accuracy of retrospective reports with landmark events. *Memory & Cognition, 11,* 114–120.

Loftus, E. F., & Zanni, G. (1975). Eyewitness testimony: The influence of the wording of a question. *Bulletin of the Psychonomic Society, 5,* 86–88.

Madigan, S. A. (1969). Intraserial repetition and coding processes in free recall. *Journal of Verbal Learning and Verbal Behavior, 8,* 828–835.

Matarazzo, J. D., & Wiens, A. N. (1985). *The interview: Research on its anatomy and structure.* Chicago: Aldine.

McCauley, M. R., Chin, D., Fisher, R. P., & Brock, P. (1991). *Revising the cognitive interview for eyewitness identification.* Paper presented at the Southeastern Psychological Association, New Orleans.

McCloskey, M., & Egeth, H. (1983). What can a psychologist tell a jury? *American Psychologist, 38,* 550–563.

Melton, A. W. (1963). Implications of short-term memory for a general theory of memory. *Journal of Verbal Learning and Verbal Behavior, 2,* 1–21.

Memon, A. (1991). *Introducing the cognitive interview as a procedure for interviewing witnesses.* Paper presented at the Annual Conference of the British Psychological Society, Bournemouth.

Metzler, K. (1979). *Newsgathering.* Englewood Cliffs, NJ: Prentice-Hall.

Miller, G. A. (1956). The magical number seven, plus or minus two: Some limits on our capacity for processing information. *Psychological Review, 63,* 81–97.

Miner, E. M. (1984). The importance of listening in the interview interrogation process. *FBI Law Enforcement Bulletin,* June, 12–16.

More, H. W., & Unsinger, P. C. (1987). *Police managerial use of psychology and psychologists.* Springfield, IL: Charles C Thomas.

Neisser, U. (1981). John Dean's memory: A case study. *Cognition, 9,* 1–22.

O'Hara, C. E., & O'Hara, G. L. (1988). *Fundamentals of criminal investigation.* Springfield, IL: Charles C Thomas.

Orne, M. T., Soskis, D. A., Dinges, D. F., & Orne, E. C. (1984). Hypnotically induced testimony. In G. Wells & E. Loftus (Eds.) *Eyewitness testimony: Psychological perspectives.* New York: Cambridge University Press.

Paivio, A. (1971). *Imagery and verbal processes.* New York: Holt, Rinehart, & Winston.

Payne, D. G. (1987). Hypermnesia and reminiscence in recall: A historical and empirical review. *Psychological Review, 101,* 5–27.

Peters, D. L. (1988). Eyewitness memory arousal in a natural setting. In M. Gruneberg, P. Morris, & R. Sykes (Eds.) *Practical aspects of memory: Current research and issues.* New York: Wiley.

Prior, J. A. & Silberstein, J. S. (1969). *Physical Diagnosis.* St. Louis: C. V. Mosby.

Putnam, W. H. (1979). Hypnosis and distortions in eyewitness memory. *International Journal of Clinical and Experimental Hypnosis, 27,* 437–448.

Pylyshyn, Z. W. (1981). The imagery debate: Analogue media versus tacit knowledge. *Psychological Review, 88,* 16–45.

Raaijmakers, J. G. W. & Shiffrin, R. M. (1980) SAM: A theory of probabilistic search of associative memory. In G. Bower (Ed.) *The psychology of learning and motivation: Advances in research and theory, 14,* New York: Academic Press.

Rand Corporation (1975). *The criminal investigative process.* Vols. 1–3. Rand Corporation Technical Report R-1777-DOJ. Santa Monica, California.

Reiser, M. (1980). *Handbook of investigative hypnosis.* Los Angeles: LEHI.

Rochester, N.Y. Police Department (1981). Preliminary investigations manual. In J. Grau (Ed.) *Criminal and civil investigation handbook.* New York: McGraw Hill.

Rock, I., & Harris, C. S. (1967). Vision and touch. *Scientific American, 216,* 96–104.

Roediger, H. L., III, & Payne, D. G. (1982). Hypermnesia: The role of repeated testing. *Journal of Experimental Psychology: Learning, Memory, and Cognition, 8,* 66–72.

Roediger, H. L., III, Payne, D. G., & Gillespie, G. L. (1982). Hypermnesia as determined by level of recall. *Journal of Verbal Learning and Verbal Behavior, 21,* 635–655.

Rogers, C. R. (1942). *Counselling and psychotherapy: Newer concepts in practice.* Boston: Houghton-Mifflin.

Rohrlich, T. (1991). "The Christopher Commission." *Los Angeles Times.* September 1, 1991.

Rosch, E. (1973). Natural categories. *Cognitive Psychology, 4,* 328–350.

Sanders, G. S. (1986). *The usefulness of eyewitness research from the perspective of police investigators.* Unpublished manuscript. State University of New York at Albany, Albany.

Saywitz, K. J. (1988). Interviewing children: A psychological perspective. *Family Advocate, 10,* 16–20.

Saywitz, K. J. (1989). Children's conceptions of the legal system: "Court is a place to play basketball." In S. Ceci, D. Ross, & M. Toglia (Eds.) *Perspectives on children's testimony.* New York: Springer-Verlag.

Shepard, R. N. (1975). Form, formation, and transformation of internal representations. In R. Solso (Ed.), *Information processing and cognition: The Loyola symposium.* Hillsdale, NJ: Erlbaum.

Shepard, R. N., & Metzler, J. (1971). Mental rotation of three-dimensional objects. *Science, 171,* 701–703.

Siegman, A. W. (1978). The meaning of silent pauses in the initial interview. *Journal of Nervous and Mental Disorders, 166,* 642–654.

Smith, A. F., Jobe, J. B., & Mingay, D. J. (1991). Question-induced cognitive biases in reports of dietary intake by college men and women. *Journal of Health Psychology, 10,* 244–251.

Smith, M. (1983). Hypnotic memory enhancement of witnesses: Does it work? *Psychological Bulletin, 94,* 387–407.

Smith, S. M. (1979). Remembering in and out of context. *Journal of Experimental Psychology: Human Learning and Memory, 5,* 460–471.

Smith, V. L., & Ellsworth, P. C. (1987). The social psychology of eyewitness accuracy: Misleading questions and communicator's expertise. *Journal of Applied Psychology, 72,* 294–300.

Stone, A. R., & DeLuca, S. M. (1980). *Investigating crimes.* Hopewell, N.J.: Houghton Mifflin.

Timm, H. W. (1983). The factors theoretically affecting the impact of forensic hypnosis techniques on eyewitness recall. *Journal of Police Science and Administration, 11,* 442–450.

Tulving, E. (1974). Cue-dependent forgetting. *American Scientist, 62,* 74–82.

Tulving, E. (1983). *Elements of episodic memory.* Oxford: Clarendon Press.

Tulving, E., & Thomson, D. M. (1973). Encoding specificity and retrieval processes in episodic memory. *Psychological Review, 80,* 352–373.

Tversky, B. (1969). Pictorial and verbal encoding in a short-term memory task. *Perception and Psychophysics, 6,* 225–233.

Underwood, B. J. (1983). *Attributes of memory.* Glenview, IL: Scott, Foresman.

Visher, C. A. (1987). Juror decision making: The importance of evidence. *Law and Human Behavior, 11,* 1–17.

Webb, J. T. (1972). Interview synchronicity: An investigation of two speech rates. In A. Siegman & B. Pope (Eds.) *Studies in dyadic communication,* New York: Pergamon.

Wells, G. (1988). *Eyewitness identification: A system handbook.* Toronto: Carswell Legal Publications.

Wells, G., & Hrcyiw, B. (1984). Memory for faces: Encoding and retrieval operations. *Memory & Cognition, 12,* 338–344.

West, R. (1985). *Memory fitness over 40.* Gainseville, FL: Trial Press.

Weston, P. B., & Wells, K. M. (1970). *Criminal investigation.* Englewood Cliffs, NJ: Prentice-Hall.

Wickelgren, W. A. (1969). Auditory or articulatory coding in verbal short-term memory. *Psychological Review, 76,* 232–235.

Wicks, R. J. (1974). *Applied psychology for law enforcement and correction officers.* New York: McGraw Hill.

Yarmey, A. D. (1979). *The psychology of eyewitness testimony.* New York: Free Press.

Yuille, J. C., & Cutshall, J. L. (1986). A case study of eyewitness memory for a crime. *Journal of Applied Psychology, 71,* 291–301.

Yuille, J. C., & Kim, C. K. (1987). A field study of the forensic use of hypnosis. *Canadian Journal of Behavioral Science, 19,* 418–419.

Yuille, J. C., & Tollestrup, P. A. (1990). Some effects of alcohol on eyewitness memory. *Journal of Applied Psychology, 75,* 268–273.

AUTHOR INDEX

211

SUBJECT INDEX